W9-CPA-051

Stay Home and Mind
YOUR OWN BUSINESS

How To Manage Your Time,
Space, Personal
Obligations,
Money,
Business,
and Yourself
While
Working
at Home

Jo Frohbieter-Mueller

BETTERWAY BOOKS
CINCINNATI, OHIO

Stay Home and Mind Your Own Business. Copyright © 1987 by Jo Frohbieter-Mueller. Printed and bound in the United States of America. All rights reserved. No part of this book may be reproduced in any form or by any electronic or mechanical means including information storage and retrieval systems without permission in writing from the publisher, except by a reviewer, who may quote brief passages in a review. Published by Betterway Books, an imprint of F&W Publications, Inc., 1507 Dana Avenue, Cincinnati, Ohio 45207. 1-800-289-0963.

97 96 95 94 93   5 4 3 2

Library of Congress Cataloging-in-Publication Data

Frohbieter-Mueller, Jo.
    Stay home and mind your own business.

        Bibliography: p
        Includes index.
        1. Home-based business. — Management.   2. Small business. — Management.   3. New business enterprises.
    I. Title.
    HD62.5.F76 1987 658'.041 87-15922
    ISBN 0-932620-83-3 (pbk.)

Cover and book design by Deborah B.Chappell
Illustrations by Jon Siau
Typography by East Coast Typography, Inc.

*This book is dedicated
to Wayne P. Mueller,
for untold reasons.*

Contents

Introduction

Yes, you can make it at home. The challenge of being one's own boss and being directly responsible for operating a business is drawing people back to their homes. The chance to try ideas, to be creative, and the opportunity to work alone or with family and friends in pleasant surroundings are other motivations to work from home. Operating a home business or cottage industry is one way to earn a living without joining the crowd in pinstriped suits or being caught in the early morning rush hour. It is a way to earn a living while watching your children, flowers, self-esteem and personal wealth grow. It means working where you can control your schedule and your environment. It is pursuing a new adventure. Who could ask for more?

Working from home will affect your life in many ways. You will experience the pleasures and pressures of living and working under the same roof. You will discover you're the boss, and quickly learn that living with the boss means living with a host of responsibilities as well as opportunities.

It takes a lot of verve and nerve to start a business, and you must be determined and excited about its potential and willing to put in the energy and hours needed to make it work. Your business will call upon many hidden abilities. Just as a muscle expands when it is used, so will your capabilities expand as you flex your will, mind and body — all of which will be called upon to run a business. And it helps to have a healthy ego — to think you can — because a certain amount of "Can Do" is needed to get a business up and running.

A home business is not for everyone. The very reason some people want to work at home is the same reason others shy away from the idea. Some like the hustle and bustle of a busy office, and they like being surrounded by fellow workers, while others prefer a quiet, less hectic workplace. Some folks flourish when left to their own devices while others want to be told what to do and to avoid risks. A home business could be a disaster for the faint-hearted.

COTTAGE INDUSTRY — YOU JUST THINK IT'S A NEW IDEA

"Cottage industry" is derived from an old European term that describes work done at home, usually for an employer. The best known cottage industries flourished in the Swiss Alps where mountain-folk, isolated by snow and ice, made parts for the famous Swiss clocks and watches. Their isolation ended when the warming sun of spring melted the ice and opened the roads into town; whereupon they emerged from their cottages, took the winter's work to an assembly plant, and were paid for their labor — their cottage industry.

More recently, "cottage industry" has become synonymous with "home business", "worksteading", or "working from home" and is defined as any income-producing job or business operated out of the home, including workers who are self-employed and those employed by others.

Working at, or from, home is a phenomenon that has come full cycle. Before the industrial revolution, people worked in and around their homes, farming and making most of life's necessities. The industrial revolution brought people to the cities with the promise of a better life, and men went to work in shops and factories. With the onset of World War II, an army of women left their homes for factories and offices to replace the men who left for war. Many of these women kept their jobs and remained in the workforce after the war was over. Now, some of the children and grandchildren of those who sought employment among the smoke stacks, typewriters and assembly lines are questioning the value of working away from home. They resent the loss of independence and the sometimes unpleasant and hazardous working conditions found in factories and offices. They have begun to realize the best workplace is their own home. These people are swelling the ranks of this country's burgeoning cottage industry. According to a study done by AT&T, 50 percent of the population will be working at home by the turn of the century.

DIFFERENT SEGMENTS OF OUR POPULATION ARE COMING HOME TO WORK

A home business appeals to a variety of age groups and life styles. Urbanites, suburbanites, and rural dwellers work from their homes and apartments to earn a living. Even the families of military personnel have learned that certain kinds of businesses can be packed up and moved along with the kids and household items each time they are transferred. Many new home business owners have been working in offices, factories and shops, and they are ready for a new experience of their own making. A large number of homemakers are now starting home businesses. Starting a business is a way for them to enter — or reenter — the business world without giving up the independence they have grown to enjoy.

Some people start a home business as a second or post-retirement career. The 9-to-5 job might start losing it's luster after several decades and a change is needed, or perhaps there is still a lot of energy and ideas left when it's time to line up for the proverbial gold watch. It's rather nice to retire to a fresh start — a second career that's just a step away from the coffee pot on your kitchen stove, one that will allow you to go fishing or take a longer lunch break if you wish.

After a lifetime of rigid schedules and duties, military retirees have discovered it's fun to be their own boss. It is also more productive to create work by starting a new business than to walk the pavement looking for a job. And they have several advantages going for them. In the first place, most armed forces personnel retire at a relatively young age. They still have the energy and spunk needed to make a business work. Secondly, they receive retirement benefits, allowing them to keep the home fires burning while they strive to make their businesses profitable.

There is a general impression that women are primarily involved in home businesses, but a recent study found that 51 percent of the people currently earning money at home are men. Thus, this is not a women's issue. But women, and especially mothers, use the home-based work pattern because working at home enables them to perform their other duties, including childcare, with less stress than a job outside the home. Flexible hours allow women to enjoy moments and years working in pleasant surroundings while nurturing their children during their formative years or caring for grandchildren, a spouse or a parent. According to "Risk to Riches", a 1987 report on women entrepreneurs, women own a quarter of the small businesses in the United States, and they are starting them at three times the rate of men. By the year 2000, they are expected to own half this country's small businesses. Many of these women operate out of their homes.

Some families use their home business as their primary source of income. Children and parents might work together to make their business successful. Women, tired of juggling home and work schedules, find they can provide for themselves and their children, or supplement their spouse's income with a home business. Some use home-based work to provide a continuous income. For example, a teacher might tutor or do freelance writing during the summer months, while a farmer might manufacture leather belts or raise earthworms or bedding plants during the slow winter months. Others use home businesses as a way to "moonlight". A librarian might spend evenings editing magazine articles or revving up a home computer for her work as an information broker. A carpenter who works for another company throughout the week might spend weekends making small wooden objects to sell at craft fairs.

UNLIMITED BUSINESS OPPORTUNITIES ABOUND FOR HOMEWORKERS

Many home entrepreneurs pursue occupations traditionally associated with home-based work such as tutoring, sewing, refinishing furniture, and producing arts and crafts.

With increasing numbers of young mothers returning to work, child care has become a viable cottage industry. The Bureau of Labor Statistics has estimated that 50 percent of mothers with children under the age of six will be working outside of the home by 1990, so we can expect child care to remain a strong field for home businesses.

Some families operate small manufacturing businesses out of their garage or basement, using inventions or designs of their own or those created by others, while other home businesses are service oriented. Currently there is a growing industry linked to the high-tech market. As high-technology becomes available and affordable and computers become increasingly "user friendly," even larger numbers of people will be attracted to the advantages of doing computer work at home. Even now, some home workers are processing purchase orders, or doing accounting, tax return preparation and inventory control for an employer whom he or she rarely sees in person. The completed work is telephoned, via telecommunications, to the company's central computer. Other computer owners work from home and, using word processors, write books, publish newsletters, or write articles for newspapers and magazines.

RUNNING A BUSINESS IS A JOB!

Successful home business entrepreneurs aren't born. They're made — at home! And the making involves lots of hard work. Many current books excite the would-be entrepreneur with phrases such as "the road to wealth," "get rich quick," "a wealth base," and "100 businesses you can start for less than $100." These books mislead their readers. It takes work and more work to make it work! A home business isn't a get-rich-quick scheme, but it IS a good way to live and a good way to work. To operate a successful cottage industry requires a thorough knowledge of your craft or trade. It takes strategy, and planning, and you must abide by the local, state and federal laws under which you conduct your business.

USE THIS BOOK AS A REFERENCE

This book contains much of the information and direction you will need to start and sustain a home business. It gives you tips on how to succeed and warns you of the many danger areas to avoid. It will help you to determine if you are socially, mentally, and economically equipped to operate a home business and show you ways to protect your time while maintaining a semblance of normalcy around the household. It gives you encouragement and urges you on.

Many of the subjects are addressed to women who plan to operate a business at home, but that is not to imply men can't do the same. I directed the book toward women because, not only do I understand their point of view better, but I also believe they can be caught in a bind, trying to be all things to all people while remaining true to themselves. Building a business at home is one way to accept the new role of the career woman without giving up the tradition of homemaking. It is a way to combine the best of both worlds while being at the forefront of our evolving society.

As you study each chapter, keep in mind how the subjects and ideas relate to your own home and how you might convert the suggestions to your own use. Next, plan your attack and get to work.

Don't expect instant success — it doesn't happen. No matter how much advice you gather, it takes time to make a business work, and still more time to yield a profit. And then it takes persistence to keep it functioning. That's just part of the fun and the challenge of being your own boss. Each business is different, and you will need to find what combination of factors yields success. But keep trying, and keep looking for opportunities. And remember, the success of your business is directly related to your energy, planning, persistence, skill, ideas, flexibility, discipline, and dedication. Can you do it? You BET you can!

Part I

**Managing Your Time,
Space, Home, and Self
...While Working at Home**

Why a Home Business?

Is something driving you — do you have a dream? Let's hope so, because a great deal of energy is released by dreams, and you can use that energy to propel your dreams into reality. Are you in pursuit of the American dream — that is, to enjoy your freedom and work where you want at a job of your choice? Since you are reading this book, your dream must include owning a business. Approximately 10 percent of all American workers work for themselves instead of for others. Around 11 million, or approximately half of the self-employed, operate a business from their homes.

GOALS

Before you begin your home business it's important to clarify your goals. Clearly defining goals will help you understand what you want out of your business, and knowing that, you can direct your energies to fulfill your specific expectations.

We all have different goals and values. One person might long to work alone on painting or sculpture. Maybe you are longing for the chance to manufacture and sell something you have invented, or perhaps to market things other people make. Perhaps you want to write magazine articles or become the best caterer in town, or organize book shows or bring entertainment to your city.

Some of us want to establish a big business and earn a lot of money, while others of us would be happier with a small business and ENOUGH money. It is important to understand yourself and identify the values that control your life if you are to meet the goals that will make you happy. But is "being happy" one of your goals? It may not be. Perhaps "being important" has a higher priority for you than "being happy". But then, if "being important" is a high priority and is attained, won't "being happy" naturally follow? It might, but not necessarily. For instance, the stress caused by the work needed to "be important" may destroy your marriage or health and negate your happiness. On the other hand, another person might have a totally different notion of "importance". Indeed, he or she might view himself as "important" if his family is content and he or she has played an integral part in building that contentment. Tune in to yourself in order to understand your goals. If you are to meet your goals, you must first understand them.

Long-term as well as short-term goals are needed in order to get a project underway and to keep it on course. Long-term goals should be established first, and short-term goals can help you achieve them. If you know where you want to be in one, five or 10 years, you have a much greater chance of getting there. Goal posts along the way, indicate where you should be by the end of the day, week, month or year. Although long-term goals are more general, short-term goals are just as important. Short-term goals may include nothing more than a mundane list of jobs, such as "call printers about stationery", "pick up tax forms", and so forth.

Having emphasized the importance of goals, I hasten to add that goals are little more than a framework on which to hang your hopes and direct your energies. They are something to get you started, but they are made to be changed. You need to be flexible in your goals and expectations in order to seize unforeseen opportunities. Build a "flexibility factor" into your plans, allowing your goals to change as you develop new ideas and new opportunities arise.

Study the lists below and adapt them to fit your dreams.

Long Term Goals

Long term goals are more general.
  To show a profit within a given time period
  Integrate business life with home life
  Develop skills and use talents
  Attain a certain level of income
  Be a leader
  Gain recognition for business acumen

Contribute to the economic well being of society, self, and family
Convince friends of your abilities
Attain a feeling of accomplishment
Enjoy living

Short Term Goals

Short term goals — i.e. tasks to be accomplished — are designed to help long-term goals become realized. Jobs that must be done to get a business established include:
Name business
Design logo
Find work space within your home
Find financing
Develop a work schedule
Contact suppliers
Send out news releases
Explain business ideas to family

REASONS FOR A HOME BUSINESS

Personal Feelings Are Important

Maybe you have been working "out there", beating your head against the wall trying to earn a living and hating every minute of it. You might feel your work doesn't allow you to use your talents and capabilities. Life has become Frustration. You've watched your boss mess up business deals you could have handled, and you start to think, why not? Remember playing "follow the leader" when you were a kid? The nicest part of the game was taking turns — after being a follower, you got to be the leader which was much more fun.

But why start your business at home? Why not open a business on Main Street and watch all the pretty girls go by? Be absolutely honest with yourself. There is strength in understanding motives. Some of us would love to be right in the middle of the action. So why are you contemplating setting up shop at home?

Maybe you need space. If you are a creative person — an artist, writer, or inventor, — you surely need space; not the kind of space to set up a table or chair, but the space of time, of isolation, of emptiness that can be filled when the mind and hands have the opportunity to work together. That special kind of space is not found in the bustle of the business world, but it CAN be created and savored in one's own home.

Maybe you need the security of home. In a sense, home is a refuge. You can try and fail without being exposed to the public eye. You can try again and again, and keep trying until you succeed. Many people who start a home business have been away from the business world for an extended time, and they are apprehensive about their ability to perform. While working at home they can gain the confidence needed to compete in the marketplace. For example, many women who have spent years tending the nest and nurturing their children now want to return to work but don't know how to get a job. Some of them start a business doing what they know best, maybe with a hobby or a long standing interest in sewing or cooking. As their businesses grow, these women discover they no longer want to find a job. Working at their own business at home fulfills their needs in a way that no "outside" job could.

Home businesses are especially appealing to those who have physical disabilities that prevent or inhibit them from working elsewhere. A home office or shop can be outfitted to meet their special needs. They find that a home business can make them vital, contributing members of their communities.

Earn Money at Home

Most people, when questioned, say they want a home business to earn money. How much money do you have in mind? Do you want your home business to be your primary source of income, — or will it supplement another income? If vacationing is your motive for operating a home business, you should know that time for travel shrinks as a business grows.

Cottage industry supplements other sources of income such as social security or investment returns. Since this type of income does not require expending time to earn it, you have more time to contribute to your work. You may visualize your home business as a way to start a large business, beginning under a protective shelter and expanding as opportunities develop. Just how big of a venture would you like to control?

You may consider earning money as a by-product of your home business — something that happens as a result of doing what you want to do. For example, even if making money is not the force that motivates you to write stories or paint portraits, it will become important as your work progresses, because financial reward is our society's way of recognizing accomplishment. Whether you are thinking small or large, determine how much money you hope to earn with your home business, and make that one of your goals.

Responsibilities Can be Met by Working at Home

Are you caught in a situation where you can't leave home, perhaps because the responsibilities of caring for a child, spouse or parent? Surely, working at home is a logical way to both be at home and earn money.

Sure, we can get a job in a big fancy office and pull on pantyhose or tie a tie each morning before taking our little ones off to the sitter. But why? Why spend each day working in an office, nursing a headache and stewing over how your child is being cared for when you'd rather spend time working at your home business, nurturing your growing child while stewing a favorite recipe.

You can do both — run a business and raise a family. Of course, your business responsibilities must be limited when your children are small and demand a lot of your time. During this period, use your time and energy to develop your business, make contacts, or get your business off the ground at least on a part-time basis. When your children are a little older, your business will be poised, ready to take off.

Caring for an elderly parent or a disabled spouse can require a lot or a little time. In some cases, it's only necessary for someone to be available in case of an emergency. At other times, this kind of care can be time consuming and exhausting. A home business accommodates the demands on your time and energy, with the business growing as more time becomes available.

A Family Business Can Help Families Grow

Children and parents can work together to make a business grow into a successful enterprise. Each member of the family contributes work and ideas and shares in the profits. You can be sure that children participating in this type of arrangement will learn what it takes to make a buck, how our economic system works, the real meaning of supply and demand, and a host of other valuable lessons. Schools may teach our children "readin', writin', and 'rithmetic", but they fail miserably in teaching the basic skills needed to earn a living. That is why so many students emerge from their formal education oblivious to the working world they are about to enter. But a child who has been raised in a home where business is a part of the household will have a significant advantage in the business world.

Working with the family has another invaluable benefit. You learn to REALLY talk to each other and to work together.

It's not "Do you have a clean shirt?" or "We'll be leaving for Aunt Nell's wedding in a couple of minutes," but instead, "How do you think we should handle this problem?" In our society, with so much to pull generations apart, sharing a common goal, such as making a business succeed, can strengthen family relationships.

Save Time and Money by Working at Home

Have you ever figured how much time you spend going to and from work? Even if your work is only 15 minutes from home, it takes 30 minutes each day for travel time, or 150 minutes each week, or 7,800 minutes each year, equal to 3.25 forty-hour weeks. If you work at home, you have that much extra time either to enjoy a morning run or an extra cup of coffee. You could even take a three week vacation with the time you would otherwise spend fighting traffic. Also, if you have been working for somebody else you may not be aware of the number of times the boss or owner is called back for emergencies or little jobs. When you are the owner and boss, you are the one called back; unless, of course, you work in your own home.

Commuting not only costs time, but it also costs money. Auto repair and fuel can slice into your income. When you work at home, the family can often manage with one less vehicle. But look at these even bigger savings. A home business actually reduces the amount of taxes you pay because you can deduct the use of your home as a business expense. The cost of childcare for women working away from home sometimes makes working an exercise in futility, but women working at home avoid this expense

The Chance of Success is Better for Home Businesses

According to Dunn and Bradstreet's "Business Failure Record," 27 percent of small businesses fail within three years and a striking 82 percent fail within 10 years. That is, only 18 percent of small businesses survive for 10 years. However, the chance of succeeding is much greater when a business operates from a home, largely due to its economic advantages. Besides the advantages mentioned above, there is the advantage of not having the overwhelming expense of rent. Home businesses use available space, and there is no need to rent or buy office or production space. You might need to make a few adjustments, and even go so far as to move a wall or enlarge a porch or garage, but that expense can't compare to renting or buying business space. We've all witnessed the demise of new businesses that never seem to get off the ground because they are overwhelmed with expenses before they begin to attract many clients or customers. These failed entrepreneurs have probably incurred devastating debts that will take years to repay. But even more crushing than the debts is the impact of failure. The ego and enthusiasm of many of these people is so badly damaged that they will be reluctant even to consider another venture, but will spend their lives dreaming of what might have been.

Enjoy Pleasant Working Conditions

We build our castles to fill our needs, using colors and shapes that enhance our lives. We work hard to earn money to make our homes lovely, and we ought to be able to enjoy the fruits of our labor throughout the working day.

We all have special "escape valves" built into our domestic lives, and these can be extended into our working lives if we work at home. When stress starts to build, it's a matter of shifting gears and seeking a momentary diversion. Make a trip to the water cooler — your kitchen sink, or step outdoors for a breath of fresh air. If you work in a large office, you would probably get a headache if you stepped outside for a brief stroll through the traffic. Office politics and noise do not distract you when you work at home. Don't be misled — there are PLENTY of distractions at home, but at least you can deal with them as you see fit.

THE PITFALLS OF WORKING FROM HOME

A home business isn't for everyone. When you have your own business, you either make it work or you don't earn money. The challenge can frighten the less adventurous or those who are a little short on self-confidence or plain old guts. It is also bewildering to those who simply can't figure out how to go about getting started. And a home business is not the answer for someone who must have an immediate income, because, after starting a new business, it usually takes time to work out the kinks and start earning money.

Also, a home business isn't for the person who lacks determination and isn't willing to devote the extra hours and energy needed to make it work. There is no denying you will work harder at your own business than at somebody else's, especially as you strive to get the business started. Most of the large companies operating across our land were born in garages and basements and parented by people who had a dream just like you.

Guard against letting the advantages of a home business become disadvantages. Home business owners want the flexible hours and the freedom to follow their own schedules, but it's very easy to abuse the non-structured day. This can lead to either of two extremes. On the one hand, frequent breaks can become a pattern and interruptions might be permitted to garner increasing amounts of work time. On the other hand, since there is no official starting and stopping time, it is important to guard against work without end. To combat either extreme set up office or work hours and make a resolution to keep them. Make a habit of getting to work on time and also quitting on time.

Isolation can be another disadvantage, and it surprises people who have longed for moments of solitude. Surrounded by colleagues who talk non-stop, chew and pop gum, and smoke throughout the day, we long for the peace and quiet of a home office. But too much peace and quiet can be deafening. Even though Grandma might be knitting in the living room, and your kids are playing within hearing range, you will feel isolated if you do not find peers.

Isolation tends to exacerbate bad habits. It is very easy to waltz over to the refrigerator when lonesomeness or the slightest hunger pang hits, but don't do it. Concentrate on controlling unhealthy urges and unproductive habits and resolve to fight isolation with healthy habits. There are ways to fight isolation, as you will learn in Chapter 8.

Another disadvantage of working at a home business versus a large organization is the loss of benefits. Many people I have talked with didn't appreciate the benefits they received from their previous employer until they had to pay for an array of services and benefits. Insurance is a good example. If your spouse subscribes to a family insurance plan where he or she works, you will be covered, but if you both work in your home it is essential that you investigate options and purchase insurance coverage. This and other benefits are discussed in later chapters.

Options for Earning a Living at Home

Options for earning a living at home are being introduced early in this book to help you select a tentative business so you can apply the information that follows to the business you are considering. As you read this chapter and evaluate different kinds of businesses, keep in mind your skills, goals, and special circumstances. Above all, select a business you will enjoy — one that will allow you to do the things you like to do. Don't consider a business that can make a profit but isn't the kind of work you like. After making a tentative selection, remain open to changes or to "fine tuning" your choice. Even after your business is underway, it is wise to stay open to changes and take advantage of unforeseen opportunities.

As an example of an unforeseen opportunity, here is the story of Marsha Tinley, who made certain business plans but later changed them when it became apparent she was missing a good market. Marsha intended to open an infant-care center and, to get started, shopped at yard sales and purchased several baby beds, high chairs and other equipment. Her business attracted several customers, but she found that when her own children returned home from school each day, they invariably had several other children in tow. Marsha spent her afternoons smearing peanut butter sandwiches for the neighborhood kids while trying to juggle, feed, and change the infants in her care. On many occasions she nursed an ailing school child whose parents were at work. And then she realized she was providing free care for a lot of children. Several months into her infant-care business, Marsha had her own yard sale and got rid of the baby beds and high chairs. She then purchased a couple of day beds, tables and an assortment of toys and now runs an after-school childcare center. To make her business more profitable, Marsha also offers care for children who aren't well enough to attend school and who cannot go to school as on snow days or extended holiday breaks. Needless to say, her own children are delighted with their "built-in" playmates.

Home businesses can be divided into three main categories: manufacturing, service, and those based on creative work. Another option for home workers is working for someone else.

Manufacturing, or the making of new products, accounts for much of the activity in our economy. After new products are manufactured they must be sold, thus giving rise to the wholesaling, and then retailing businesses, and as the products are used, many of them need to be serviced. Service businesses do not make new products, but rather maintain or distribute already existing ones. Service industries also include a host of occupations that maintain buildings and grounds, and promote the well-being of our population through activities such as medical treatment, governing, law enforcement and education.

Some lines of work are in a gray area, between manufacturing and service, and it is the place where the work is performed or the quantity produced that determines if it is manufacturing or service. If a woman bakes pies in her home and sells them at the market, she manufactures pies, but if she bakes them in somebody else's home, where she works as a cook, then her work would be considered a service.

The desire to do a specific kind of work is what attracts some people to a home business. Others haven't the slightest notion of what business they might start, only that they either want or need to work at home. These people remind me of the would-be writer who wants to write a book, but doesn't know what to write about. It is necessary to focus on a possible business, learn about it, decide if it can be mastered, and find out if it there is a need or a market for it. If the answer to each of the questions above is yes, then the stage is set for the first step toward making a business commitment.

Entrepreneurs have a distinct advantage if they have a business established elsewhere and move it to their home. Healthcare professionals, attorneys, consultants and others who have a going business take home their list of clients or contacts and give their business a running start.

You may be thinking you must start from scratch as you build a home business, but you don't. We all have a multitude of skills, experiences, hobbies and interests, and it is essential to build on your background as you create a business.

MANY HOME BUSINESSES OFFER A SERVICE

The number of home businesses that deliver a service is rapidly growing. This kind of business is especially appealing because there is no need to make a heavy investment in machinery or raw materials. In fact, many service businesses can get underway with a few minor pieces of equipment, stationery, business cards and advertisement.

There are several things to consider as you narrow your focus on the kind of service you might offer. Jot down the things you like to do. List the jobs you have had, equipment you might have, where you live in relation to other business activities, and include special skills and education. Now let's try to find a service business for you.

Take Advantage of Your Location

The place of business has been settled — you plan to work at home. The location of your home could be the basis for your business. Where do you live? Who passes your house? Is there extra ground around your home?

One of the women I met at a homeworker's networking organization has made a business of packing lunches. Cressie Mosburger lives near a company that employs several hundred people. The lunchroom facilities are inadequate and she noticed that many of the office workers left the building for lunch. Cressie developed a line of sandwiches and snack foods and started selling them from her back porch. She attracts customers by placing flyers on the windshields of employees' cars. Now the employees buy food at her home and go elsewhere to eat it. Cressie saw a need and filled it.

If you live near a stadium you might consider renting parking space on your side lot, or selling snacks, umbrellas, or whatever seems to be needed by the passing fans.

Do you live on a farm? Some of the things you take for granted would be an exciting experience for the city-bound. A lot of people don't even know what a farm is anymore, and some of these people and their children might like to spend a day or two on a farm. You might make a business of having weekend guests who mend fences, milk the cows, slop the pigs, retrieve warm eggs from under sitting hens, and pick the berries or shuck the corn. They might pay to do your work! Of course you will have other work, including cooking for guests, and changing and washing linens.

If you have extra land, you might consider laying out garden plots and renting them to people who want to grow their own vegetables or flowers. You could earn more income by offering to turn the soil or preserve their excess produce. Or, you might use that extra land to offer pony rides. If there is space in the barn, you could stable horses for city folk. And if there is a lake on your land you could stock it and open it for fishing.

Use Your Job Skills to Create a Business

Generally, any type of work you have done for an employer can be employed by you to develop your own business. What are your skills and how can they be converted into a home business? A bookkeeper with a large firm can use those skills to develop a bookkeeping business at home; a professor can spend evenings and weekends serving as a consultant; an auto mechanic can run an auto service business; a secretary can form her own secretarial service; a draftsman might draw plans for homeowners wanting to remodel, and so on. The list is seemingly endless, covering the many skills that are used to keep the business community and our society functioning.

You can use your skills even if you haven't worked a single day outside the home. If you have raised a family, you know how to cook, clean, sew, decorate, and care for children. You probably have been involved in cake sales, scout activities, PTA meetings and parties, not to mention resolving personality conflicts, nursing egos and illnesses, and encouraging child and spouse development. All these skills can be put to use in a home business and are sorely needed by various segments of society.

Use a Hobby or Special Interest to Start a Business

Practically any hobby can be converted into a successful home business, and there are many people who do for money what other people do for fun. Hobbies can be very expensive, but when they are used as a business, they make money rather than cost money. The following list suggests some hobbies that make good business ventures.

● Shutter bugs spend a fortune gathering photographic equipment and supplies to feed their hobby, but they can also use their skill and equipment to develop a nice photography business. Photographers can take in-house photos for passports or engagements, and out-of-house photos at weddings, graduations, baptisms and other memorable occasions.

● A special interest in antiquing, going to estate sales and attending auctions can be the impetus needed to start an antique business. You might combine it with furniture refinishing and chair caning to make the business a more profitable operation.

● The love of animals can lead into breeding and/or training dogs, cats, or horses.

● An expertise in dance, tennis, singing, baton twirling, golf, or cooking (to name a few) can lead to teaching classes or private lessons. ("Giving" is a misnomer, it should be "selling" private lessons.)

● If interior decorating is your hobby, your home can be used to demonstrate the kind of work you do as you set up an interior decorating or custom decorating business.

● If you have an extensive collection of tapes and the necessary sound equipment, you might consider becoming a disc jockey and providing music for receptions, school dances and community parties.

Design a Business Around the Equipment You Have

Look around the house and you might discover you already own something that can be used to start a business. A boat can be used to give rides on a nearby lake or be rented out to fishermen for other outings. A van might be used to make deliveries of people or things. Or, the van could carry equipment for other work, such as ladders and paint for paint jobs, plumbing fixtures for plumbing work, or cleaning equipment. It could be used for a courier service. A swimming pool can be opened for lessons or swimming sessions. A well-equipped kitchen begs to be used for baking, preparing meals for the home-bound elderly, and other food-based operations.

If you have been gathering power tools, maybe it's time to start making money by putting them to use. A chain saw could be used to start a business clearing wooded areas, trimming trees, or cutting firewood. An air compressor might be used to paint furniture, sand blast or clean equipment. Each power tool in your workshop can probably be applied to some kind of home business.

Your family room can become a childcare center, and your computer could become the key to a writing business. And don't forget your mailbox. Mail order businesses are a viable way to make money from home. Resources to help you start some of these businesses are given in the Appendix.

A Service Business Can be Built on Helping People

People seem to be busier now than they have ever been. Even though our homes are loaded with energy and time-saving gadgets, we barely have the time to use them. We are so busy working, running between jobs, social events, and volunteer projects that many people have precious little time to do some jobs that must be done. The movement of women out of the house and into the workforce has created a need for more service businesses. These women have left behind sinks full of dirty dishes, loads of laundry, dirty windows, tubs and carpets. There are also children that need love and care, cars that need servicing, lawns to be mowed, and families to feed. That represents one heck of a market. Service businesses are quickly filling the niche created by working mothers, and many of these operate out of homes. In fact, there is a curious exchange occurring among working people: as more women go to work outside their homes, they are creating more business opportunities for women who work from their homes. Working women are also influencing the restaurant and fast-food business as they stop to pick up a pizza or a bucket of chicken on their way home from work. They also need a dinner out after a hectic day at the office. It is not surprising then that the service industry is booming, and that the division of labor is becoming more defined as women join the outside workforce.

Men are also using more services than they once did. This is because our economy is providing us with more disposable income, and since we have more money, we are more inclined to pay for work we used to do for ourselves. This provides a great opportunity for service businesses that offer to help people with tasks they either can't or don't want to do.

Use Your Experiences, Background or Knowledge to Start a Business

Don't give away information you can sell. I have a physician friend who was regularly accosted at parties and social happenings and asked for advice. The rash, swollen lymph nodes, and hacking cough all represented potential customers, and when he offered free advice he was losing business. This doctor has become very adroit at avoiding on-the-spot medical treatment. He now enjoys his outings without these intrusive encounters and also without losing business. Of course, an emergency is met, but routine questions and complaints are dealt with during office hours.

You might be surprised to learn that what you know is in demand or has a market. If you have sold articles or books, other writers will want to know how to sell them. If you run a successful business, other people will pay to find out how you got started. If you catch fish, where and using what? If you organized a church bazaar, you can tell us how you did it. Whatever you can do, you can sell the information. Give lessons, lectures,or seminars. Write a book or be a consultant. Cash in on the knowledge you have worked to acquire.

Use Your Personality to Run a Sales Business

Sales is included among service businesses because it distributes manufactured products to the marketplace and to consumers. It is a service to both manufacturers and consumers. Sales is a truly big business — approximately 2 million retail stores operate in this country, in addition to door-to-door, mail order sales, and roadside stands. Sales can include operating your own marketing business and functioning as a sales representative, or running a retail shop and selling products from your home or studio. It also means the distribution of goods through parties, such as those given to demonstrate Mary Kay cosmetics or Tupperware. You can open a resale shop in your garage; or again, you can sell by mail order.

Where can you acquire merchandise? What kind of commissions can you expect? Take a look at a few of the books listed in the Appendix and in Chapter 18 to learn if this might be something you would enjoy doing and how to go about doing it.

A MANUFACTURING BUSINESS MIGHT FIT INTO YOUR HOME

Large profits can be realized in the manufacturing business. Manufacturing includes the conversion of raw products into finished merchandise and assembling parts to make a completed product. Manufacturing sometimes involves a substantial outlay of funds to purchase machinery and raw materials, but some manufacturing can be accomplished with only a modest investment in machinery, using a labor intensive process instead. I have an acquaintance who has built a large business on labor-intensive manufacturing. Dick Sinclair, who retired from the military only several years ago, and his wife operate a gift-manufacturing concern that started as a home business, but now employs several hundred people. During his tenure in the service, Dick's wife, who is an artist, designed small wooden objects that she and their children made and sold to friends and military acquaintances. Little did this family realize that they were laying the groundwork for a successful and very profitable business.

After Dick retired from the service, the family kept on making the wooden pieces. They also developed an aggressive marketing plan, using a network of sales representatives to market their products throughout the country, and were soon overwhelmed with orders. Unable to keep up with the demand for their merchandise, the Sinclairs hired a few helpers to cut and paint the items. The business grew even more and the number of helpers increased dramatically. In an effort to control overhead, about 75 percent of their employees still work at home; the remaining 25 percent work at company studios and offices that have been recently established. While the company grew larger, the Sinclair children grew older. Now they are young adults and are in charge of various departments within the operation. This is a good example of a very successful family business that grew with the family.

To Machine or Hand-Make Products; That is the Question

There are several things to consider in evaluating products you might manufacture. How much labor is required for the manufacturing procedure? How much equipment will be required? How expensive is the equipment and the tooling up procedure? Is a strong market available or does the market need to be created? And importantly, can the product be developed, made, and marketed at a profit?

Many home manufacturers produce items that use labor instead of machines. There are probably two principle reasons for this phenomenon. In the first place, it costs a great deal to purchase manufacturing machinery and not all home businesses can afford this initial expense. But perhaps the more compelling reason is most of us don't understand the procedure of setting up a machine-based manufacturing business. But we DO know how to make something by hand because we've spent our lives doing just that.

If you are considering handcrafting products, it's well worth it to consider the ramifications of this type of business. Many of us have an unrealistic notion of handcrafted items and how they are produced. When we pick up a handcrafted doily in a shop we visualize a little Granny, rocking and humming as her needles click away. That vision might inspire you to buy that doily, but it is not necessarily an accurate scenario.

Handcrafted items easily fall into at least three different categories. The first category is handcrafted one-of-a-kind pieces. These compositions usually have a satisfied artist-craftsperson somewhere in their background, and the creations are a source of pride and pleasure to both the maker and the purchaser. They are usually quite expensive.

In the second category are the items crafted by people in

typical Mom and Pop homecraft businesses. These craftspeople might use a pattern they have found in a magazine or elsewhere, although some of them work from patterns of their own design. Many items are made from the same pattern. These craftspeople usually sell their own work at fairs and flea markets, and since they sell directly to the consumer rather than to a retailer, they determine the price and can usually get a fair return for their work.

The third hand-crafted category consists of items made by employees of a company that mass produces merchandise from a mold or pattern. These pieces are sold through catalogs or in shops. This entails a totally different crafting procedure. These items are not crafted by the hands of the designer (although the original one was), but by the hands of an army of people who are usually working for less than acceptable pay. Many work at home under contract with another party, and it is called "piece work", meaning the individuals doing the work are paid a fixed fee for each piece they make.

As a result, they try to crank out the pieces as quickly as possible in an effort to earn a living wage. When we admire and buy these handcrafted items, we tend to deny the impoverishing wages paid the workers who have produced them, yet we know in our gut that the low prices asked for the lovely pieces mean they were probably produced under unsatisfactory conditions. Such mass produced handcrafted pieces might be viewed as symbols of repression, and that certainly takes the joy out of having them decorate our homes.

On the other hand, maybe it's not as bad or as unfair as it appears at first glance. Crafting items at home may be the only work some people can do, either because they are unskilled at other jobs, or because they are confined to their homes due to other responsibilities or a physical impairment. And there will always be individuals who would rather do handwork than spend idle days. Some handcrafters like to work while watching afternoon soaps or sitting outside under a shade tree. And still others, retired couples for instance, spend evenings working together with a common purpose, enjoying their togetherness. While these people don't earn a goodly amount, they do, nonetheless, have the opportunity to earn money for their time and effort. Also, these workers don't have the expenses associated with jobs outside of the home, and for this reason they can work for less compensation.

How does all this affect you? If you are planning to produce and market a handcrafted product as your home business and intend to use a group of laborers to produce it, you will be forced to make some hard decisions. In truth, you will find yourself caught in an ethical/business bind. In Chapter 3 you will learn that my family's home business is based on handcrafted products produced by workers in their homes. We quickly discovered we couldn't pay our workers enough for their work and still recover a profit. To pay what we considered a fair wage would have required us to charge more for the product than shops were willing to pay. Still, our workers wanted the work and gladly accepted what we offered. Yet, we agonized over the dilemma. We nearly stopped producing our handmade products because of this conflict until we realized we would have only heightened the problems of our homebound workers — to stop production would have left these people with no work and no pay, rather than work with inadequate pay. We remain uneasy with the arrangement, but find ourselves caught with no obvious alternative. This is a good example of the kinds of problems you will be forced to deal with as you develop your home business.

I must add that the number of people tucked in garages, sewing rooms, basement workrooms and behind dining room tables is much greater than the IRS or the rest of us realize. They could well be the elusive Fifth Column of our economy.

Deciding on a Product to Manufacture

There is a wide range of products suitable for home manufacturing including printed paper products, small toys and decorative household items, miniatures, pottery, needlework and wooden objects. Concrete and plaster products, confections and specialty foods are also products that could be manufactured with little machinery but lots of hands.

Home manufacturers might make products they design, products designed by others, or they might make a component used by another manufacturer.

Manufacturing products you design requires that you are attuned to the times, sensitive to trends, alert to changing markets, AND, that you have a style that can capture a corner of the market. That is, you need to have a combination of the artistic and engineering senses.

Design a product to make a profit. The design you use will determine if the item is economically feasible. In the first place, each item you produce must compel consumers to want it — it can be either cute, lovely, charming, or useful — but it must be something people will be willing to purchase. Just as importantly, it should be designed to be made efficiently. There must be absolutely no wasted movement or materials. It takes a great deal of thought to develop a product that is desirable and at the same time designed for the greatest efficiency in construction. When designing a product, keep in mind it will be made over and over again, perhaps thousands and thousands of times. Time spent in perfecting a design is a necessary investment because this will save time, money, and energy when it is produced, and that might make the difference between making a profit or losing money.

Manufacturing products designed by other people is another way to get into this lucrative business if you lack the skills and creative talents needed for product design. But you must be careful. It is unlawful to use the intellectual property of someone else without permission, although this is done regularly as when Mickey Mouse, Raggedy Ann, and others are copied. Hire a designer. Artists working from their homes are willing to freelance this type of work. Art suppliers and instructors can direct you to freelance artists who can design products to manufacture.

Manufacturing articles other than crafted items can be very profitable, but how do you find a product and a market for the product? You will need help and there are several places to look for ideas. Government-owned patents are available on a non-exclusive royalty-free basis. Many of these are for products that require a large initial tooling-up process, but it could be worth the cost if the product offers the prospect of a profit and long-term marketability. Information on government-owned patents may be obtained from the U. S. Patent Office, Department of Commerce, Washington, D.C. 20231.

Private patents are also available for licensing or sale, and these are listed in *The Official Gazette* of the U. S. Patent Office. The *Gazette* lists new patents only once, as they become available. The *Gazette* is obtained from the Superintendent of Documents, Government Printing Office, Washington, D. C. 20402.

Another source of ideas are the shows where inventors show their wares. These are fun to attend even if you aren't looking for a new product; just to see the array of "things" people invent. These shows also get you to thinking about marketable designs and, for that reason alone, are worth attending. They are usually sponsored by the Chambers of Commerce in large metropolitan areas. To learn when and where such events take place, write to the Office of Inventions and Innovations, National Bureau of Standards, Washington, D. C. 20234.

Another type of manufacturing operation involves producing a component used in a product manufactured by another company. A small manufacturer might make the knob used on the gear shift of a certain make of car, or some other component of a multifaceted product. These items are subcontracted to small manufacturers. Contact manufacturing businesses if you are interested in this type of operation.

MAKING AND SELLING ORIGINAL COMPOSITIONS FROM HOME

Creative people work with original ideas or they put old ideas together in new combinations. There are creative people working in every field trying to figure out a better way, whether it's a better way to bat a ball, to package candy, or to shoot a satellite into orbit. These people have accepted the responsibility for improving our lot, for helping humanity rise above itself. In the context of this chapter, creative people are identified as painters, sculptors, potters, composers, authors, and inventors of new technologies.

Most people who create original compositions work for the joy of creating, identifying and defining a new concept and putting materials together in a new way. But these people also have to eat — they need to earn a living. Fortunately, a home business can be built around creative work.

Making original art and craft objects has been a traditional home business partly because creative people tend to shy away from crowds and stay away from the ordinary. Working at home provides the time, space, isolation and freedom needed to explore new ideas and make new creations.

If you are driven by a desire to make original compositions, you must also learn how to make a profit from your work and develop a few business smarts. Business-wise artists orchestrate their careers to create a demand for their work: for example, an artist who lives and works near a tourist area can open a studio/show room at home and tend shop while working. Seeing the artist at work is often the catalyst that brings a sale. If you are contemplating a life of creative work, you might consider moving to this type of community because it will not only bring you in contact with potential customers, but also with colleagues who have similar interests. But you don't need to be located in a tourist area to sell your work. Arts and crafts can also be sold through an agent who will place the works in galleries or other appropriate places for viewing and sale. Other outlets include art shows and art markets, or a co-op of several artists operating a gallery. In the next chapter you will learn how an artist gets customers to her remote studio to watch her paint and to buy her works.

I "run" with an artsy crowd and have for many years. I have watched them ply their trade, and, my conclusion is that the best artists don't necessarily earn the most money, maybe because they are better at art than at business. The most successful, if measured by works sold, are the feisty little gals who have pieces hanging in exercise clubs, the airport terminal, restaurants all around town, dinner clubs, concert halls, libraries, and even on rented panels in large shopping malls. The reason they sell their work is because a lot of people see it. Also, since they have more sales, they can let a piece go for less than the artist who rarely sells anything. And you can be sure these aggressive ladies never let an art show pass without entering some of their work to gain more exposure, possibly win a prize and build their reputations.

Writing is another popular home business based on creativity. This field is similar to arts and crafts in that competition is stiff, and it takes more than a good composition to get published and earn money. A writer must be very aware of the times, keep abreast of the news, and write about topics of interest to a specific audience. But knowing how to market written material is just about as important as knowing how to write it. If you are planning a writing career, find other writers. Join a writer's guild and use the successes of other writers to spur you on and help you to learn how to use marketing tools and how to sell your work. (See "Writing" in the Appendix, and Selling Written Work in Chapter 18).

WORKING AT HOME FOR ANOTHER BUSINESS

Working from home doesn't exclude working for others. If you don't want the responsibility of operating your own business but would like to work at home, then you should seek out a business that hires home workers. It has been estimated that 2 to 3 million people are currently working at home for an employer, and the number of companies hiring people to work in their homes is rapidly growing because this allows a company to expand without adding office or production space. In effect, they can enlarge without growing pains. There is also evidence that home workers are more productive than their counterparts who work in the corporate offices. Some companies operate through a network of home-based workers and have very few "in-house" employees. Information-based companies are especially adaptable to this arrangement. Some newspaper journalists rarely see the office but send their stories to the editor's desk via telecommunication. Reservations for hotels and community events are often taken by a home worker, and some mail order companies may not have an office to work from. Other kinds of work you might do for another business includes product assembly, writing computer programs, and functioning as a sales representative. It is now a common practice for corporation sales reps to work from their homes or apartments, with the company providing their sales people with computers for telecommunicating with the home office. Some companies even subsidize the rent of their sales personnel who work from home, and the company encourages them to rent larger apartments so a room can be devoted exclusively to the business. Yes, that sounds like a lot of money to be putting into a sales force, but these people are the key to making the business profitable.

If you aren't interested in any of the jobs listed above, the best chance of getting a job working from home is to convince your present employer of the advantages of your working at home. But don't barge in some morning and lay this idea on the boss. Build your case. First, work to become an invaluable employee. Next, start taking a little work home at night, and return in the morning with the job done to perfection. Increase the amount of work that goes home, and ask, for instance, if you can work on a special project at home where there are fewer interruptions. Always return with exceptionally good work to show your supervisor. After it becomes obvious that you are just as effective at home as you are in the office, ask if you could work at home a couple of days each week. You do have a little leverage. It takes money and time to train personnel and even though there are a lot of people out there who might want your job, it is in the company's best interest to retain you and reduce turnover. Consistently work to convince your superior you can do your job at home. If you are allowed this, keep in contact with the main office. It's risky for your career to spend all of your working time at home, because you can miss out on special projects, and gradually lose your position in the pecking order. Schedule certain days in the office to make your presence known, to hear shop talk, and to catch up on what is going on. And don't hesitate to ask for instructions for your homework since your supervisor will not be around to give you directions.

If you cannot convince your current boss to allow you to work at home, then look elsewhere. Freelance work is one way to get started with a business, and as your work load increases, you will gradually become their "relied upon" home worker. But beware! If you get started this way, you can become a full-time worker without the benefits of other full-time employees. In fact, pay schedules and work benefits for home workers must be clearly defined. For instance, how many hours will you work; how will you be paid; and what benefits will go with the job? Can you move to the office if you want, and will you continue to be promoted if you aren't in the office? Whose equipment and supplies will you use? These are all questions that need to be addressed.

Resource: *Work-at-Home Sourcebook: Over One Thousand Job Opportunities Plus Home Business Opportunities and Other Options.* 4th ed. Lynie Arden, 1992. Live Oak Publishers, 1515 23rd St., P.O. Box 2193, Boulder, CO 80306.

3 A Review of Several Successful Home Businesses

This chapter describes several successful cottage industries, including at least one for each type of business discussed in the previous chapter. Whether you are leaning toward a manufacturing or a service business, or considering making and selling original compositions or working for an employer, try to visualize yourself in the businesses described below to see how they appeal to you. As I talked with the people reviewed in this chapter, I noticed they all have a lot of energy and enjoy being responsible for making their businesses work. That enthusiasm and fun seems to draw customers to them and is partly responsible for their success.

A MANUFACTURING BUSINESS
Printed Tree, Inc.

Printed Tree, Inc. is our family business. It has convinced me there is no place like home to hang out a shingle and bring in the bread.

I never realized people could make so much money at home. My husband, daughter and I operate a hand-crafted gift products business from the basement of our home. Before starting this business, Wayne and I were perfectly content doing our regular work — he is a college professor and I am a freelance writer — and we weren't particularly interested in the business world. Our daughter Janet majored in business and marketing in college. She interned at a gift manufacturing company during her senior year and discovered that manufacturing can be a good way to make money. She watched closely during her internship, learning how to produce and market merchandise. When she

saw the account books and realized the significance of those
black numbers on the balance sheet, she decided to start her
own manufacturing business. Knowing that it would take more
time, energy and money than she could offer, she asked if we
would join her in this venture. We agreed and became equal
partners. Little did we know how that decision would change
our lives.

Janet lives in an apartment several miles from our home,
and my husband and I live in a quiet neighborhood surrounded
by lovely neighbors and where kids and dogs abound. We have
converted our 1200 sq. ft. finished basement into our business
quarters. We feel it is important to keep our business activities
within the confines of our home, that neighbors remain
oblivious to our activities, and that the character of the
neighborhood is not changed in any way by our cottage industry.

The business we developed involves the manufacture of
handmade products that we sell through sales representatives
and mail order catalogs throughout the country. To get started
we selected the name, PRINTED TREE, INC., simply because
it has a pleasing ring and sounds rather noncommittal, yet it
might suggest various paper products ranging from books to
greeting cards. The truth is, we didn't know where we were
headed, the kinds of products we might manufacture, or in what
direction the company might evolve. We needed a name that
was flexible.

The company was incorporated immediately (cost $36.00
— we did the legal work, see Resource in Chapter 11) in order
to protect our personal lives and property. After calculating
that about $3,000 would be needed to get underway, we each
bought $1,000 worth of stock, using personal funds to buy the
stock rather than borrowing money from a lending agency.

Next, a logo was designed to fit the company name, and
with the logo and name in place, stationery was printed costing
a total of $65.00 for 500 sheets of letterhead and 500 envelopes.
Chores were divided and our jobs were defined: Janet was put
in charge of marketing, I took responsibility for product
development and inventory control, and Wayne took over all
office work.

While I concentrated on developing a product, Janet ran
an ad (cost $15.00) in the trade magazine, *Gifts and Decorative
Accessories*. She advertised for sales reps to carry our lines. What
lines, you're probably asking? We still didn't have any products
to sell, but since we knew the lag time is several months between
placing an ad and getting responses, the advertisement alluded

to a line of potpourri products, since we thought the first lines would include potpourri. Meanwhile, Wayne and I prowled the stores and craft shows for ideas. When we thought of a possible product, we asked for it in many stores and were delighted when the clerks said, "Sorry, we don't have anything like that." This was exactly what we had hoped to hear because it indicated a unfilled niche in the marketplace. I put together many trial products, and the three of us discussed their potential. It took a lot of talking to get our business up and running. Some days we would actually get hoarse and tired from talking. When evaluating a possible product, several things had to be considered: Was there a market for the product, and did it have a favorable chance of good sales? Were the needed materials readily available and was the cost reasonable? Was the product designed for greatest efficiency in construction and with little lost material? And, could it be made and sold for a profit? We finally decided on several products and we were on our way.

Suppliers were needed and we discovered a wonderful way to find them. There is a set of books housed in most libraries, called the *Thomas Register,* which gives invaluable information about who produces what in this country. Many of Printed Tree's suppliers of raw materials were located through this source (and were contacted through their free 800 telephone numbers.) Other suppliers were found by going to stores and copying the names and addresses from items for sale. Using our newly printed business stationery, we started contacting businesses who might be suppliers. I'm sure my finger got shorter those days as I dialed the number of many companies listed in the *Yellow Pages* in an effort to locate supplies and services. While many of these companies did not carry the specific items we needed, some offered advice as to where they might be found. This search and discovery also included looking for the best price for each item needed.

Next, catalogs had to be prepared for the sales reps who would be answering our advertisement. The catalogs needed to show the items manufactured by Printed Tree with descriptions and prices. We quickly discovered that a catalog containing glossy pages with colored photos was too expensive for our fledgling company. Also, the minimum order for printing these fancy catalogs is rather large, and once printed, it would be difficult to change the products. We sensed that flexibility was the key to surviving the early stages of business. We refused to get tied to anything that could inhibit our ability to make quick changes.

As an alternative, samples were made of all the products we planned to offer and, using our 35 mm camera, we took colored photos of them. A full roll of film was taken of each of the products and multiple copies were ordered when they were processed. This provided enough photos to put together sales sheets showing the Printed Tree products. Information sheets explaining the products and their costs were typed and copied. The color photos, along with swatches of fabric were pasted onto the information sheets, and the completed sheets were slipped into clear, heavy plastic folders — the type that could be added to the sales rep's catalogs. The total cost of assembling these sales catalogs was $93.00. We put a lot of energy into making them look good because this would be our first contact with the sales reps, and we wanted to impress them so they would accept our line for marketing. Also, the sales reps would use these folders to sell the products to shop owners and buyers. We tried to visualize how the reps would use the folders, thinking though the process of entering a shop, opening their portfolio, and trying to get orders for merchandise. We designed our folders to attract attention. An example of the thought that went into the process: We bought plastic folders a fraction larger than most on the market so that, when thumbing through the whole portfolio, our folder would stick out from the rest and might make the buyer pause to look at the merchandise.

By this time we began feeling an urgency to get some merchandise ready and an inventory built. Some supplies were gathered — lace, cotton prints, ribbons, potpourri ingredients, plastic bags for the finished products, and "headers" to clip on the tops of the bags (cost $640.00.) We started sewing and stuffing. At this point we could not afford to hire workers so we spent MANY hours making the items, building up quite an inventory to sell. Meanwhile, the magazine ad had appeared, and we were getting a good response from sales reps who were curious about, and possibly interested in, selling the Printed Tree line. We had prepared POLICY AND COMMISSION sheets (we pay 15% commission to sales reps), and sent them, along with the photo/product information sheets, to selected reps who answered our ad. A road kit containing samples was also sent to each rep. We studied the resume and the territory covered by each of the reps and began hiring. We realized the importance of hiring effective sales reps because they are given exclusive rights to sell in a given territory. That area is lost as a market if they are unsuccessful. We found it worthwhile to give the reps a "try," and if they failed to sell enough, replace them with someone else.

Not all of our products sold well. (That is an understatement, as you will shortly learn); so we kept changing them, eliminating and adding, until we settled into a steady pattern of sales. That's easier said than done. I can't help but laugh when I think of one of the first products we put out. It was my idea and I was absolutely certain that it would rival hoola hoops and Raggedy Ann. It didn't. Very simply, the item was called Bosom Buddy. It was a small lace bag on a satin cord filled with a delicate potpourri. It was trimmed with tiny ribbons and was to be worn like a necklace and hang at the bosom; thus, the name Bosom Buddy. Now isn't that clever? Sales don't lie. I still can't believe that not a SINGLE one sold! Obviously it was a bad idea. Thank goodness our other products sold well or we would have been forced to close shop. From that experience we learned the importance of testing the sales potential of a new product on a limited market before introducing it into the national market. To get a feel for the market, we now make a few samples of each new product being considered and try selling them to shops in our hometown. The response to a new product is immediate and sometimes very surprising. A product that we think could be a "hot item" might not merit a glance from buyers, but when buyer after buyer picks up a product, turns it over and feels the cloth and maybe even sniffs it, we know it's time to gear up for production. New products that sell well in the test territory are added to the nationally marketed line. If a product does not sell, we dump it, move on, and never look back. We've learned that "good" ideas don't necessarily sell — that people tend to shy away from unfamiliar items and buy things they feel comfortable with, things that are variations on a well-established theme.

Money was tight at first. Many things are needed when a business gets underway, from scales for weighing shipments ($65.00) to a seemingly endless array of supplies (tape, boxes, postage) — and everything costs money. And since we were the new kids on the block and had no credit rating, everything needed to be prepaid or paid for when it was delivered (COD). And there is a long lag time between buying supplies to make products and actually getting the money from selling those products. During this period (which in retrospect was very brief, only five months) we barely hung on, and wondered if we would ever see a profit. During this period the three of us made everything that was sold, which was a very large task. Finally the profits started to come in and the whole operation smoothed out. That was the point when we began hiring workers to make the items, and the long hours eased into regular work hours.

Hiring Workers for Your Business

Hiring workers is straight forward. A listing in the 'Help Wanted' section of the local papers brings an amazing number of responses. We advertised for part-time workers with sewing machines to work in their homes, and for retired men to build wooden objects in their own work shops. Although the work isn't hard, it must be done well since we sell our products for a good price, based on the premise that they are of good quality. Therefore, we need workers who take pride in the quality of their work. Which of the people who answers an ad and wants a job will do the best work? It's hard to tell, so we take a lot of chances. Most of the people we have hired try hard to do good work, but we've had to replace a few who couldn't or wouldn't do an adequate job.

After hiring a helper, we teach the person how to make the product and supply them with the materials and equipment they'll need. This part-time help, working in their own homes, has allowed our business to grow and flourish without adding overhead. Also, by providing the supplies and having our helpers work in their own homes, we are freed from paying taxes and benefits for the workers. They are responsible for their own taxes, since we, in a legal sense, are buying back finished products.

Keep the Neighbors Happy

In order to keep movement in our neighborhood to a minimum, supplies are delivered and finished products are picked up at the homes of the helpers. The only unusual activity that neighbors can observe is a daily visit by the UPS truck, when the truck is loaded with boxes destined for shops throughout the country. No sign is in the front yard, and we aren't even listed in the telephone book. To have our business listed would be like hoisting a flag, informing everybody, especially the neighbors, that we are operating a business at home. Even though this type of operation isn't illegal in our community, we find it's a good idea to keep the neighbors happy by keeping a low profile. Also, it costs a few more dollars to have a business listing in a telephone book, and since we sell through sales reps, a listing would yield very little extra business.

When you come into our home there isn't a single clue that it houses a very productive cottage industry. Every business item remains in the basement in order to keep our business lives separate from our personal lives. Also, we entertain frequently, sometimes on the spur of the moment, and do not want papers and other business-related things within the living area.

Yes, it works. We are continuously updating products and building territories. We have very little overhead, therefore the profits are building. Our business has spawned other cottage industries, because, as it has grown, we have hired an array of helpers — from ladies who sew to woodworkers who build display units, and tax consultants who keep us out of trouble. All these people are working in their own homes.

So what's the problem? We have come to a crossroad. The business has grown faster than anticipated, and is taking more time than we thought it might. We must decide if we will give up our other work and devote full time to our cottage industry, or if I will continue to write (which I love), if Wayne will continue to teach (which he loves), and hire more help for Janet. Another alternative is to keep the company small, but yielding a steady income. We are wrestling with this decision as of this writing.

A BUSINESS BASED ON CREATING AND SELLING ART
Steinkuhl's Art Studio

It's not an ideal location, and you wouldn't expect an art studio in such a remote area to be successful, but it is. Evelyn Steinkuhl paints and sells her work in a studio at the back of her home. It is off the beaten path, and might seem inconvenient for customers to visit, yet they come and they buy. Evelyn obviously enjoys people, and her warm easy manner and enthusiasm for her work keeps customers coming back to watch her paint and to buy more of her paintings. She has built a clientele by developing a style that is readily identifiable and by capturing well known scenes and architectural landmarks in her paintings. She knows how to play to the crowd and is riding the wave of nostalgia that is currently sweeping the country.

Steinkuhl was a "weekend painter" during the years she was raising her children, but after they left home she began concentrating on her painting and opened a studio. Her husband Ray enlarged and remodeled her studio and, more importantly, encouraged her as she tried to find her niche in the art world.

Making and selling artwork has been a cottage industry since before recorded history, when art wasn't sold for money but traded for goods and services. The industry has changed through the ages, and today it is perhaps the most widespread of all home businesses.

One of the problems with earning a living by making and selling original art is that it takes a great deal of time to produce an original composition, and then it can be sold only once, unlike manufactured items in which a pattern is used to clone an article many times over. An increasing number of artists are looking closely at the art market and, in an attempt to beat the "one piece equals one sale" formula, are having their work copied so a single composition can result in numerous sales. Painters are capturing a larger market by having prints made of their work. These do not cost nearly as much as the original, and most customers are perfectly content to own a print.

Evelyn Steinkuhl recognized the limitation of selling original art and reasoned she could generate more profit if she had prints made of her paintings. When she completes a piece that she thinks will have wide appeal, she has prints made of it.

The printing process is quite expensive, and Evelyn considers each printing a gamble. She has calculated that approximately fifty prints must be sold to cover the cost of one thousand prints; however, those sold after the first fifty are "gravy" and the potential for profit is significant. She considers this a gamble worth taking. Sometimes a "limited edition" is printed, after which the plates are destroyed. Limited edition prints are made on heavy, high quality paper and signed by the painter. Some may also be numbered, and these bring a higher price than those without a number. Both the prints and the original are put on the market. The price of the painting is influenced by the number of prints that have been made from it, with each print adding about one dollar to the cost of the original. Thus, a painting from which a thousand prints have been made would go for around a thousand dollars.

Steinkuhl's subjects have contributed to her success. A family might want "the old home place" captured in oils, and everybody in the family clamors for a copy. A large extended family might buy as many as several hundred prints.

A painting of a church draws even more interest, with the members of the congregation anxious to buy prints. The original is usually sold and hung in the church. This is especially effective when a new church is being planned or has been built. True to human nature, interest in the old church increases after it is torn down, and the painting of the original church gains a prominent place in the new building.

Steinkuhl also paints series — a group of pictures on a theme. This practice encourages those attracted to her work to buy more than one piece. A series might consist of some old well-known local buildings such as the railroad station, firehouse, and courthouse. Or she might paint the same building or scene through the four seasons. Another big seller is a series of covered bridges. Some collectors not only buy one of each print within a series, but they want the same numbered print for each picture within the series. This takes a little bookkeeping, but the extra effort results in both sales and satisfied customers.

Steinkuhl sells the prints and the originals from the studio in her home, and her work is shown in most of the galleries around town. She also shows and sells at art fairs. She offers her customers the option of buying prints with or without mats or frames, but has found that most customers prefer a piece that is ready to hang or give as a gift. She does all of her own matting, and her husband makes many of the frames.

Evelyn admits frankly that she doesn't win at many art shows, but she concentrates on producing what people are willing to buy. Blue-ribbon art show winners watch in dismay as she laughs all the way to the bank.

A BUSINESS BASED ON COMPOSING MUSIC
A Country and Western Music Writer
Makes (Radio) Waves

Don't expect this to be an instant success story. It's the story of a young woman who decided where she was going and formulated a plan to get there. Many others have had the same destination but have failed to reach it because their plans weren't detailed enough to show alternative pathways should something block their road to success.

Sharon Sanders Rudolph grew up in Nashville and has heard "country" for as long as she can remember. At an early age she knew she wanted to write country and western music and dreamed of hearing her music played over the radio. Sharon's work has been recorded by leading country and western singers, including Barbara Mandrell, Dave and Sugar, Zella Lehr and Judy Lyn. Now when tooling along the highway, her pride swells when she hears a familiar number come across the air waves.

Sharon is married with two small children. She works at home, composing music while perched on a stool behind a piano with a microphone and a tape machine recording her work sessions. If a session yields a good phrase or a nice progression of chords, they are taped to be used in a new number. Sharon usually writes both the words and music, but occasionally puts someone else's words to music.

She knows she must be be honest with herself and evaluate each new piece with detachment. After taping a new number, she gets in her car, takes a ride, and plays her music. She knows it's good if her reaction is to turn it up, but she also knows that if she'd rather change stations, it's time to erase the tape and try again.

You might be interested to know how one goes about presenting music to a recording studio. Many successful composers don't know how to read music or play an instrument. The notes are rarely written on a musical staff but are recorded on tape, while the typed words accompany the tape to the publisher or producer.

Publishers insist that the quality of the tape will not affect their decision to buy, but many writers put a lot of money and energy into producing a slick, professional-quality recording. Recording studios can provide background music as well as a singer if the writer doesn't want to perform. It costs about $400 to make a tape of three songs, and many composers spend a hefty sum trying again and again for that big break. Only a very few ever sell one of their numbers and recover some of their expenses. Still, the lure of the big break keeps them trying.

This is a tough market. It's much harder to sell and record music than to publish articles. The reason is simple supply and demand. New articles must be bought every day to fill the hundreds of magazines that are published each month. Once published, the editors need more material to fill the next month's issue. Music has a much longer life span, and a very limited number of new songs are needed by the recording studios.

There are reasons for Sharon's success. In the first place, she writes good material, but other people's good material remains unsung and unheard. The difference is the thoroughness of her marketing procedure.

The trick is to meet the movers and shakers of the country music industry. But before you can step into their offices you must know who these people are, who buys music, and which recording stars they represent. Sharon keeps track of who makes the decisions in the publishing companies, makes appointments and drives the 100 miles to take her tapes to the right people. She also makes it a point to know their secretaries since a secretary can be her key in getting to the boss.

She is determined to get a hearing for her work. Her tapes are usually played while she sits in the office with the publisher. She can explain bridges and emphasize the features that can heighten her chance for a sale. She also mentions artists who might use her songs. From her research she knows who needs new music. Her work is not lost among scores of tapes arriving in the daily mail. Most writers spend a bundle preparing a demo tape of their new songs, then mail it to Nashville, say a silent prayer and wait. Most of these tapes never get a hearing.

Sharon keeps her name in front of the publishers by dropping them a line whenever she has any sort of success, such as an airing on The Nashville Network. Sharon's career shows that patience is needed. It may take a lot of time before something is picked and used. For example, she recently received a nice check for a number she had submitted to a publisher years ago. The song had been unused until the right artist came along, whereupon it was recorded, and she received the royalties. On the other hand, a new song might be used immediately if it happens to match the sound of a recording artist who is looking for new material.

Some composers not only write music but also dream of becoming a singing star. They attempt to sell their voice along with their music, and this is a much more difficult package to sell. Sharon is only interested in hearing her songs recorded by an established vocalist. Sharon can sing but being a recording star means living and breathing the music world, going on the road to promote, and residing in Nashville. That life is incompatible with staying home, raising her kids, and being a partner in marriage while continuing to write music. Her goals are more realistic than those of the star-struck youngster who is ready to chuck their whole life style for a chance at stardom. Sharon admits that becoming a recording artist is a possibility, and she is keeping her "looks" intact in case she will move into recording when her children are older. But for now she is doing exactly what she wants to do — raising a family while staying home and minding her own business of writing country music.

DISTRIBUTORSHIPS:
Nancy and Mary Kay Show a Profit

Nancy Ahrens was teaching school when she decided something had to change. The rigid schedule was beginning to wear thin. She found herself wanting to stay home with her children but also wanting to earn a little money. Starting her own business meant too much responsibility and too much investment of herself and the family funds. As an alternative, she looked into serving as a distributor for another business. As you know, some companies such as Tupperware, Undergarment Wear, Avon, Herbal Life, and Shaklee market their merchandise through home-based distributors.

These distributorships offer flexible schedules, tried and tested products, name recognition, and training programs. A very small investment can get you started. A distributor has his own business, but with the support and benefits of a larger organization, or, as a promotion brochure reads, "Work for yourself but not by yourself."

After investigating several possibilities, Nancy decided to represent Mary Kay Cosmetics. The "start-up" kit, a small suitcase containing an assortment of cosmetic supplies, cost $85. Besides this, she ordered a modest inventory so she could sell products at her first show rather than take orders and deliver the merchandise at a later date.

Nancy has been selling these products for nearly a decade. She works 15 to 20 hours each week and makes as much as she did when she taught school. Each week she strives to have three skin care classes or "parties", and she meets each Monday evening with her "unit", which is composed of women she has recruited to sell the products and to whom she gives continued career guidance. Nancy also does private facials, either in her own home or in the client's and she takes reorders by phone.

The purpose of a skin care party is to sell cosmetics. The hostess invites guests and serves dessert, after which the guests are taught how to care for their skin and apply makeup. The hostess receives free merchandise, based on the amount her guests purchase and the number of bookings for subsequent parties they make.

Nancy likes to work at home. She would rather give skin care classes in her own dining room than drive across town with a satchel full of cosmetics to work in somebody else's home. So she offers each hostess an extra bonus if they invite guests but arrange for the party to take place in Nancy's home. The hostess is responsible for dessert but little else.

Nancy sells products to the women who attend her skin care classes. A class of five or six women might spend an average of $125, and she receives a whopping 50 percent of the total order. She also earns from four percent to 12 percent on the orders written by the saleswomen she supervises. Her percentage is based on the number of active recruits and the amount of their monthly sales, so she tries to keep her recruits happy and working. Her saleswomen earn their money through their own skin-care parties and private facials. A new recruit can expect to give three parties each week and to sell around $125 worth of merchandise at each party. She will earn 50 percent of her sales or around $187.

There is a reason for Nancy's success. She has made an effort to develop an attachment between herself and her customers — she offers a personal touch. After looking her clients in the eye from a distance of 12 to 15 inches while applying the various lotions and potions used during the facial, and helping them apply the products, she feels she begins to know the women. She keeps in touch with these new acquaintances through little notes or a recipe she might pop into the mail. You can be sure this personal attention yields increased sales.

Nancy has a well-equipped office in her home, with a photocopier, answering machine, filing cabinets, beauty kits, and clusters of cosmetics between the stacks of papers and mailings. The only evidence that this office has served another purpose are the slightly faded toy soldiers still marching across the wallpaper.

Companies which sell through home-based distributors have different approaches to marketing. Most do not limit their distributors to a particular territory, but allow them to sell wherever they can find a customer. Some companies are more innovative than others. In a company with a multi-level or pyramid structure recruits earn on the basis of where they are on the pyramid. Other companies, such as Mary Kay Cosmetics, allow their distributors to earn money through their own retail sales and through the sales of the workers they recruit but there is no deep pyramiding. This latter plan is a more equitable program and is more stable for the people involved.

If you consider this type of work, look at the marketing approaches of the various companies you might represent and study their products. Talk to someone who has sold the products but preferably someone who is no longer with the company. If they are still working for the organization they may try to sell you on the idea of joining, as one of their recruits and, consequently, you may not get an impartial evaluation of the company.

If the company sells a consumable product such as cosmetics, vitamins, or detergent, you have the opportunity for reorders. If the products have a reputation for durability and even have a lifetime guarantee (such as Tupperware), then the chance for reorders is reduced, although customers who have a good experience with the product will sometimes buy more for themselves or to give as gifts. Other companies (such as Avon) stimulate sales by incorporating "collector's items" into their merchandise. Like lambs to the slaughter, buyers line up to lay out cash and start collecting, not because the product is worth collecting but because of the magic of semantics and because they are in the habit of following without thinking. As you consider the various businesses, look for one that will not only produce the sales and profit you expect, but also one that fulfills your expectations of a satisfying home business.

A SERVICE BUSINESS
The Speedometer Shop

My parents, at 83 and 77, are working every day in their home business, a speedometer repair shop. Retirement and the prospect of sitting idle didn't appeal to my Dad, Ed Frohbieter. Dad owned and operated a large auto repair shop and employed numerous mechanics, parts men, and office help. At the age of 70 he started thinking about what part of his business he might like to take along into retirement. He sold the main part but retained a very defined unit — the speedometer repair portion. His experience with the auto service industry taught him just how many speedometers needed repairing, and he knew that very few people had the skill and equipment. As he grew older he could do this "sit down" work easier than other auto mechanic jobs.

The Speedometer Shop is located in a garage behind my parent's home. A few changes were made to accommodate the business. A two-car garage was enlarged to twice its original size, and the walls were lined with shelves to hold the many parts needed for the repair work. A heater and several extension telephones were installed, along with a refrigerator, running water, and a toilet and sink, the latter items being added to keep the traffic, dirty hands and feet confined to the shop and out of the home.

Most of the tools and special equipment needed came from Dad's original business. Not only did he take the equipment from his earlier business, but he also took his customers along.

Dad deals only with auto repair businesses not with individual car owners. Mechanics bring in the defective speedometers — ones they have removed from cars they are working on in their shops. Consequently, there is never a car with a raised hood in the driveway or customers standing around waiting for a job to be completed. Thus, the business fits nicely into a residential neighborhood.

Mom plays an integral part in the family business. She is responsible for bookkeeping, billing, and picking up parts needed to complete the repairs. Her office is tucked into an extra bedroom that converts into a guest room when one of the kids or grandchildren comes to visit. She does her business chores between household work and social activities. And she keeps a steady stream of food going to neighbors and friends, many of whom are much younger than my parents, but who still need a little help. The only outside help Mom and Dad use is a tax consultant.

This couple is financially comfortable and doesn't need the added income brought in by the speedometer repair work, but they seem to enjoy being a part of the working world. In the 13 years since Dad sold his larger business and started working from home, The Speedometer Shop has been nicely integrated into their lives. They meet the challenges of operating a business while enjoying a more relaxed working day, a quiet moment at morning tea, and a short nap after lunch. There is time to go fishing and time to take an extended vacation in their recreational van and, since their customers are specific auto repair shops rather than the general public, they can quickly give notice when they will be gone for an extended period.

Their work has kept this couple young at heart, financially comfortable, and actively participating in the business and social world. Thinking back over his working life, my Dad might wonder why he struggled so mightily to run a large business when the smaller one he is now operating is so much more pleasant and comes with fewer headaches. The expenses of his large business — including shop space, equipment, and payroll — continued whether business was good or bad, while his home business has little overhead, no payroll and a steady stream of customers. At 83, Dad is thinking he might take a partner, someone who might be interested in learning the business and buying it when he is ready for his second retirement.

A "SPECIAL OCCASION CAKE" BUSINESS
The Cake Lady

Doris Schumacher runs a cake baking service from her home. She bakes wedding cakes the likes of which this part of the world has seldom seen. As a result of her cake-baking and cake-building prowess, her reputation has spread, and her services are in such demand that among the first things a newly engaged couple does is to contact The Cake Lady to reserve her services for their special day.

Doris lives in a rural area, but close enough to town for the bride-to-be and her mom to make the sojourn to her bakery. She greets customers and guides them to a table in the center of a spacious indoor cactus garden. It is here where pictures of her cake styles are shown, prices discussed, dates are reserved and plans are finalized. This lady has such an outgoing personality that you feel as if you've known her for years after that first meeting. It's not uncommon for a customer who has admired one of the plants in her flower garden, to leave with a piece of root tucked in some wet paper toweling, ready for transplanting.

When Doris started her cake-baking business, she baked in her household kitchen and baked well into the night to meet the looming deadlines. But she quickly realized she had stumbled onto an unfilled niche and enlarged her operation to take advantage of the business opportunity. Her husband became a business partner when he retired, and they built a special building for their business which is conveniently located down a short path beside their home. It is equipped with two standard-sized ovens and a complete kitchen. This building is needed to provide enough oven and decorating space, but it also allows them to maintain a semblance of order and serenity in the family home, and to keep out the heat of baking. (It functions somewhat like the "summer kitchens" of long ago, where our grandmothers canned and baked on hot summer days.)

Most wedding receptions occur on weekends, therefore, the cakes for these receptions must be baked late in the week. Doris uses the early part of the week to clean and put order into the kitchen, order supplies, and make sugar ornaments that will decorate the cakes. She and her husband begin baking early Thursday morning, and they continue baking into Friday. A large part of making a wedding cake is decorating it with the flourishes — sugar flowers, and swags of icing — and this begins after all the cakes have been baked. Working together, she and her husband function as a cake-decorating assembly line designed to save time and motion. After the last sugar rose is in position, the cakes are partially assembled and prepared for delivery.

A specially appointed van is used to deliver the exquisite confections. There is no room for error — each cake must arrive on time and in perfect condition. Many cakes must be delivered within a very short time span, so a route is laid out and arrival times are planned to the minute. Each cake is delivered in several parts and assembled to form the complete cake after they are safely within the reception room.

It's a thriving business, and Doris and her husband are making a nice profit because they deliver good service. The only advertising they do, other than business cards, is to participate in an annual "Bridal Show" where Doris sets up an elaborate display of their wares. This show gives them the opportunity to demonstrate their specialties including cakes built around fountains, fresh flowers, and lights. Most of their clients are acquired via a grapevine of pleased customers passing the word. The Cake Lady has all the business she can handle, with some bookings as far ahead as two years for special events like golden anniversaries. She is often forced to turn away customers.

Doris readily admits she couldn't do the work alone. She needs her husband's help, and they work together daily. This is the feeling of a great many other men and women who work at home. I have found a large number of homeworkers have the support and help of their mates, and this seems to make their work less demanding and more fun.

This cake baking business is a good example of someone who has taken advantage of known skills and converted them into a profitable business by expanding the skills, taking a partner, enlarging the business facility, and growing to meet a receptive market.

By contrast, another woman started a "Special Occasion Cookie" business that failed. As I compare the cake and cookie businesses, I feel the reason one failed and the other succeeded is the difference in the cost of the products. Specialty cakes command a handsome price, but we aren't willing to pay very much for a huge cookie no matter how fancy it is. We are willing to pay more for wedding and special occasion cakes because they are used for once-in-a-lifetime events, while large fancy cookies are used for parties, usually children's parties, and we don't tend to spend that kind of money for kid's party food, especially since the cookie is often only one of several party foods.

The six businesses that have been reviewed represent a diversity of business types, each fulfilling distinctive goals. They came into being via various routes and have met different needs. As I interviewed the entrepreneurs, I noticed they share several common characteristics. They are positive people who obviously enjoy their work. They are quick to spot opportunities and willingly accept help and suggestions from their mates, and each one of them feels a sense of satisfaction in making their business succeed.

And One that Failed... the Reasons

It's a little misleading to relate the stories of several successful businesses and a single failure because statistics show that more businesses fail than succeed. But this book was written to help you *build* a business and therefore the emphasis is on success and not failure. Nonetheless, it is instructive to study a business that failed, if for no other reason than to understand the importance of planning for success, watching for weaknesses, and correcting a problem before it destroys the business.

Tolstoy's *Anna Karenina* begins with the line, "Happy families are all alike; every unhappy one is unhappy in its own way." That line can be changed a bit and applied to businesses: "Successful businesses are all alike; every unsuccessful business is unsuccessful in its own way." Or so it seems. Actually, while each failure has its own idiosyncrasy, the reasons for failure fall within basic categories such as financial, personnel, product or service-related problems, and so forth. The following review focuses on a business that failed for several reasons and suggests ways that it might have been saved.

A MANUFACTURING BUSINESS
The Clock Works

Terry was a metal fabricator at a local manufacturing company. He was paid an hourly wage and made a reasonably good income. Terry had spent many years "on the line" and had seniority, so he was surprised and shaken when he got a pink slip. The line he worked was being shut down because of slow orders, and there were rumors that the whole section where he worked was to be phased out. At 32, with a wife and two kids to support, he could lose little time looking for a job.

Looking for work was a new experience for Terry. He was just a kid when he started working with the manufacturing company and had never known unemployment. As he made the rounds of several small factories in the area, he quickly discovered that the other men who had been laid off along with him were also making the rounds, vying for the same few jobs in town. It wasn't long before he realized the chance of finding a job in his line of work was very slight and he would need to find another way to earn a living.

Terry was good at building things. He knew how to work with wood, and he instinctively knew how to put things together. He had grown up in front of a workbench and, as an adult, spent many leisurely weekends making handcrafted items that he and his wife gave as gifts. More recently, he had been making clocks after happening upon an inexpensive supplier of clock works. He designed many different styles of cases and clock faces to go with the works. The one for his son's room used small baseball bats for hands, and the clock for his mother was made on a miniature washboard. He also made a clock face from an old phonograph record, and for the very modern, he designed a desk clock from a computer floppy disk. Many of the clock faces he designed suggested hobbies. Some looked "country", others were art deco, and still others were contemporary.

When his efforts to find a job failed, he wandered into his shop, looked at the diversity and quality of his clocks and thought, why not? And with that his business was born.

It didn't take much to get underway. Terry had been collecting tools for years and had mastered the skills to use them. He had already developed an assortment of unusual clock designs, so the only things he needed were wood and different sizes of clock works. Even though he had no income, he could manage to buy these few supplies. Without much ado, Terry was making clocks and he became totally absorbed in the process of manufacturing an assortment of the unique timepieces.

Days turned to weeks while Terry kept busy at his workbench making clocks. When his inventory began to fill his workspace he knew he had no choice but to get out of his shop and start selling. After all, the reason for this work was to make money.

He hadn't thought much about how to sell the clocks, but knew other craftspeople sold their products at craft fairs. He thought he might do the same, selling a few at flea markets and at the local craft shows and fairs that took place in his hometown several times each year. He also planted a sign in his front yard, with a huge clock face that told passing motorists the time of day. He expected some of the motorists to stop for a closer look and perhaps buy a clock. He also intended to sell some to gift shops for resale.

Terry liked making the clocks but hated trying to convince a shopkeeper to carry the various styles he made. It was deflating for him to have his clocks rejected because he was used to being surrounded by friends who praised his work and enjoyed receiving the clocks as gifts. Neither did he enjoy the crowds at craft fairs. He had hoped to demonstrate clock making while tending his booth, but spent his time trying to keep an eye on kids who wouldn't keep their hands off the clock hands. And he didn't sell many clocks at the fairs. At several fairs he barely made enough money to pay for his booth rental. His best avenue for sales proved to be the big clock ticking away in his front yard, beckoning customers in for a closer look.

Sales seemed to be going rather well, and although he didn't get any big orders, a steady trickle of business kept coming in. That is why he was perplexed when, after several months, he realized his profit didn't seem equal to his efforts, and he began to feel "the faster he worked the behinder he got." Terry had not yet put pen to paper and worked with the numbers, and when he finally did figure income and expenses, he was in for a big surprise.

Terry's clocks fell more into the realm of craft items than quality clocks, and they wholesaled for an average of only $8.00. When he sold them at fairs or from his home he got the retail price, which averaged $16.00 each. If he sold equal numbers at the wholesale and retail prices, the average price he received per clock was $12.00. The supplies needed to make a clock cost $4.00; therefore, his profit was around $8.00 each. Sounds good enough. But then he calculated the number of clocks he must make in order to have an income of $16,000 per year. Without including overhead expenses such as electricity for the woodworking tools, boxes and packing materials, travel to and from shows and stores, and many other incidentals, he calculated he would need to make 2,000 clocks each year. There are approximately 250 working days every year (365 minus weekends and holidays), so Terry would need to make 8 clocks each day. He thought he could do that. But some days had to be spent selling rather than making clocks, and those overhead expenses couldn't be dismissed, so they were added to the calculations. At the very minimum, Terry figured he would need to make from 15 to 18 clocks each woodworking day in order to earn only $16,000 per year, and that profit would be realized only if all the clocks were sold. The numbers were sobering. He knew he couldn't make clocks that fast, but even with the data before him, he proceeded as if everything might somehow work out.

After a few more months it became apparent that the stockpile of clocks was growing, but the income from the small amount of sales was totally inadequate to support a family. In an effort to increase sales, Terry's wife started calling on gift shops. She learned which clocks were the most appealing to the shop owners and started making sales. She even expanded her territory to include all towns within a seventy mile radius of their home. But it was a tough job and after a particularly exasperating day she decided she could earn more money working in an office. Using one of the contacts she made while peddling her husband's wares, she found an office job. When she stopped her sales efforts, it became clear that The Clock Works really didn't work.

Terry wasn't willing to give up. He liked making the clocks and he had developed many clever designs. But how do you sell this kind of thing? He knew one of the shopkeepers rather well and asked how other companies sell their products. He was learning about sales reps and marketing procedures when, nine months after his layoff, he was called back to work. The frustration of the past months could be measured by the speed with which he dropped his tools and fled to the security of a regular paycheck.

The story might end there, but it doesn't. Terry had failed to make his business work, but he had experienced the pleasure of spending his days at his workbench. He remains convinced that his clocks will sell if they are marketed correctly. Now, with a paycheck taking the pressure off the business, he is doing the legwork he should have done before the business was ever started. He is preparing for success by developing a marketing plan. He has also looked closer at the prices he charged and has adjusted them to more reflect the materials, time, and overhead needed to make them. He is putting together a professional-looking promotion and sales kit of printed materials to present his line of clocks, and he plans to promote his business on a part-time basis. If the business grows as he suspects it might, the next layoff will find Terry working at a successful home business.

Managing Your Time

How much time do you have "on your hands"? Isn't that a strange expression? Every moment of every day is probably filled. So where do you expect to "find enough time" to run a business? As you sit and consider alternatives, "time marches on," and you have probably learned that "time waits for no man." But "these are the times that try men's souls,", and as a result of our modern economic situation and "at this point in time", many of us need to "find time" to earn money at home. As you get your business underway, don't let your work consume your life, but "take time to smell the roses."

Our literature and lives are filled with expressions about time. The one that immediately comes to mind is Benjamin Franklin's statement: "Do not squander time, for that is the stuff life is made of." Franklin also said, "Remember that time is money." If we reach far into our past we find Aristotle saying, "Time is the most valuable thing that a man can spend," and a few centuries later Dante wrote, "He who knows most, the loss of time most grieves." In the 16th century Rabelais wrote, "Nothing is so dear and precious as time," and finally, Napoleon told one of his aides, "You can ask me for anything you like, except time."

Everybody has the same amount of time each day. You can count on 24 hours or 1,440 minutes, and it's what you do with those precious minutes that will determine who you are, what you are, and how successful and happy you are. Some people use their time without thinking about it, while others plan how to spend their time by defining the goals they want to accomplish.

It's interesting to think about this idea of "spending time." We each have a time account like most of us have a bank account,

but there are distinct differences between the two. In the first place, you can't save time in the same sense that you can save money. As each moment passes you have one less moment left in your life, so respect your time as a piece of your life. You have *no choice* but to spend your time, but you may choose to save your money. Once spent, time cannot be replaced, whereas it's a matter of time before you can replenish your bank account. People who go from store to store trying to find the best sale in town are sometimes delighted at the amount of money they have saved, yet are seemingly oblivious to the more valuable asset they have spent — their limited time, that non-renewable resource. Clearly, time is the most valuable commodity we own. If you really want a bargain, don't worry about "saving time," for that is impossible, but try to get more for your time: plan, define goals, organize, make routines.

As you start your new business you will discover the myriad of jobs you must do demands that you spend your time wisely — that you learn to MANAGE YOUR TIME. Time management should become a way of life. Just being aware of the concept of time management will make you sensitive to lost moments and alert you to "time bargains." It is worth it to consciously incorporate time management procedures into your day.

ORGANIZE YOUR TIME

Organize your work to accomplish more in a given amount of time. This requires you to make some decisions. First, you must define exactly what you want to accomplish, to establish objectives, to SET GOALS. Goals were discussed in a general sense in an earlier chapter, but when you are trying to get organized, your goals must be very specific. In the case of a home business, your daily and long range goals will include both home goals and business goals. Setting out goals in mind only is not good enough because unwritten goals remain nebulous thoughts, not clearly defined. Your goals need to be written down, to be read and edited until you are satisfied they truly reflect your objectives.

After deciding upon a destination, TURN GOALS INTO TASKS. Household tasks might include preparing dinner, and maybe shopping, while business tasks might be getting orders out, finishing letters to clients and the like.

Having decided on the tasks that need to be done, make a decision as to which ones are the most important; that is, SET PRIORITIES. If getting out orders is more important than preparing dinner, and only one of the two can be done, then start working on the orders. You can invite Colonel Sanders to dinner.

Having defined goals and turned goals into tasks, the moment is at hand to find ways to "save" time. There are several techniques to maximize your efficiency, allowing you to get more accomplished in a given period of time. Each will be discussed in detail below.

MAKE A WORK SCHEDULE

When would you like to work? You have a choice! One of the reasons many people start a home business is because they want the opportunity to choose the times they work.

Some people plan their work schedules around their peak performance time. Morning people get out of bed alert and anxious to start working while the sun is still trying to get up and the family hasn't begun to stir. The household is quiet, the telephone silently rests in its cradle, and the only sounds to be heard are the early morning birds and maybe the hum of a computer or the rhythm of a sewing machine. These people will have the best part of their day's work done by the time the rest of the world starts moving around.

Others like to work late at night, again when the rest of the household is tucked in. Night people might spend the day caring for their family but save their creative work for the solitude of night. It can be a startling revelation to these people, when forced to be out early, to see households with lights streaming from the kitchen window and cars on the road with occupants obviously comfortable with this part of the day.

And then there are people who work throughout the day, following much the same schedule they would follow if they worked away from home. The difference is that now, working at home, they have the option to plan household and work tasks to better fulfill their personal needs and preferences.

The nature of some businesses dictates working schedules. I have a friend who operates a learning center for children — children who are either having trouble in school or who are especially advanced and need extra mental stimulation. This service can be offered only when the children are not busy at school, so she starts work just before the school day is over, filing and preparing records, and works with children throughout the late afternoon and early evening.

Work can be planned around another priority. Mothers

might spend their daytime caring for small children, and start their business-related work when their husbands relieve them after THEIR work day. A special interest might also play a part. One of my networking friends is a long-distance bicycle rider and she starts to work after returning from her daily 20- to 30-mile ride.

A rigid, formalized schedule is followed by some work-at-homers, while others prefer a less formal, but nonetheless, organized schedule. In either case, the work will get done if a ROUTINE is established and followed. Let's look at what might happen when a routine is broken. Consider the night worker who has established a nightly work pattern and reaches peak performance in the wee hours of the morning. If this worker is busy with a big project and works late into the night, and then, breaking the pattern, gets up early the following morning to continue the work, less work will get done in the long run. By the end of the second day, when the night worker is normally moving into prime work-time, he or she is too exhausted from getting up early, and prime work-time is lost. Even while a big project is in progress, the best way to bring it to completion is to follow a schedule religiously and concentrate on the project, leaving less urgent tasks to be done after the project is completed.

Plan how many hours you will work and schedule specific hours. You should be acutely aware of the time it will take to run a home business. You will probably need to work many more hours than when you worked for somebody else, so plan to make this commitment, and give your business that extra push it needs. How many hours? You might need to devote as many as 10 to 14 hours, maybe even more, to your business each day as it gets underway. If you don't have that much time to give to a business, that's OK. Your business will grow slower if you can devote only a small part of each day to it, but starting slowly isn't such a bad idea. It allows you to develop your work patterns and your product, and to integrate your business into your daily life.

IT'S TIME TO GO TO WORK

Homeworkers sometimes have a problem getting to work because there is no bus to catch or car pool to meet. On a cold winter morning the snugly comfort of your bed seems to offer a refuge from the chill that lingers in the household, and it is very tempting to crawl back between the blankets after turning up the thermostat. Twenty minutes lost. Or, just one more cup of coffee might get the blood circulating. Fifteen minutes lost. After dressing for work, you might remember the plants need watering. Twenty-two minutes lost. And you really should fold the wash in case the kids need some socks for school. Twelve minutes lost. If you aren't careful you can squander the entire day doing odds and ends. If a job needs doing, or if you want to do other things before going to work, it should be on your schedule. But don't use it to avoid getting to work.

It might be necessary to fabricate a morning ritual that moves you from being a homebody to being a business person. Just having a starting time, an hour to report to work, is enough for some people, but it is easier if a starting time follows a regular happening of some sort. You could go to your office or shop after the morning news, or you could take a brisk walk or an early morning jog and then immediately start your day's work. Or, kiss the kids and spouse goodbye before reporting for work. Select a signal that works for you, and use the same signal each morning to start your business day.

PLAN YOUR DAY

Getting to your office or shop is but part of the battle; you must also get your work under way. Each morning is a new challenge, and sometimes you'd probably just as soon not be challenged. After all, the house might still be a little chilly and, in the dead of winter, it's probably not even very light when you start your workday. You might sit down, stare at the walls and wonder, "What am I doing here?" Well, you've got a job to do and the best way to get started is to do the same thing every morning. First, clean off your desk. You should have left it clean when you stopped yesterday, but if you didn't, clean it first; don't start the day with a bunch of clutter. Find a place for everything on your desk — reports, correspondence, articles from magazines, notes about ideas.

On the bottom of the pile you will probably find your calendar. Begin your day by referring to your calendar. Keep only one calendar to schedule both family and business activities and tasks. Some people carry a small calendar in their purse or coat and use a large one at their desk. It can be a mistake. Two calendars can be misleading because the dates recorded in one rarely get transfered to the other. Use the type of calendar book that has a whole page for each day, but one that is small enough to carry to meetings and appointments. As soon as dates become known, put them in the calendar. Record school holidays, vacations, doctor or dentist appointments, sports events, social events, club meetings, business meetings, client's appointments, deadlines for projects and so forth. Also note dates when payments are due, bills should be sent, and correspondence written. Use your calendar for planning your day, week, month, and year. When your calendar has been used, and another one started, save the old calendar as a record of the past year's activities.

As you start each workday, list the tasks you hope to accomplish on that day. Include phone calls you should make, the main projects of the day, odd jobs, things to think about or read. Refer to yesterday's list, and if something was left undone, add it to the current list if it's still valid. Study the list and number the tasks in their order of importance. Next, in the corner of your schedule, jot down the dinner menu. If a roast needs to be thawed or jello needs to set, be sure to look after it during your morning break.

To get your mind in gear and your body functioning, it is helpful to leave something unfinished the previous day so you can start working without much thought. I have found it helpful to stop the day's work in the middle of a sentence if I'm writing, or with orders partially packed, if I'm filling orders. By doing this, it is easy to get to work the following morning and once started, one thing leads to another.

As your day unfolds, cross out each task after it is completed. This gives you that wonderful feeling of accomplishment. On many occasions I've forgotten to write down something that needed to be done, but after spending time and energy doing it, I wrote it down and crossed it out AFTER it was done. This is not only my reward system but a way of record-keeping.

GET MORE FOR YOUR TIME

There are a lot of "time saving" techniques, but first, in order to save time, you need to know where you are losing it. Think through your daily procedures and try to identify lost moments. The following are possible ways to save time:

1. Use time-saving devices. A conventional telephone takes five times longer to dial than a touch-tone telephone. Be sure to use a telephone with an extensive memory, allowing you to program and redial frequently called numbers. Other time-saving devices include a dishwasher, computer, fast printer, microwave oven, food processor, and tape recorder.

2. Organize information and materials. Time is lost

searching for things. Organize information from telephone numbers and addresses to suppliers and sources of information. Use filing procedures that give easy access to the information. For instance, a telephone number or address can be recovered more quickly from a Rolodex file than a file box containing 3×5 cards. Keep a filing cabinet with clearly marked file folders. Occasionally check the file and discard outdated material, or at least remove it from the active file and place it in an inactive file where it can be recovered if necessary.

Keep frequently used supplies and information at arms length, but place materials used less often outside the work area. Supplies used simultaneously should be kept together. An example is the assortment of items needed to ship orders. Boxes, packing material, tape, mailing labels, record book, information stamps, stamp pad, and rate card should all be in one area so shipments can be readied without unnecessary movement.

Have a specific place for each piece of equipment and every supply, and make a habit of returning the item to the same place each time it is used.

3. Do two or more things at once. We do a lot of things that don't require our undivided attention. Watch the news while emptying the dishwasher, fold the wash while waiting for a computer printout, fill the bobbins while your hot glue gun heats up, read while you're on the "john," make phone calls while taking a cigarette break.

4. Keep a record of how you spend your time. We have a tendency to think other people waste our time, and fail to recognize we are our own worst time wasters. People can waste our time only if we allow them to do it. Determine when you are not using your time well by keeping a record of how you spend your day. Eliminate time-wasting activities such as reading junk mail, writing a letter when a call would suffice, procrastinating, over-extending a coffee or lunch break or delaying decisions on unimportant matters.

5. Turn tasks into routines. Anything that can be converted into a routine will save time. Henry Ford made the assembly line a part of our industrial work pattern because he convincingly demonstrated that it could save time. You can develop your own assembly line while working alone at home — functioning first in one capacity, then moving to the next task, and repeating it until the product or process is complete. If you need to make fifty dolls, divide the process into a sequence of steps that can be done over and over again as a routine. It may not be quite as satisfying as making one doll completely before moving on

to the next, but the time saved makes it an acceptable tradeoff.

6. Practice saying "no." You will be tested. When it becomes apparent to others that you are working at home, you will be asked to do an assortment of jobs from baking cookies for Johnny's class party to leading the singing at a church meeting. Of course you should bake cookies when it's your turn, but after you have baked them, then it's the next person's turn, whether that person works at home or in a fancy office far away from home. And lead the singing at the church meeting? No, you weren't even planning to attend. It will take just a few "no's" for the callers to learn you aren't available for their endless missions. I am still stung when a well-meaning but thoughtless person asks me to do something, "since you don't work". They've GOT to be kidding!

7. Keep a list of small chores: a stack of letters that need stamps, a pile of folders that need filing, papers that need collating, and nails to file. Quick little household chores — from writing a thank-you note to peeling potatoes — each can be done while waiting for a call or an appointment or during the few spare moments that are "between-times." Use those little segments of the day to clear away an assortment of small tasks.

8. Think "efficiency." Your attitude toward time will influence how you use this limited resource. If you have slipped into the habit of procrastinating or "goofing off," make a conscious effort to break the habit. This can be done by making a schedule and refusing to allow other activities to keep you from it.

MAKE YOUR TELEPHONE WORK FOR YOU

Although it was briefly mentioned above, this special section is devoted to the telephone because it is so important to a home business. The telephone connects you to people. It connects you to both the business world and to your friends and family and can be a time-saver or a time-waster.

Whenever possible, "let your fingers do the walking," and don't go if you can call. Save your feet, time and patience by spending a few minutes working the *Yellow Pages* when you are looking for information.

The calls you make can save you time, but the calls you receive can be time consuming. Whether your caller is a customer or a friend wanting to pass the time of day, be prepared to deal with the other end of the telephone line. Learn to control the length of your conversations, and get back to work. Guard against long-winded talkers. It's very easy to get "caught" by someone who doesn't have a schedule to keep. When you feel a conversation should draw to a close, either thank the caller for contacting you or say, "It's been nice talking with you," and hang up. But some people persist. I keep a timer on my desk for these people, and when I can't think of another "out," I let the timer buzz and say, "The timer is buzzing, I must go," and quickly hang up.

Your first contact with a potential customer is very often through the telephone. If the contact is successful, it can bring business, but if your telephone technique and manner do not project a professional image, the caller might take their business elsewhere. So, work on your phone delivery.

If a business caller wants to make an appointment to discuss something, try to handle the matter over the phone. If a meeting is necessary, be sure the caller knows that only a given amount of time can be scheduled, and when it takes place, adhere to a time schedule. Rely on body language to end a meeting — stand up, close your folder and glance at your watch. Thank your visitor for coming as you lead the way to the door.

When you are busy and can't get to the phone, it's helpful if the children can take calls. They should be taught exactly what to say. Do not allow children to answer the telephone if they are too young to project a business attitude or if they are unable to take messages accurately.

If you use the home phone for your business calls, answer during business hours with the name of the business, like "Good morning. Cakes and Catering. This is Mrs. Wilson speaking. May I help you?" After hours, when the business is closed, answer as you do for all personal calls to your household. Answering calls differently when you are working and when your business is closed will help establish your business hours. Of course, some people who work from home do not have specific working hours and are willing to take business calls at any time. In this case, you might answer, "Good morning, Mrs. Wilson speaking."

Maybe you should consider subscribing to a business line. There are two big advantages to this type of service. First, your business name and phone number will be listed in both the White Pages and Yellow Pages. While a business line costs about two and a half times more than a private line, the listing in the Yellow Pages is targeted advertising that could bring enough business to pay for the added expense many times over. The second advantage of the business line is controlling after-hours calls simply by not answering or by taking the calls on an answering machine (answering machines are discussed later) and then returning the calls when you go to work the following day. Many businesses are conducted exclusively via the telephone, and they surely require a business line, but it would be of little advantage to a business that makes contacts through the mail and rarely uses the telephone. However, if the telephone company learns you are operating a business from your home but do not have a business line, they will make every effort to install one although they have no legal way of forcing one on you.

Various kinds of telephone equipment and services are available to you. A custom calling package that includes three-way calls, call waiting, and call forwarding can be arranged to alleviate some problems you might encounter, especially if your business uses a telephone extensively.

Three-way calls, as the name implies, allows you to interact with more than one party. This is valuable when conferences are needed between several people. "Call waiting," another telephone company service, allows you to interrupt an ongoing call to take another one, but using this service can be "touchy," as callers are sometimes insulted when you leave them waiting to answer another call.

Even if you don't need a business line, and you don't want to put out money to pay for the extra services, you should consider buying two pieces of equipment. The first is a memory phone. The memory feature allows you to "program" your telephone so you can dial frequently called numbers by pressing a single digit. It is worth the extra few dollars it costs.

The second piece of equipment, a telephone answering machine, allows you to control the telephone rather than the reverse. This machine records the messages of incoming callers and plays them back on command. Telephone answering machines are becoming standard equipment for busy households and businesses, and in a sense these set you free because you don't need to stay within hearing distance of the telephone ring. They offend or intimidate some callers, but if your greeting is brief and upbeat, most will leave their message. Be sure your message to the caller sounds professional. When you are preparing your recorded message, write it and practice reading it until it sounds exactly like you want. A message might go as follows: "Thank you for calling The Balloon Connection. We are unable to come to the phone, but if you will leave your name, number and message, we will return your call as soon as possible." This message does not say you are gone, and therefore possibly invite robbery, only that you cannot answer the telephone.

One nice feature of an answering machine is a control that allows you to hear the caller's message without answering the phone. You can turn on the answering machine and screen the incoming calls when you don't want to take the time to answer calls. If one of the calls is important and you wish to answer, the machine can be switched off and you can talk to the caller. You can return the remaining calls when and if you want.

As you replay the recorded messages, make notes about the callers, their telephone numbers, and other pertinent information. After listening to all messages, list the calls in the order of importance, and return them when you have a few spare moments.

Before dialing, jot down the points you wish to discuss and make sure you cover the list before finishing the conversation. Never let a secretary or the party you are calling put you on "hold" unless you have some routine work at your fingertips.

If you must be away from your shop or office for an extended time, then you might consider "call forwarding", which is a telephone company service that allows you to transfer calls coming into your home to another telephone number. The calls are forwarded to an answering service or to someone who has agreed to take your calls, maybe a friend. It only requires that you dial a prefix and the forwarding number when you wish the calls to be transferred. A similar procedure redirects calls back to your telephone. A small fee is charged for call forwarding, and it can be done on a daily basis if you're gone from the house much of the day, or for a long time like a vacation. The advantage of this service is that the caller speaks with another person rather than a recorded message, and that person can respond to questions and take messages. You can call into your answering service periodically throughout the day, or you can buy a paging device that allows your answering service to contact you when calls need to be answered. It's a good idea to keep apprised of the quality of your answering service by occasionally calling in and acting like a customer. Who is on the other end of the line taking your calls? Somebody else with a nice little home business! This service can be found in the Yellow Pages under "telephone answering service."

If you use the telephone frequently, you will discover it can be very expensive. The cost can be reduced if you follow these tips:

1. Dial direct. The savings over operated-assisted long distance can amount to 60 percent of the call.

2. Use 800 numbers when possible. An increasing number of companies have 800 listings, and you can get a directory from the phone company that lists the 800 numbers nationwide.

3. Call on off-hours when the rate is lower. Call East before 8:00 am because it will be later on the East Coast and people will be working, but make your calls to the West after 5:00 pm because the workday will still be in progress. Be sure to complete the calls before the regular rate goes into effect or the entire call will be charged at the higher rate.

4. Check bills for errors. There are a surprisingly large number of errors in phone bills, and the only way you can be sure of the calls you have made is to keep a running record as they are made. Keep a pad by your telephone for this purpose. If you are overcharged be sure to contact your telephone company.

5. There are now several long distance phone companies serving America. Their rates and types of service vary. You have undoubtedly chosen one, but in light of your business needs, it might be worth reevaluating them and select the one that is best for you.

WAYS TO HANDLE INTERRUPTIONS

Interruptions are a part of living. While it is an interruption to go to your child's school play, would you want it any other way? Isn't this one of the reasons you are working at home, where you have the OPTION to take in these events, rather than in an office or shop where you must stick to the work schedule even when your heart and mind are elsewhere? However, you will be considered fair game when you work at home — to be called, invited, requested, and dropped-in on. You must convince your friends and neighbors that you are a serious business person. Some of them will be "put off" when you deny them access to your time, but you have no choice but to be protective of your time if you intend to get your work done.

Interruptions can be categorized into the expected and unexpected. Forewarned is forearmed, and, anticipated interruptions such as social happenings or family activities can be looked forward to and enjoyed or expected and rejected. Unexpected interruptions can be a wagon full of wonderful-looking melons for sale in the neighborhood or an emergency like a surprise storm that sends you scurrying to secure animals, home, and property.

Some interruptions are pleasant, while other are just the opposite. When working very intensely, it's a pleasure to hear from a friend or spouse who wants to run out for a quick lunch. On the other hand, it's certainly not pleasant when something malfunctions within the household and you must stop work to find a repair person, or worse yet, make the repairs yourself.

Some interruptions are necessary while others are quite unnecessary. When the school nurse calls because a child is ill, most mothers are quickly out the door, but that same child will be considered a pain in the neck when he unnecessarily interrupts you.

Interruptions can come from anywhere. You might think it easier to reject an interruption that comes in the mail, but it's not. In fact, when you receive a letter asking you to chair something or the other, or give a lecture, it may be more difficult to brush aside the request than if you are approached at a gathering or called on the telephone. The request warrants special attention since it was put in writing. However, a written request gives you an opportunity to plan a way to reject it gracefully, and it is usually to your advantage to write a "Sorry, but I can't" letter before you are contacted for an answer, thereby denying the person the chance to persuade you to change your mind.

The mail will bring interruptions you simply can't ignore — invitations to weddings (buying a gift is a major interruption), showers, parties, and benefits for all kinds of organizations. At the very least, you need to send regrets, and even that takes your valuable time. The mail will also bring news about stocks, new laws, and all kinds of legal and financial matters you must deal with.

The doorbell! Other than hide behind drawn curtains, you can't very easily ignore the door bell. The interruption can be as insignificant as a neighbor wanting to borrow a little wood for a early winter fire but it could be somebody who wants to come in and visit. If the caller gets past the front door, DON'T SIT DOWN or you might get stuck for at least 15 minutes. Chat a bit, then say you are busy, but you will get back to them when you have a chance, all the while walking towards the door.

What about your children or spouse? They may have legitimate reasons for needing to interrupt you. Who decides

— you or them? It's not a bad idea to have ground rules on what constitutes a legitimate interruption and what is not acceptable.

Your children should clearly understand they must inform you of an emergency. Discuss different kinds of emergencies with your children, but since you can't possibly anticipate every situation that might arise, make certain they understand that other crises that haven't been discussed can also be reasons to interrupt.

If you work in a home office or other defined area where you can close the door, this may be enough to indicate that you shouldn't be disturbed. However, let your children know when you will be available. If they are small and can't tell time, it won't mean much if you tell them they can come talk with you at so-and-so time. Instead, set a clock outside your office, and beside the clock place a clock face that shows when they can come in for whatever reason they like. Expect your children to test you and attempt to bend the rules, but if you are CONSISTENT in handling them, they will respond to the scheduled shared time. (It has been assumed in the previous discussion that you have arranged for childcare, and their basic needs are being met.)

KEEP FOCUSED ON WORK

At times your house may seem like a zoo, with dogs barking, kids running, neighbors calling, repairmen hammering, and you might whisper in desperation, "Why me, Lord?" Well, it IS you and it's up to you to make it work. You've got a business to run, and if you find yourself surrounded by chaos, you will need to develop a tough attitude and an impenetrable determination to accomplish the tasks at hand. This is the time to pull out the goals you wrote down earlier. Read them. They are good goals, and the work you are doing is what is needed to reach those goals. Those written goals are invaluable in times of stress because they are the only tangible evidence you have that you really are working for something. Do what must be done to reach the goals, whether it's reaching for a couple of ear plugs, asking someone to run interference for you, or hiring better childcare.

The schedule you prepared is also valuable in times of stress. It's easy to keep on schedule when your surroundings are serene and nothing interferes with your work, but when your household seems to be rumbling under foot, the written schedule can help you keep your chin up, fortify your determiniation, and keep you working toward your goals.

YES, THE WORKDAY ENDS

It's time to change hats — to move from being a business person to being all those other people you might be — spouse, parent, cook, housekeeper, a person with interests, friends and activities. It is very easy to become a workaholic when you run your own business. Still, you are more than a business person, and other responsibilities and pleasures require your time and attention.

Stop work on time. Stopping work on time is just as important as starting on time, and sometimes just as difficult. It should be a part of your schedule. You might build quitting time around another obligation, such as picking up the children at school or running a few errands. This type of activity is useful because it clearly defines the end of the workday and gets you out of the house, away from those last-minute jobs you might feel compelled to do.

If you're an incipient workaholic, working at home might aggravate your tendency to try to do everything today. Frank Knight, a telecommunicating product marketer for Nynex Corporation said, "There's always something to do, and as soon as you think about it, there's no reason not to do it since your office is down the hall." Frank discovered he was working 60 to 70 hours every week until he made a conscious effort to change his work pattern. It's very easy to slip into an "all work, no play" pattern, and it takes an effort to prevent this from happening. When quitting time comes, you might be in the middle of a project or finally getting to something really important. Let it wait until tomorrow or you will become trapped by your work. Wind down your work with a ritual that will prepare your work space for the next day's activities. Dump the trash basket and tidy up your work area. Flip to the next page on your calendar and check to see if there is anything special on the agenda that will require you to dress differently when you get ready for the office, or anything that will require special preparation. Close the door, then leave. You are on your way home from work!

You have a few extra minutes since you don't have to fight the traffic. Do something you enjoy. Kick off your shoes and have a soft drink, or take a walk and pick a few flowers for the dinner table. A few paragraphs back I wrote that your house might be like a zoo and now I'm suggesting you take time to pick flowers? Yes, if possible. Obviously, if you are caught in the middle of an overactive household, you will have little choice but to forget the flowers and put a little structure back into the home. And that's hard because you may leave one kind of work only to get involved in another.

Maybe YOU know when work time is over, but the rest of the world isn't quite sure. Have specific work hours and post them. Since you run your business from home, it is hard for clients to know what time is off limits unless you tell them. And again, consistency is the key to making your schedule work. It is important to CONSISTENTLY tell customers who show up after hours, when you seem available, and ask them to return when you are open. You may lose some business with this approach, but only you can determine if your private time is worth the lost business.

CLUES THAT YOU ARE OVERWORKING

Here are some clues that suggest you are working too much.

1. Do your friends call less than they used too? That's good, up to a point, but when you find you have more business acquaintances than friends, it's time to look closely at the direction of your work.

2. Overworking often makes one feel tense and lose their sense of humor. Hang loose and enjoy this adventure you call a business.

3. If you find your relationship with your spouse, children, or other housemates deteriorating, slow down and take another look at your priorities.

4. Are you willing to spend a weekend totally away from business? If not, pull out your schedule and reorganize it. Program at least one non-workday each week, preferably two.

5. Do you still take time to enjoy special interests? You need these diversions to rekindle your spirit and keep you whole.

Perhaps you feel you have to overwork to run a business and devote time to friends, spend weekends playing, enjoy family, pursue special interests, but this is not true. Rome wasn't built in a day, and your business doesn't need to be built quickly if it jeopardizes the reasons you are working in the first place. It will take longer to build a business when you participate fully in living, but it's worth slowing down and being a whole person.

Resource: *Time Management for Business People.* Allan H. Smith, 1988. Success Publishing, 2812 Bayonne Dr., Palm Beach Gardens, FL 33410.

Managing Your Space

While physicists concentrate on the Laws of Thermodynamics, and economists wrestle with the Law of Supply and Demand, we, the house and apartment dwellers, can formulate our own law, and that is the Law of Diminishing Space. It's well-known to anyone who has tried to keep closets and garages tidy, your possessions expand or contract relative to the amount of available space — and the storage space needed is always a little less than the space available.

You are thinking about going into business at home, but your house is already bursting at the seams. Where will you find the room for an office or shop? I grew up in a home filled to overflowing, but there was always room for one more person, either at the table, or overnight, or competing for the ear of my parents. Looking at our overstuffed home you would have thought we couldn't possibly find room for anyone or anything else, but we did many times. And I learned something. There is always room to do the things you want to do, whether it's feeding a vagrant, offering a friend refuge — or setting up a business.

If 10,000 people read this book, there will be 10,000 different ideas about where a business might be tucked into a household. Some of us live in tiny apartments in the middle of metropolitan areas, while others live on vast farms far removed from populated regions. Yet it is the rare home that has a room sitting empty, waiting for a business to fill it.

But, you WILL find or make the space you need. You might find it in a corner in the laundry room, a breakfast nook, or maybe an underused den. If you can't find space in your home, then it might be necessary to create new space. Whether you use already existing space or create new space, it would be unwise to make drastic changes in your home until you know what you need. It isn't necessary to have the desk nailed in place or the philodendron plant on the filing cabinet before the first batch of letters go out or before your first customers start calling or coming up the walk. As you are getting underway, try to JUST get underway — just enough to function as a business. It takes time to learn what is actually needed, and it's best to let your space evolve as your business grows.

Let's assume you have found the space for starting your business. Is it legal to use it? Is it legal to operate a business, to make and sell things, meet with clients, have an employee — to do what you want to do in your own house? That depends upon what you want to do because laws govern what we do in our homes and the land surrounding them. It is important to know these laws and understand how they relate to your proposed business before too many plans are made.

This chapter will explain the types of laws governing the work you can do in your home and on your property. It will also help you reorganize your space to make room for your business.

IS IT LEGAL TO WORK AT HOME?

Public zoning laws and private covenants address the issue of businesses within the home, and it would be wise to learn how they can affect your business before setting up shop. Public laws on the local, state and federal levels both restrict and protect you. The private covenants of homeowners associations can influence the types of business you can undertake.

Zoning Laws

Property is divided into zones based on the activities and buildings there, and zoning laws control property use. Many zoning laws were written long ago to keep smokestacks, trucks and congestion out of residential neighborhoods. There is still a need to protect these neighborhoods from intrusive changes that detract from the quality of life, but the early laws may thwart the development of some home businesses that would not be a detriment to their neighborhoods.

Land is generally divided into four zones — residential, commercial, industrial, and agricultural. Most people interested _in setting up a home business live in either residential or agricultural zones, although a few might find themselves in either the industrial or commercial areas.

Agricultural zones are generally non-restrictive. Virtually all home businesses can operate within them. The population is usually sparse in these areas, few neighbors would be annoyed by a business or would protest against one. In fact, the most prevalent home business in an agricultural zone is none other than the family farm.

Commercial zones present a different twist for home entrepreneurs. Living accommodations are acceptable in most commercial zones, but the emphasis is different. Instead of working where you live, you live where you work. It was once very common for owners of small shops to live upstairs or at the back of their store. Of course, there are some advantages to this arrangement. Most notably, the family's presence affords some protection for the business, but this arrangement is no longer very common.

Most of us live in residential zones where houses line the street and the only apparent business is an occasional ice cream vendor or a truck farmer selling produce, (both need a vending license, by the way). At least that is how it appears to the untrained eye. Actually, today's residential neighborhoods are buzzing with business activity. What do the zoning laws say about running a business from home? They vary from city to city. Some cities have no residential zoning laws, while others have very restrictive ones. It is very important for you to determine the zoning restrictions of your neighborhood.

What Zoning Laws Affect You?

As you plan your business venture, call on the local Chamber of Commerce. That is what the organization is all about — to promote commerce. They may not answer all your questions, but they are very good at telling you who to contact, and often have a number for you to call close at hand. If you call them about the zoning laws in your town, they will probably refer you to the local planning commission, which may be a county or city office. They might also refer you to the city or county zoning board, or perhaps the Secretary of State.

These offices usually forward information on zoning restrictions, and there is no need to explain why you are interested, only that you want to know the zoning codes. Listed below are the types of restrictions you *may* encounter.

1. The home occupation must be conducted entirely within the dwelling by a person who is a resident member of the family residing on the premises, and with no additional employees.

2. The floor area devoted to the business may not exceed

25 percent of the floor area of the dwelling.

3. An outside entrance may not be provided solely for the home occupation.

4. A display of goods or services relating to the home occupation must not be visible from the exterior of the home.

5. No manufacturing is permitted.

6. A zoning use permit must be issued by the zoning commission for each occupation.

That's how a zoning code might read; now let's interpret it. After talking with personnel in several offices that deal with zoning permits and home businesses, I'm convinced we are caught in a time warp — some laws remain on the books but no longer reflect the changing economy and are rarely, if ever, enforced.

Number one above states that only a resident can work in the business, but the zoning law for the area allows for a variety of occupations that require a second person. For example, a dentist needs a dental assistant and maybe a secretary, yet according to the zoning rules, these are forbidden.

Number three above refers to an outside entrance. If you pursue the issue, you will learn that if the dentist has an office on a side porch or side wing, an outside entrance is permissible IF it was there BEFORE the business was started, but an entrance cannot be added to facilitate business activity.

What about number four that prohibits a display of goods or services? If you pay for the zoning use permit, which is a straightforward procedure with a small fee, then you can hang out a shingle. A shingle of specific size, but nonetheless, a shingle (2 sq. ft. maximum in some areas).

And number five prohibits manufacturing. This is so loosely worded that it could even prohibit making original art work, since the word "manufacture" originally meant to "make by hand." When questioned, the zoning officer I spoke with wasn't sure if original art could or could not be made at home.

Should you even bother about zoning restrictions or should you go about your work and mind your own business? The truth is, zoning commissioners rarely go looking for trouble. According to the zoning personnel with whom I spoke, the laws are sometimes archaic, rarely enforced and sometimes unenforceable. Through the years they have been inconsistently interpreted and there is a lot of "give." However, they encourage applying for a zoning use permit but admit that only a very low percentage of home business operators actually apply.

What happens if you are found to be operating a home business without a permit? You would then need to apply for one, but there is rarely a penalty for not having one. The usual reason a home business is notified that a permit is needed because a disgruntled neighbor has called the zoning board to protest a questionable business activity.

The impact of a home business on a neighborhood varies greatly. A business conducted in front of a computer will go unnoticed while one that involves clients coming and going could cause neighborhood congestion, and therefore, neighborhood protests. If you are careful about the way your business affects the neighborhood, you probably won't have any legal hassles. However, it doesn't hurt to keep a good relationship with neighbors and keep business activities to yourself as much as possible. It would be foolish to allow news of a big contract to spread throughout the neighborhood, although that can happen very easily just by mentioning it in casual conversation. You would be shocked at how quickly this kind of news travels from door to door, and behind one of those doors a neighbor could be building a private vendetta that could endanger your business. So keep your business activities to yourself or share them with someone other than the neighbors. Unless you thoroughly know and trust your neighbors, this point cannot be overstressed. But, if a neighbor is also engaged in a home business, your revelation of a similar home use should cause no concern and could lead to a valuable source for networking.

If the zoning board receives a complaint about your business, an investigator might drive past your residence or park on the street for awhile to observe how your business functions to determine if the complaint is valid. A letter will be sent to you if you are violating the law, indicating that you have a specific time in which to respond to the complaint. If the matter is not resolved after several more encounters, the zoning board will take you to court to force you to comply with the zoning restrictions. The court could put you out of business if you are found to be in violation of the law.

Special Use Permits

You can apply for a special use permit if your business can't function when encumbered by the restrictions of the zoning code. This is handled by the zoning board and requires a public hearing. There are two ways to approach the zoning board for a special use permit; you can either quietly pursue the permit and hope the neighbors don't protest or you can actively solicit their support.

Although there is a public notice about an impending hearing, it may not attract much attention if the permit would not bring a significant change to the neighborhood. An example would be the dentist who needs a dental assistant on the premises. It's difficult to imagine that a band of neighbors would get up in arms over a dental assistant (but you can never be sure about something like this). Go prepared to assure the board that the special use will not adversely affect the neighborhood. By the way, I have asked several professionals if they have a special use permit that enables them to have outside help, and not a single one of them even knew it was required. And it's worth noting that, having been informed, none of them rushed out to get this special permit.

You should find out how your neighbors feel about your proposed venture if you are asking for a special use permit that would allow activities that could affect them. If they are not opposed, ask for their support. There is a much greater chance of winning approval if the neighbors support your request.

Filing for Rezoning

You must file to have your property rezoned if your business requirements are greater than those allowed in a special use permit. This procedure is time consuming and may cost several hundred dollars. The procedure is explained in an information packet available from the zoning office. Rezoning requires a public hearing, a filing fee, the cost of publishing the intended rezoning, a legal advertisement, and the cost of sending a notice to anyone who owns property that touches the property under question. If the property is not rezoned, you have no other recourse than to change your business plans or move to a commercial area.

Private Homeowners Covenants

The zoning laws discussed above are all public issues, but private issues must also be considered as you undertake a home business. Some condominiums, apartments and houses located in areas controlled by Homeowners Associations have activity restrictions placed upon the occupants. These organizations are usually quite adamant about keeping the pact, so you should determine if your property is subject to these restrictions. They are usually noted in the property deed. However, just because a restriction is in a deed doesn't necessarily mean it is legal or that it is even constitutional. If you have questions, it may be wise to seek legal advice for an interpretation.

Other Restrictions

Besides your local government, state and federal governments also have guidelines and rules that may affect your business. State laws vary, but you can learn the restrictions by contacting the office of your Secretary of State. You will learn what can and cannot be manufactured in home businesses in your state. For example, some states prohibit preparing food to be served in commercial establishments. (Most states prohibit home businesses from making drugs, poisons, children's toys, and children's clothing. If you are planning a manufacturing business, it is imperative to learn of these restrictions.)

The federal government also has some control over home businesses. Some laws were written in the 1940's and are currently being updated. The federal laws were written to prevent sweatshops and other demeaning conditions, but they also reflect a strong union lobby which pushed through an array of legislation to prohibit manufacturing of such products as women's clothing, mittens, jewelry, embroidery and many other items. Many of these laws are no longer valid. There may be some changes in the near future.

The laws were intended to protect employees, but were loosely constructed and now are having an impact on the home businesses sprouting across the land. The groundswell of people involved in our changing work patterns is forcing the legislative bodies to reconsider some of these old laws. Also, modern technology has revitalized the question of what can and cannot be done at home. Labor unions have a vested interest in controlling or containing the extent of home work, and the AFL-CIO is attempting to get a law passed that would prevent using such a common tool as a telecommunicator or device from home. But do not fear, the homeworker's lobby is strong and is presenting a convincing rebuttal. You can be sure the debate will continue.

TAX BENEFITS
Know the IRS Requirements
BEFORE Designing Workspace

One of the advantages of working from home is that you can save money on renting business space, and also on taxes since a deduction is allowed for your home workspace.

It's worth the effort to qualify for these deductions because they amount to a significant savings. All direct expenses for the business portion of your home are deductible including paint jobs, new carpet, new lighting fixtures, and the cost of normal repairs. Also, you can deduct a percent of other costs. The percentage is based on the portion of the total household used for business purposes. These expenses include gas, electricity, water, telephone service, household supplies, real-estate taxes, rent, trash collection, insurance premiums, cleaning expenses, and mortgage interest.

Now is the time to learn what is required to make it tax deductible, so you can plan your workspace to fulfill the requirements. To take a deduction for using a part of your home for business purposes, that part of your home must meet two qualifications. First, it must be used exclusively AND regularly for business purposes, and secondly, it must be used as your principal place of business or as a place to meet clients or patients. The space in question must be clearly defined and set apart from non-business areas. The IRS is quite firm and unyielding about these requirements.

Exclusive Use

"Exclusive use" means that you engage a specific part of your home ONLY for the purpose of carrying on your trade or business there. If, for instance, each morning after breakfast you clean off the breakfast table, get out your typewriter, set it on the table and spend the rest of the day typing, you can NOT claim the deduction because the table is not used exclusively for business purposes. However, if you eat breakfast in the diningroom and leave the breakfast nook permanently set up for business, this would constitute exclusive use.

The only two exceptions to this rule are: 1) the use of part of your home for the storage of inventory or 2) as a partial use day-care facility.

The exclusive use exception is granted for the "storage of inventory exception" if all of the following is true:

1. Your business or trade is wholesaling or retailing products, and
2. The inventory is needed for use in your trade or business, and
3. The storage space is used on a regular basis, and
4. The space is identifiable as a storage space.

In other words, if you meet all the above tests, the goods could be stored in areas used for other purposes too like kitchen cabinets or trays under beds.

The space used for a day-care facility is the other exception to the exclusive use rule. Here, deductions are based on the percentage of time and percentage of the area used. For example, a child-care, elderly-care or mentally or physically impaired-care facility operates for eight hours each day (or, one-third of a 24 hour day,) and the site of this care is the family room. If the family room is 30 percent of the floor area of the home, it would qualify for 1/3 (portion of day) of 30 percent (percent of area); i.e., a 10 percent deduction.

Regular Use

Regular use means that you use the exclusive business part of your home on a continuing basis. It does not need to be used each day, but only on a regular basis, such as every other evening, or every weekday morning. The occasional or incidental business use of your home does not meet the regular use requirement, and you would be unable to claim the deduction even if that part of your home is used exclusively for business purposes.

Principal Place of Business or Place for Meeting Patients or Clients

The second qualifying condition for taking a deduction is: the part of your home you claim for a deduction must be your principal place of business. Of course, you can have a principal place of business for each of the businesses you engage in. If you work outside of your home during the day but have an alteration and custom sewing business at home in the evenings, then your home work space would be the principal place of business for your home sewing occupation. The area also qualifies if the space is used as a place to meet with patients, clients, or customers in the course of business. Examples are a doctor or dentist seeing patients, an insurance salesman meeting clients, or a piano teacher selling lessons. Again, when used as a principal place of business or to meet clients, it also must be used regularly and exclusively for business purposes to qualify for a tax deduction.

Free-Standing Structures

A separate, free-standing structure such as a barn, studio, garage, shop, or trailer on your property is deductible if you use the structure exclusively and regularly for your business. Unlike your home, this structure does not need to meet the previous qualification — it does not need to be your principal place of business, nor do you need to use it to meet clients or patients. For instance, a manufacturer of yo-yos might use his shop to store boards and saw them into smaller pieces. He then takes the small pieces of wood into his basement where he spends most of his time shaping and finishing them. Both the separate free-standing structure and his basement would qualify for deductions if they are not used for other purposes.

FINDING A PLACE TO SET UP SHOP

Where can I set up shop, where?
Will the kids get purple jelly on the papers that I type?
Will the neighbors watch and wonder why the walls are moving out?
Will the lights be shining brightly in my office late at night?
Will the mailman start to wonder "What's this business on my route?"
Where can I set up shop, where?

Many things should be considered as you seek a place to house your business, including the amount and kind of space needed for your proposed work, your personal needs and preferences, and the need to blend your business with other responsibilities.

Take a look at your space and try to visualize how to best use it for your home business. Remember you can probably get started with much less than optimal conditions. Don't spend time and money creating the perfect home workshop or office before you have tested the market. You need only enough space and equipment to get started. You will learn what is needed to run a home operation as your business begins to grow and you can then shape space to best fulfill your needs. So, as you begin, go minimal.

Kind of Business

Different businesses need different kinds of space and the space you have available can influence the type of business you undertake. The typical office requires very little space — room for a desk and chair, typewriter or word processor, supplies and filing cabinets, telephone, and little else. A business based on office work would fit nicely into an apartment or into even less space than most other businesses need.

By contrast, a manufacturing business usually requires a large area. Space is needed for the manufacturing process, for the storage of raw materials, and for the finished products. Also, an office is needed for records, correspondence, and sales promotion, and another area is needed for packing and shipping.

The manufacturing process can be noisy and dirty, if heavy machinery is used, or quite and clean, if products are crafted by hand or items are fabricated on a sewing machine or other small machine.

Service businesses cover such a spectrum of activities that it is difficult to cover the range of diversity with a few remarks. Some service businesses require very little space, while others consume an entire yard, basement or garage. A service might operate from an office-like setting, a studio, or even from a pick-up truck.

Personal Needs

What do YOU need in the way of workspace? Personal needs should be considered as you look at possible places for your business. What do you like? Do you need a private or secluded place to work? Are you content in an area far removed from family activities, or would you be happier in the middle of the action, watching the pot boil and within earshot of the kids? Would the noise and activity drive you to distraction? Will your responsibilities include keeping an eye on a child while you are working, or will you need to work where you can see customers or shipments arriving at the door?

How do you feel when you go into a basement? Some people become depressed when they work below ground, while others don't mind. Windows, with a view of the outdoors, are important to some people, while others are perfectly content to work in a closet.

Do you mind sharing workspace or do you prefer a private location, where no one will bother you or even see your work? Would it distress you if someone used your desk after you finished working or would you prefer to leave your papers out so you can easily pick up where you left off?

Too many questions? You need to answer all of them before deciding where to spend your working hours. Only then can you select the best workplace and avoid an area that is totally incompatible with your needs and responsibilities.

Other Considerations

Will clients visit or call at your home, and will your family and home be secure if strangers are around? If clients must come — and they surely must if yours is a people-oriented service — make an effort to locate your business so they remain confined to the business area.

Will "outside help" work in your home? This is usually prohibited by city zoning laws but if you live in a rural area you might use a number of outside helpers. Can the workers do their jobs without invading the family's private living quarters?

You will need to provide toilet facilities if clients or outside help come to your home. It would be best to have the work area near a toilet so that customers remain apart from the private areas of the home.

USING AVAILABLE SPACE

Let's assume you know the kind and amount of space needed to operate your business. The next task is to find the space and convert it into appropriate workspace without adversely affecting the family living quarters.

Take a Look at Each Room

Take inventory of your space. Walk through your house and try to imagine what might be. Study each room, then peek in the garage, basement, and attic. Let's take a closer look to find usable space but first a word of advice. Respect private space. There are areas within a home and on the lot that must not be violated if harmony is to prevail in the household. One rule must not be broken: don't move in on somebody else's territory. The kids need that area under the stairs to get away from the family and as a private retreat. That "empty" counter space is a planning center, and that workbench you might be eyeing is where weekend projects come to life. Don't covet those places used and enjoyed by others as possible places for your business activities.

Strive to keep living space and work space separate, even though they might be juxtaposed, and don't allow business space to dominate your household. While on the prowl for a work area, watch for nooks and crannies to store inventory and equipment, preferably places that are out of the way, yet easily accessible.

Finally, as you search the premises for your business location, keep in mind the "exclusive use" requirement needed to qualify for a tax deduction. Remember that a part of a room can qualify, but that part must be clearly defined and separated from the nonbusiness part.

THE LIVING ROOM

How often do you use your living room? Some families

reserve the living room for special occasions, somewhat like the parlor of the past, and it sits empty most of the time. If the living room in your home is rarely used, consider converting a corner of it into an office. The desk and other furnishings could be compatible with the decor, and arranged so "the office" can be "closed" at the end of the workday and blend into the rest of the room. The living room would work nicely if you have clients calling and need to meet them in a formal setting. However, it would not meet the exclusive use test and therefore, would not be tax deductible.

THE DINING ROOM

In small homes, the largest surface in the whole house might be the dining room table. Some families use it only for special meals while others use it as their center of activity — for meals, sewing, studying, working puzzles and gathering. If you don't have many other choices, you can make the table your center of operation. Do what you must to make it work, and if necessary, keep supplies in a suitcase; unpack each morning when you go to work. The dining table could also be used for meetings, or several people could sit around it and work. It's amazing what you can make do when you are determined.

THE KITCHEN AND BREAKFAST NOOK

Kitchens range from small efficiencies to huge "country" kitchens. If you have a medium to large kitchen, you might find a corner for an office or a place where you can sew, paint or do whatever your business requires. A kitchen office is especially handy for someone who has a food catering or food products business because this keeps the operation confined to one area of the house.

A business that involves catering, food preparation, or canning specialty foods can overtax a home kitchen so it is important to be organized. Since the kitchen must double for both business and home cooking, a schedule is needed to accommodate both needs. Storage space should allow you to keep supplies and equipment separate, clean, organized, and handy.

Many older homes have that delightful room, the breakfast nook. These are sometimes bright, airy areas, surrounded with windows, and set apart from the rest of the kitchen. They make perfect offices and sewing rooms. I work from a breakfast nook, having converted it into a writing room, with computer, printer, desk, telephone and answering machine. This room is in the center of the house and from this vantage point I can look out over the neighborhood, hear what's happening in the house, and begin dinner when I need a break from my writing.

BEDROOMS

Every bedroom is probably full if you are raising children. However, if your children have left home, you probably have an extra bedroom that you have converted into what we euphemistically call a "guest bedroom." This might be a nice work area. It's probably near a bathroom and off the beaten path, so if you need privacy or want to keep your work away from the main part of the house, an extra bedroom would be an excellent choice. Keep the bed or replace it with a fold-out sofa so the room will easily convert to a guest bedroom when needed.

Your own bedroom is another possibility. It is probably the most private part of your home — one rarely seen by visitors — so there is little need to put things away after work. Your bedroom would not be suitable if you need to meet with clients.

FAMILY ROOM

Many home businesses operate from the family room. This is a bit surprising since the family room is supposed to be the family sanctuary, a snug refuge from the world where the family can relax, play, snack, and talk. On the other hand, if the whole family is involved in the home business this might be the best gathering and working place. Family rooms are usually near the back of the house and often have an outside door handy for clients or for bringing in supplies.

THE BASEMENT

A basement can work for many types of indoor businesses. It might need some sprucing up, but the potential is there. If your basement is finished, then it's only a matter of reshaping the space to meet your needs. If it's unfinished, with bare floors and block walls, you will need to convert it into a suitable office if you greet and meet with customers, but a manufacturing business would not need a finished look and could function without cosmetic finishing.

Basements have several problems that need to be dealt with. 2If you have a basement office and meet with clients, use an abundance of lights and a plethora of plants to make the office warm and bright. A wall of drapes with back lighting will give the illusion of sunlight trying to peek through.

Basements can also be cool and damp. Use textures to combat the coolness. A carpet will take the harshness from a concrete floor, and textured fabrics should cover the chairs or sofas. Heaters and dehumidifiers will help to control dampness.

ATTIC

If the basement isn't suitable, move in the other direction — up to the attic. Some attics have finished floors, walls and ceilings, while others are just the framework of a room. If the attic has at least seven feet of head room it can be converted into work space. Can you get to it? Do stairs lead to the attic? If not, you can add stairs. Indoor stairs may take up valuable space, but stairs can be added to the outside of your home without reducing usable space.

PORCH OR BREEZEWAY

A porch makes a wonderful office or workroom. The ceiling, floor and at least one wall are already in place, so it's a matter of adding the remaining walls to make a room. If your business will have clients or customers coming and going, the porch would keep them from the house proper. A side porch is more adaptable than a front porch because it is removed from the normal household activities, and family visitors would not need to pass through the office to get into your home.

A breezeway, the space that connects the garage and house in some architectural arrangements, also works nicely for an office or studio. It is usually bright with windows, has an outside entrance, and is removed from the home's front entrance.

GARAGE OR SHOP

An attached garage or shop might fulfill the space needs of your business. We generally think of those areas as being rough and unfinished, but many businesses need just this setting. If you plan to do auto repair, you will obviously need to work from your garage, but even office work can be done in a corner of a garage.

Garages can also be used for storage and cleanup. I have a friend who runs a carpet cleaning business. He used to store his rug-cleaning equipment in his basement, which meant the bulky machines had to be taken down after each day's work, cleaned, and brought back upstairs. After several months of this backbreaking labor, he enlarged his garage and now drives his truck into the garage, rolls the equipment off the truck, cleans it over a drain, and rolls it back into the truck ready for the next job.

CONVERT EXISTING SPACE

Converting space into different configurations might change available space into business space. A room can be divided by screens, drapes, bookcases, or furniture. Remodeling by using movable partitions costs little and is not permanent.

Consider how a divider might function in your business. If you need a wall for storage, design a partition that can serve both as a room divider and as a storage unit. The unit could have storage compartments on either side — the business side might contain folders, books, and supplies, while the other side might house a television, toys or other household items. Or, the unit might provide business storage on one side, while the other side could be painted to match the walls with pictures added to make it blend with the room. The "rooms" on either side of this partition will feel larger if the partition itself does not reach the ceiling, and its stark lines can be softened with plant vines flowing down from the top shelf.

Screens can be objectionable because they are such obvious room dividers, but there are ways to make them less so. A screen won't look like it's sitting in the middle of the floor if furniture is placed against it. Also, a divided room will feel larger if the screen has open areas that allow air and light. This gives a totally different feel than a solid screen.

Furniture can also partition a room into different shapes, and because it does not extend as high as wall units or screens, it gives a visual perception of space, making the room feel bigger.

REMODEL AVAILABLE SPACE TO FIT YOUR NEEDS

Remodeling permanently changes your home and can be quite expensive. Carefully analyze your space needs before undertaking a remodeling program.

Remodeling might include such changes as erecting a wall to make two small rooms from a large one, or knocking out a wall to make a single large room. It also includes enclosing a breezeway with outside walls, or adding an outdoor stair to a second floor workroom. As you plan your remodeling, let your imagination run free as you dream of possible ways to reshape your space into functional work areas.

MAKE NEW SPACE BY ADDING ON

You can add space to your home by going up, out or down. But creating new space in this way means spending a significant amount of money, and again, I caution you not to make drastic changes until you are sure they are justified by the economics of your business. Even though you are sure you need the addition, don't spend the money until your business can support such extensive renovations. It's better to spend your money on supplies and equipment than on bricks and mortar during the early phase of business development.

When your business can financially support a renovation, raise your sights and look ahead. Make changes to accommodate what your business will become, not what it is at the moment.

Go up by raising the roof, or making dormers. Go out by adding a wing, room or porch. Go down by digging a basement under your home.

SEPARATE STRUCTURES

A barn, shed, garage, shop, guest house, trailer or other structure apart from your home might work as business space. You may recall The Cake Lady worked from a building beside her home, and The Speedometer Shop was housed in an expanded garage at the back of a city lot. Many home businesses are conducted from a separate structure on the home lot. There might already be a building on your lot that can be adapted to your business or, as you know your business needs, you might wish to design and construct a separate building. You may recall in the section about taxes, that, unlike areas within your home, a separate structure is tax deductible if it is used exclusively and regularly for business purposes, EVEN IF IT ISN'T your primary place of business or isn't used to meet with clients.

Managing Your Non-Business Responsibilities

MAKING CHOICES

Time and energy are your most valuable resources, and you must develop strategies to tap them wisely as you manage your non-business responsibilities. Plan to trade in some of your old responsibilities as you assume new ones. Instead of personally doing all the household and childrearing chores, manage them by finding alternate ways of getting the jobs done. Decide what are the most important non-business roles you play — parent, wife, housekeeper, cook, mentor, friend, helper — and apply your limited time to those with high priorities.

The terms "supermom" and "superdad" refer to people who attempt to do it all — function in the traditional capacities and also work — but these people often get burned out and lose interest long before their job is done. It's much wiser to recognize that you can't do everything yourself and arrange for help in handling family obligations as your business grows. The following two-liner carries a valuable message; commit it to memory for help when your life turns hectic.

Do the things you do best,
Hire someone else to do the rest.

One approach you might take is to divide your responsibilities and tasks into three groups. The first group is the most important and includes the things you cannot delegate such as being a parent or spouse. The second group would take in tasks that can be ignored without upsetting the household (for example, forget the fresh baked bread), and the third category

103

consists of tasks you might delegate to others. Since you will be busy with your business, it is reasonable to expect family members to share your load. If they are too busy, unwilling or unable, it may be necessary to hire child care, housecleaning and laundry services, thereby using someone else's cottage industry to complement your own. It's the old division of labor approach, and if ants and bees can master the process, surely we too can put it to good use.

FAMILY OBLIGATIONS

Family obligations are directed toward your children, spouse, and maybe a parent. Plan to integrate family obligations with your business schedule. Family obligations run deep, and each of us feels different obligations because of how we were raised. Someone raised in a family that rarely dined together may not feel the need to gather the family each evening for dinner, and those nurtured by a mother always at home may feel a twinge of guilt as they drop off their children at the sitter on the way to work.

Childhood experiences may have the opposite effect. Someone who spent their childhood being cared for by a parade of baby sitters might be unwilling to leave their children with a sitter, and many adults are more than happy to trade the family table-talk and home-cooked meals for pastrami on rye eaten from a tray in front of a television.

Clearly, we are complicated creatures who respond to our own set of obligations, and although we're never quite sure how they got a grip on our consciousness, we're not able to escape their intrusion into our lives. Still, family obligations can be a stabilizing factor. This tug from our past helps to hold families and society together; it gives us a chance to keep one foot on solid ground while we look to the future — for a spot to put our other foot. As you start your business at home, you will be on unfamiliar ground. It would be wise to use the solid ground of family ties to steady your movement into unknown territory, but it could be difficult for you and your business if you do not recognize your limitations and reject some of your past roles as you acquire new ones.

Parenting

One of the advantages of working at home, and one reason many people return home to work or start a business, is that it gives them the opportunity to have a closer relationship with their children. According to a 1985 Census Bureau and Department of Labor report, over half of the mothers of school age children work full time outside of their home, and as a result, latchkey kids are the rule rather than the exception. "Latchkey kids" are children who return from school to an empty house, carrying a key to unlock the door. The latchkey phenomenon has far-reaching consequences that are causing parents, especially mothers, to look for a way to earn money, yet care for their children. According to a survey conducted by Diane Hedin at the University of Minnesota, children left alone for extended periods are mildly depressed, and leaving them alone causes apprehension in their parents. Hedin's study found "the switchboards at the corporations across the country light up after 3 o'clock with mothers calling home, and kids checking in with their parents." Apparently parents use the telephone to supervise their children from afar. When latchkey kids were asked if they did things they wouldn't want their parents to know about, 16 percent said they drank beer or wine, 20 percent reported being involved in some sexual activity, and one third use the telephone to make crank or obscene calls.

These kinds of reports are causing concern among working parents, and it is not surprising many welcome the chance to return home to work. This enables them to be at home with their children, or be home when they return from school and still have a business in motion. That is an enticing combination.

If you have been working away from home, your children will probably be delighted to have you greet them when they return home from school, however, if you've never left home but are changing your life by starting a business, they might wonder what the fuss is all about. In either case your children will need to get used to seeing you in different roles. They will get different messages as you go from being a parent to being a business manager, and they may be confused as they try to find a way to respond to you in your various capacities.

Don't become overwrought about your children interfering with your business, or your business interfering with your children. There is time for both, so relax and let them both be important parts of your life. Expect your kids to be kids, and that means noise, running, questions, snacks, interruptions, crying, kissing, listening, scolding — the whole ball game. If you can't be an effective parent while working at your business (and you probably can't in many kinds of businesses,) then be a parent when the kids are around and quickly resume your role as a business person as soon as they are occupied or elsewhere. I have spent years doing just that. While getting the family off to work and school, I looked and sounded like a mom and a wife, but the minute the house was empty, I became writer, speaker, and scientist, with a different set of colleagues, different tone of voice, and a different wardrobe. Occasionally, when the roles overlapped, I would catch a strange look from the kids as they wondered "what gives?" Children aren't overly impressed by accomplishments, and they have a wonderful way of bringing us back to reality.

Many homeworkers try to accommodate both family and business but struggle to separate the two. Some attempt this separation by distance — putting their business in remote corners of the house — or by closing doors when working on the business, but a few steps or closed doors aren't effective deterrents for little ones who want your attention. It's much easier to separate your business and children by TIME — working on your business when the children aren't at home or when they are busy, and being a parent after school and on weekends. (If your children are a part of the working staff, as explained later, the above comments aren't applicable.)

Single Parents

Most single parents who read this are probably single mothers trying to make a living at home. These women are caught with two pressing needs; the need to be a full time parent and compensate for the missing parent and the need to make a living. They work at home to try to fulfill their dual role of homemaker and breadwinner. Single parents are confronted with several problems that are difficult to overcome. First, it takes a while for a home business to start making money. A couple can get through this lean period because one can continue working outside the home while the other gets the home business going. A single parent does not have this financial cushion. Also, couples can share household tasks, and what they can't do might be done by outside help. A single parent can call on the children for help, but must still carry a very heavy load. With the financial problems that often plague single parents, they are unable to hire outside help but instead must work harder, faster and smarter to get things done.

Children of single parents can either help or hinder their parent's work. Small children need a lot of care, but older children can literally take the burden from their parent by either caring for smaller children or by helping with the business. These children may be forced to grow up faster and assume more responsibility, but while a single parent might want to protect his or her children from this demanding life, there is little choice but to depend on their help and hope they can keep ahead.

Children Have Different Needs at Different Ages

While reading (and writing) this section on children, we tend to think of our own children. Some of us have babes in arms, others are just discovering their children have minds of their own, while still others are coping with the terrible (and not so terrible) teen scene. Each phase of child development requires different kinds of care and nurturing. Some phases can be very difficult to dovetail with your business, while others will complement your work.

Your children need you. While children have different needs at different ages, they need YOU at ALL ages. Don't ignore their needs while you establish your business.

THE PRE-SCHOOL CHILD

Infants still in the crib and immobile can be the easiest children to care for because you can control them! They need little more than food, clean diapers, touching, caring, and sounds. When your child is in a crib or playpen you can place him or her in your office or shop and work on your business while responding to, and caring for the child. This period is very brief, so enjoy it.

You will need to spend much more time caring for a child who has become mobile and has started exploring. This is probably the most intense period of child care and, unlike the infant cooing from a crib in your office, these tykes can destroy your nicely typed papers, or injure themselves as they crawl under desks, chairs or machinery.

You might think you can care for a toddler while building your empire at home, but small children demand an inordinate amount of time and energy, leaving you precious little to devote to your business. If your child is in this stage of development, either work on your business while he or she is sleeping, or arrange for child care so you have an extended period to concentrate on your work. Planning to work while the child sleeps isn't very satisfactory because you will not have much time to devote to your business, and you may be tired from caring for the little one and need rest.

SCHOOL-AGE CHILDREN

Once your children reach school age, you will have a solid

block of time to call your own. If your kids ride a school bus, you can count on approximately a seven-hour day, since they are in school around six hours, and it takes about another hour going to and from school.

Use this time wisely. When the house is empty, the time is ripe to work. Save your household chores until the kids get home from school since many parenting and household tasks blend well together.

It is important to take advantage of school days because there aren't as many in a year as you might think. With summer vacation, holidays and weekends, school days number around 180 days each year. Add to that the days a child is ill and remains home from school, and you can see why you must take advantage of the hours they are away.

After working through the school year to establish a going business, what happens when summer comes and your children become a presence, being children all day long, all summer long? You will need to decide if your business can be put on hold during summer vacation and on holidays. If continuity is essential to your business, you may need to arrange for child care during these periods, or it may be possible to work with the children in the household.

There are several steps you can take to help your children adapt to your work schedule and still feel there is no place like home. Since you can't oversee their every activity, have ground rules. They need to know where they can play, how much noise they can make, if they can have friends in, when and what they can snack on, and who is in charge. They need to know where they should play if you have business clients visiting. It wouldn't work for them to run through the house while you are trying to conduct a business meeting, and it takes a little polish from your meeting if you must stop to play referee. It is important to give clear signals as to what is and is not acceptable. At first you will be tested, and it may be difficult to get new household rules and patterns of play established, but if you CONSISTENTLY respond in ways that reinforce the desired behavior, the household will settle into a pattern that will allow family life and business activities to co-exist.

Child Care

If you can't care for both your business and your children, then look for alternatives. There are ways to resolve this problem. Both newborn babies and newborn businesses require undivided attention to develop properly. Your children may have already had your undivided attention, and now it's time to devote yourself to your business so it too can grow and thrive.

There are a host of child care options available. Most of the options cost money, but you can claim a tax credit by using IRS Form 2441, which allows for both in-house and out-of-house child care.

IN-HOUSE CHILD CARE

The most obvious in-house child care is that provided by an older sibling, spouse, live-in parent or relative. Children twelve years of age or older should be capable of caring for younger siblings. They will be more successful if the younger children are significantly younger. A 12-year old child can wield very little authority over a 10- or 11-year old sibling, regardless of who you say is in charge. Actually, this type of arrangement could result in more chaos than if each child is left to his own devices. On the other hand, an older child might care for young children quite well. The advantages of using siblings for child care is they are readily available, and the money they earn stays within the family, (and is tax deductible as a business expense).

A spouse, live-in parent or other relative is another possible source of child care. These people are known by the children and have a special interest in them. Of the three, the live-in parent (grandparent of the children) is the better choice if the individual is in good health and capable of coping with active children. Many live-in parents look for ways to contribute to the well-being of the household, and this would surely be an invaluable contribution. Also, the parent/grandparent would probably be available more often than your spouse — and might be more enthusiastic. Assuming your husband works throughout the day, I'm sure you can empathize with him if he is responsible for the kids after work and is greeted by a dirty diaper or a fussing child when he drags through the door. A spouse might be more effective on weekends, and this would give the live-in parent a break.

Other relatives might also be willing to care for your children. I fondly remember how my husband's maiden aunt helped us raise our son and daughter. With no children of her own, she loved to spend time with our children, and since she was retired and wasn't in a hurry to go someplace or do something, she could tell stories, work puzzles, and play with them. She became a very important part of our family when both my husband and I were developing our careers. We

appreciate those years of help and look back on them as a time of sharing each other's lives. This kind of generosity may be unusual, but still you may have a relative to call on occasionally. The problem is, occasionally isn't enough. When you are running a business, you need help consistently, maybe every day, and relatives may grow to resent being imposed upon so frequently.

Look outside your home for help, but be selective. Why hire a sitter who watches children but does little else? You need help, and you might as well hire a "mother's helper," a person who not only cares for the children, but also throws in the wash, cleans up the kitchen and oversees the household. Mother's helpers can be a godsend. Instead of leaving your business at the end of a workday and going to a house full of clutter and whining kids, you can take over from your helper, with the house in order and your children content and cared for. Yes, this costs money, but not much more than a regular sitter, and it's worth the added expense because, with this kind of backup help, you will be free to run your business, knowing that all is well on the home front.

OUT-OF-HOUSE CHILD CARE

Out-of-house child care includes private sitters, before and after-school programs, child care programs for preschool youngsters, day care homes, co-op arrangements, and in-school programs that include free after-school activities from scouting to computer classes. The biggest advantage to out-of-house care is the total privacy it affords you.

Your child will probably get more individual attention with private sitters than with other child care services, but this is the most expensive type of child care. Many private sitters have children of their own, and they select a child to care for who is near the same age as their own child so the children will become playmates.

Child care programs have been growing in popularity as more mothers join the workforce. Many of these programs are well organized, and the children spend their days learning skills as well as playing. These kinds of facilities don't provide care for sick children, whereas private sitters will usually care for a sick child. This may not be a problem since you may want to watch over a sick child anyway, and by working at home you will have that opportunity. Licensed child care programs are usually reliable, but check them thoroughly before placing your precious children in one. Several child care facilities have gained notoriety in recent years as a result of a few sick minds using them to satisfy criminal behavior, but because of these cases, there is an increased awareness of possible problems, and this has resulted in closer monitoring. The best way to find out about a program is to talk with parents whose children are enrolled, not with the directors. Learn the ratio of children to adults (the lower the better,) how the children spend their days, and how emergencies and discipline are handled.

Before- and after-school programs can be found within public schools as well as private facilities. There is usually a delivery service to take the children to and from school if the program is outside the school. You probably won't need this type of service because you will have a large block of time in which to do your work while your children are in school, and will probably be ready to take over after school hours.

Another option for out-of-house care is the co-op or trading care arrangement. Some of these are operated by a professional while others are very informal arrangements with neighbors or friends taking turns caring for each other's children. These usually cost little or nothing except your time. If you have little cash but time to spare, this option might appeal to you, but if you are already too busy, this added chore may not fit your schedule. The cost of lost productivity from time spent on child care might not be worth the money saved. Another disadvantage is that these arrangements are usually not operated on a regular schedule, (although if you find the right person, you might be able to arrange a regular schedule).

The following story relates how two women were able to help each other by trading child care. Terry Nash and Cindy Hasenfus met during a parent's night at a 24-hour child care facility. After chatting for awhile, they discovered they had much in common. Both were divorced, both had small daughters and lived on the same side of town, and each needed child care, except at different times of the day. Terry works the day shift while Cindy works at night. They realized they could trade child care and worked out an arrangement that is better for their daughters than the commercial facility and it costs them nothing. During the day, Cindy cares for her own daughter and Terry's child. Each evening, as she goes to work, she takes both of the little girls to Terry's home and tucks them into bed. In the morning Terry awakens and dresses both children, prepares their breakfast, and takes them back to Cindy's home. The two women have become close friends, and their girls are growing up much like sisters.

Children and the Family Business

In most of the previous discussion it was implied that you alone would be involved in your home business, but that may not always be the case. You may be planning a family business with you, your children and your spouse sharing the multitude of tasks. If the children will be involved, it is terribly important that they understand and accept their roles. At the same time, you should understand that children's lives change quickly, and their involvement in your cottage industry should not be essential to its success.

Do your children have time to devote to the business? If they attend school, will they work in the evening? How long? Will the business bring in enough money to pay for family labor? Will you pay your children for their work? Why or why not? How do your children feel about the family business? Could they make more money working someplace else? Would they rather work at home or at another job? If the children help, will they have enough time to "be kids" — to play, do schoolwork, participate in extracurricular activities, and still have those valuable moments of just doing nothing? If they agree to participate in the business, is their commitment written in stone or can they change their minds and work less or more than was originally planned? All of these questions should be discussed and answered before you try and involve your children in your home business.

The family may need to pull together to make your new business survive, but the children will need more than the mere promise of success to remain involved and devoted. Start paying them as soon as possible or their work and interest will quickly wane. Wages paid to children are a deductible business expense, and you don't need to pay social security or unemployment taxes for minor children. Children pay no income tax on the first $2,300 they earn each year, but you should certainly keep records of their time worked and the work done. Pay family members the approximate rate you would pay non-family members. The IRS will take issue with their earnings if you pay an exorbitant amount because it looks like they are being used to reduce business profits and avoid paying taxes. Also, the IRS will look askance at records showing a seven- or eight-year old working many hours, while these same hours might be reasonable for an older child and would not be questioned.

Which brings us to the subject of just how much and what kind of work can you expect from children? This depends on their age, personalities and capabilities. I'll never forget visiting a craft shop in the Smoky Mountains. The shopkeeper sold ceramic pieces she made while tending shop in the front room of her home. I was greeted by a precious little urchin dressed in rolled-up coveralls and topped with a thatch of blond hair. He proudly showed me his work. This child of about seven made tiny bird's nests by pushing wet ceramic clay though his water pistol to make a mound of ceramic strands. He then pushed his thumb into the pile of clay strands to make the bowl shape. His mother made birds to fit the nests. Frankly, they made a good team, but I'm not sure if she was helping him or if he was helping her!

Be realistic when assigning jobs to children. Give them attainable goals, jobs they can accomplish well and without undo stress. Carefully and patiently teach them how to perform their duties, frequently check the quality of their work, and be generous with your praise for jobs well done.

A single child helping with the business seems to work well, but when several children help, sibling rivalry can lead to squabbles and cause more trouble than their help is worth. Assign totally different jobs to the children to avoid this.

Family-run businesses with inefficient workers have a slightly different problem than other businesses. What can you do about your 12-year old son who loses his enthusiasm for doing chores during the World Series? If you can make the business work without his help during special times, let it be. However, if a child (or spouse) is an integral part of the business and is being paid for a given amount of labor, very clear guidelines must be provided so there is no ambiguity as to who does what, when, where and how.

Finally, the "happiness factor" is an important element to more and better work. Promote a positive attitude among the family about the home business, and make the atmosphere surrounding the work interesting and fun. Why not listen to a football game while you're painting something, or have cookies and milk on hand for a quick break? And if simple handwork is involved, encourage a patter of chatter and light heartedness.

Your Spouse and Your Business

A home business will cause many changes in your household, and it is helpful for you and your spouse to discuss and understand the changes that will take place. The following comments are directed to women working from home, but most of these ideas can also be applied to men working from home as well.

Let's take a look at two possible business arrangements and think about how they might affect your spouse. In the first, the business is yours and you will operate it by yourself. You'll need your husband's support and cooperation, and it is wise to seek his understanding and counsel as you get underway. Starting a business at home will bring about a role change for both you and your husband even if he isn't directly involved. He will need to cope with new feelings as he sees you grow, and he will need to face new responsibilities as you do fewer household chores. The way he reacts to your needs and the changes you undergo will depend on his character and on the strength of your marriage.

If you have been working for somebody else, you will soon discover that people treat you differently when they learn you are running your own business. They usually give you more respect, and this will increase your self-confidence and independence. Your spouse might feel a bit insecure and unneeded and resent your new-found independence, or, he might delight in your successes. If you have been a full-time homemaker, your spouse might even be annoyed as your business grows and takes you away from homemaking. Or, he might feel a little smug if your business falters and doesn't develop as you had expected. Another man would react quite differently, perhaps pitching in to help with household chores so you can concentrate on business, commiserating with you when things go awry and helping in any way he can to make the business more successful. How will YOUR husband react to your successes, failures, needs and role changes?

Although it's your business, your husband will most likely be involved in many unforeseen ways. He will probably be the one who makes shelves for your books, reads and corrects your manuscripts, helps you find the imbalance in your bank statement, oils the sewing machine, runs new wires for better lighting and so on. You can bet the poor guy is going to be involved in ways that even you can't imagine. Even so, you have to be sure that your work doesn't intrude excessively into his life, and conversely, that he respects your obligations and your schedule.

Another possible business arrangement is a family business where you and your spouse work together. With this arrangement, you and your husband will probably work together throughout the day, and you can expect your relationship to change. If you have a good marriage and enjoy each other's company, then working together should be pleasant and rewarding. Instead of having only evenings and weekends to share, you will literally spend your lives together, working toward a common goal. But don't expect this much togetherness to make things better if you are having problems in your marriage. In fact, working so close all day every day could exacerbate a tenuous relationship. The stability of your marriage and how you feel about being with each other for extended periods should surely be taken into account if you are contemplating a family business.

Another question to be considered is who will make the important business decisions? Decisions must be based on goals, but who decides which goals to pursue? Even if you agree on goals, you may disagree on how to reach them.

Who will make critical decisions if you and your spouse disagree? How will you resolve conflicts? While your business is in the planning stage, you may think this is an unnecessary worry, and that you can work out differences of opinion as they arise. This may be true, but you should be prepared for the time when a hard decision must be made and you should know who will be responsible for making that decision. In other words, who's the boss or is there a boss? Are you equal partners and can you reach decisions through consensus?

Suppose a couple is working together, making handcrafted items and selling them at craft fairs. Their products appeal to a wide market, and there is little doubt that their business could grow significantly. One partner wants to expand and begin selling to retail outlets, but the other is perfectly happy and isn't interested in enlarging the business because it would mean working longer hours. Who will decide the course of action? When one partner's decision affects the other's life, the equilibrium within a relationship is at stake, and the decision must be weighed carefully, its ramifications thought through. Decisions of importance will test your skills of logic, negotiation, persuasion and understanding.

Among other things, people in love need to be touched, kissed, complimented, talked with, listened to, and enjoyed. Relationships are always changing, either deteriorating or improving. A relationship may grow relative to the growth of the individuals and it's important that both parties keep growing so the partnership remains interesting and stimulating. Fresh ideas and experiences and new business challenges can give impetus to a marriage.

Here are some common sense guidelines to keep a marriage

alive and well, and as you work at home, it would be wise to use them to nourish your relationship and keep the spark of love ignited. Most importantly, be kind to each other. Think how your actions will affect your spouse. Keep your partner's best interests in mind as you pursue your goals. Don't get caught up in little irritating disagreements, but save your disagreements for more basic problems. Resolve conflicts as they arise and be willing to compromise whenever possible. Save time for each other, and do things together. Just as importantly, do things separately. Otherwise you may have little to discuss and develop a myopic view of the world. Don't be too serious. Relax and enjoy each other. Share each other's successes and help in times of unhappiness or distress. Talk and LISTEN to each other. Share ideas, respect opinions and keep an interest in the other's work, hobbies, and concerns.

Live-in Parents or Others

Many households include live-in parents or other relatives. These people may be well and able to care for themselves, or they may be living with relatives because they cannot care for themselves. Older people who are well but live with young families for companionship are usually anxious to participate in the daily activities of the home and help share the chores. This can be a big help for a homeworker trying to run a business. Some live-in parents might even enjoy being involved in the business since they have retired and often feel lonesome and useless. Contributing to the home business might help them regain their enthusiasm for living.

Parents who are aged, fragile and maybe a little senile are moved into their children's home so they can be watched more closely and given the help they need. They usually don't require constant surveillance, only an occasional check, and this is no problem for someone who works at home. If the parent requires more attention than you can offer during your workday, it would be wise to hire a sitter, much as you would hire child care. This is MUCH less costly than hiring an aide or a nurse. The other alternative is to hire a live-in helper and provide room, board and a small salary. This helper could care for the elderly parent and help maintain the house. There are many people willing to do this kind of work. Sometimes, they have no family and seek the companionship of others. Try advertising in the classified section of your local newspaper for such workers. College students are another possibility. They sometimes work in homes for room and board and can be found by contacting the placement office of a nearby college or university. Finding the right person to help can ease the burden of trying to manage your non-business responsibilities.

Watch for Interpersonal Problems

Interpersonal problems can easily develop should you become overly absorbed in your business. If you were working away from home, you would leave your work behind at the end of the day, but when your work is down the hall, it's very easy to allow it to filter into family life. Make an effort to stop work on time and leave it behind. While you will want to share some of the events of the day, try not to linger over every detail or discuss your business over dinner. Forget about business when you have guests or go out for an evening, and certainly don't take it to bed or you can be sure your family will begin to resent its omnipresence.

Try to sense your family's needs. It is difficult to predict what problems might arise, but be sensitive to a breakdown in communications or a growing resentment toward your work, particularly if your business starts to consume an inordinate amount of time.

PETS

Pets that make a house a home can make a business a disaster. It's essential to keep pets away from the work area if clients visit your home. You may feel comfortable with the family dog or cat, but don't expect your customers to share your feelings. Many people are frightened by all four-legged animals, and some are allergic to them, especially cats. Cats seem to have a sixth sense and head straight for the person who is allergic or who isn't a "cat person." Even if customers or clients enjoy being around animals, their presence can interrupt a business meeting or make it difficult to concentrate on business matters. It's also worth noting that whenever animals are allowed to be around business visitors, there is the problem of possible injury to a client. A docile family pet might bite a client, and this could lead to all kinds of problems and quite possibly a lawsuit. It makes sense to avoid trouble by keeping pets away from business associates, clients and customers.

Even if no one visits your home during the workday, it's a good idea to keep dogs well away from your work area. Many homeworkers give an impression to clients, whom they deal with only by telephone, that they are working from a business office. A dog barking in the background could be very embarrassing and blow your cover. A case in point is Sharon Sievers, who operates a local printing service from her home. One day, while taking orders over the phone, her dog wouldn't stop barking. When she had no choice but to tend to the dog, she told her customer that the security dogs were upset and she needed to check the warehouse, whereupon she hung up, got the dog under control, and returned the call. If you have a dog, either keep it outside or away from your business area to prevent an assortment of problems.

MANAGING YOUR HOUSEHOLD

It's not easy to hold a household together even without running a business. But since you are, or will be, there is a good possibility you will need some help. How can you get the help you need to keep the house and surrounding property intact? Some help is right there, under your own roof but other help is available too. It is useful to list jobs that must be done and determine how the work can be allocated.

Who should be responsible for what jobs? Barbara and Jim Dale work at home designing the "Woman's World" memo pads and greeting cards that are being sold in over 25,000 retail outlets across the country. They devised an unusual scheme for joint housekeeping. All chores are assigned a point value based on the degree of distastefulness. Cleaning the bath tub is worth a 10 as most distasteful, while washing dishes rated a 2. After rating all jobs, they divided the list so each had an equal "distastefulness sum." It sounds like a workable scheme, but Barbara is a little reluctant to do some of her assigned work because, as one of their note pads declares: "A man's home is his castle; let him clean it himself." Kidding aside, there are ways to share jobs and get them done without letting your business suffer.

Keeping the House Clean

If you are a white glove fanatic, forget it. Keeping that kind of house is incompatible with running a business unless you hire a full-time housekeeper. When you operate a business at home, the threshold of cleanliness takes a little step backwards. That's not to say you can expect to live in a mess, but you will have more important things to do than spend time giving the place the spit and polish treatment.

Some houses are easier to keep clean than others because they have low maintenance features. If you are anticipating new

floor coverings or window treatments in your house, make changes that are easy to maintain. No-wax floors, medium colored or variegated carpets, vertical rather than horizontal slats in window blinds — these types of features can make housekeeping less of a chore.

If you don't have time to clean house, then the best you can hope for is a little "surface cleaning" — keeping the house picked up and orderly, but you won't be able to do even that without the cooperation of the rest of the family. One rule says it all: "If you mess it up, you clean it up." If your children bake cookies after school, fine. Just make sure they clean the dirty pans and messy counters. If your spouse fixes a snack in the evening, insist that the kitchen be left in order — no crumbs, no mess, no dirty dishes. Enforcing and reinforcing the "mess up, clean up" rule will save many steps, and will put your children on the road to a lifetime of orderly surroundings.

Every member of the household must understand their help is needed to keep the house in order. Everybody over the age of six is capable of, and should be responsible for keeping their area tidy, their clothes hung in the closet or in the wash basket, and possessions put away or in use. Even children under six can be taught to pick up their toys and clothes. Each family member should be responsible for making their bed each morning, changing the sheets, replacing towels, and doing the routine tasks of keeping their bedroom tidy. If your spouse and kids aren't used to doing this, expect some rebellion. Other tasks can also be assigned on a rotating or daily basis, including taking out the trash and discarding the newspaper. Ash trays should be emptied by the person who uses them, following the "mess up, clean up" rule. The key to this training is consistency.

The two home areas that seem to need constant attention are the baths and the kitchen. The kitchen can be kept tidy if you get into the HABIT of doing one special job each day as you clean up after dinner. If your spouse or child washes the dishes or fills the dishwasher, then you can use that time to clean a drawer, wash a filter, scour a pan, run a wet mop or shine an appliance. This daily attention is needed to keep the kitchen reasonably clean.

Bathrooms are the "Waterloo" of most homes since they are the site of so much activity. It's a chore to keep them clean. If you maintain the kitchen, someone else should be responsible for the baths. One way to keep them clean is to assign, on a rotating basis, the task of scouring the fixtures, polishing the mirrors, and replenishing the soap, tissues and toilet paper. Don't trust your memory but keep a running sheet of assignments posted in the baths so there is no question about whose turn it is.

The condition of your household will gradually deteriorate if it is cleaned only superficially. Since you will probably be too busy to do the deep cleaning, it would be wise to get outside help. There are a lot of people willing to clean your house for a fee, and this is probably money well spent. A weekly or biweekly cleaning should maintain an acceptable level of cleanliness. Have a different room cleaned thoroughly at each session, with a "quick over" for the rest of the house. DON'T hire someone to clean your house and then get involved in overseeing the job or preparing the worker's lunch. (You'd be surprised how many people do this.) Instead, hire someone who can work without instruction; then make sure the necessary cleaning agents are available, and get back to minding your own business.

Shopping

Have you any idea how many things are brought into your home? Just look at the amount of trash your family must dispose of each week. Everything that goes out as trash had to come into your house. Besides the disposables, there are consumable items like food, personal items, and cleaning products. Altogether, this amounts to a huge number of items, and somebody has to shop to find, buy, and carry them home. It takes a significant expenditure of time and energy, not to mention money, to buy the array of products needed to keep a household functioning. While this task can't be eliminated, there are ways to do more shopping in less time. Whatever you are buying, buy more. Buy greeting cards by the box; fill up the gas tank, buy postage stamps by roll, hosiery by the box, and canned goods by the case. Shopping this way not only saves time, but it also saves money. You will rarely need to dash out for a can of this or that if you keep a well-stocked pantry. Also, shopping ahead gives you the opportunity to shop sales when you happen upon them rather than rushing out when a sale is advertised. Study the following tips to improve your shopping skills.

GROCERIES

Grocery shopping can be time-consuming or it can become a study in efficiency. You can tell if shoppers have much going on in their lives by watching how they move in a grocery store.

Some dally over every item as they stroll down the aisles, while others wheel their carts with a look of determination.

If you do most of the cooking in your home, you will probably want to do the grocery shopping. Keep lists. Whenever you run out of something or use the last can of something, put it on the list. Rather than shop several times a week, save time by shopping weekly.

Shop when few other people are in the store. Markets are usually less crowded during the early part of the week, but avoid Mondays because the shelves have yet to be refilled after the weekend. Also avoid the crowds and long lines of Friday and Saturday. As soon as you return home, make the weekly menu as you move the foods from the grocery bags to the refrigerator or pantry. This menu should be written on your calendar in the corner of each day's schedule. It only needs to include the fresh meat and produce you have purchased. You can fill in the other items as the meals are prepared. By doing this, you can dole out the foods so they last a week, and also, by planning menus, you can use foods in the order best suited to ensure freshness. For instance, use mushrooms, fish and seafood first, but leave hot dogs and cabbage for later in the week. If you have a roast on Wednesday, you can plan a stew for Friday with the leftovers and use a different entree on Thursday.

If a few odds and ends are needed throughout the week, either get them when you are doing other errands; send one of your children to the market, or have your spouse pick them up on the way home from work.

CLOTHING

Sorry, but you're going to need another list — the clothing sizes worn by every member of the family — shirts, shoes, pants, undies, hat, gloves, everything. Keep the list in your wallet so when you're out shopping and happen upon something you can pick it up without being concerned about the size. While you'll still need to shop for the small children in the household, the children can do most of their own shopping as soon as they have learned what it takes to earn money. Working for the home business is a good way for them to find out what it takes and knowing that, they are much better prepared to shop and make budget-wise purchases. My husband and I paid for most of our children's clothing as they were growing up, even after they earned money from part-time jobs, but when they wanted something we weren't convinced they needed, we offered to pay half the price if they were willing to pay the other half. This made them reconsider items and buy only what was important to them.

As far as clothes are concerned, your spouse is on his own. He might need a little help, but encourage him to shop for his own wardrobe. A lot of men used to get "the little lady" to buy their clothes, and it took a lot of time. Those days are long gone. A woman shouldn't have to oversee her husband's wardrobe.

HOUSEHOLD ITEMS

Incidentals can run you ragged. Light bulbs, garbage bags, laundry detergent, shampoo, toothbrushes, and scouring powder seem to be swallowed by a "black hole." Buy these things on your regular grocery shopping trip. Shop a large market that handles an assortment so you can avoid extra stops.

Bigger household articles take more time and thought. Furniture wears out and appliances stop working. It's a waste of time for both you and your spouse to pound the pavement trying to find the right item to buy. One or the other of you can do the legwork, and when a decision must be made, if it's a big decision, then maybe the two of you should look at the article together. Otherwise, trust the other's judgment and save a little time.

GIFTS

Our culture dictates we buy gifts for numerous occasions, but selecting, buying, wrapping, and shipping gifts takes an awesome amount of time and energy. It takes longer to buy gifts than it takes to buy routine household items because they don't follow a pattern. We know what to buy when we go to the grocery, but a wedding invitation can send us to the mall walking the aisles in puzzlement. Gifts usually cost us more in time than money.

With a little forethought, you can make gift buying easier. Select a standard gift to give to all nieces and nephews as wedding gifts. Also, start a collection — ceramic ducks, pot holders, whatever — for parents or others on your gift-buying list, and add to their collection on each occasion. This is much easier and takes less time than trying to think of something different for each gift-giving occasion. If possible, send out-of-town people gifts that can be wrapped and shipped from the place of purchase. A good example is the gourmet foods sold by shops that oversee every detail after you put the cash on the counter. You can also save time by starting a tradition, — send the same consumable item, like a cheese assortment every year.

CATALOG PURCHASES

Shopping by mail has become the preferred way for people who have little time to go to stores. Sitting by the phone with a credit card, you can flip through catalogs and shop nationwide. Also, once you place a catalog order, you will start receiving numerous catalogs from other companies because customer mailing lists are sold. For best results, shop only reliable companies, ones that have a return policy, and don't buy items that need to be fitted. It's easier to go to a local store and try something on rather than order clothes that must be returned.

Some large mail-order companies ship orders to their local stores where you must pick them up, while others ship directly to your home, which is obviously more convenient.

CRAWLING THE MALL

A modern shopping mall carries an assortment of goods and performs such an array of services that you can do most of your shopping and many of your errands without darting from place to place in a car. Years ago, on Sunday afternoons, our family used to "crawl the mall." At that time it was a social happening, and we spent the afternoon chatting with friends we encountered. Now, with little time to waste, we crawl the mall with a purpose, and in a single expedition can resupply the household, pick up some clothes, find a few gifts, eat out, buy gourmet foods, get eyes checked and new glasses fitted, have photos printed and do a little banking. If you haven't discovered the time-saving features of a mall, check it out!

Feeding the Family

Preparing family meals can tie you to the kitchen for long periods every day, but if family members do their share they can reduce your cooking responsibilities. In any case, food must be available for breakfast, lunch, and dinner, and maybe a few packed lunches and snacks. You can't prepare all that food and expect to run a business, and it's not unreasonable to expect and encourage self-sufficiency among family members. If your spouse or children carry a lunch, let them pack their own. And children eight or nine years old are quite capable of putting together their breakfast if cereal, toast, juice and/or fruit and milk are within easy reach.

You can expect to prepare at least one meal each day, and it will make more of an impact if you concentrate your efforts on dinner. Maybe it's old-fashioned, but some people feel its nice to have the whole family home for dinner with everybody's feet under the table at once.

You may wonder how you can put together a nice dinner while struggling to get orders out or trying to meet a deadline. The trick is to plan ahead. Each morning before starting your business work, refer to the meat and produce menu guide you wrote on your calendar after grocery shopping and spend a few minutes lining up dinner. If meat needs defrosting, pull it out of the freezer, or if it must simmer for an extended time, put it on the burner. Use every short cut you know and rely on such kitchen helpers as the pressure cooker, crock pot, dishwasher, microwave and food processor.

Include the family in dinner preparations. They will be better helpers if they know what is expected of them. One child could set the table each evening for a week, while another fills or empties the dishwasher. They can also make salad or help with other food preparation. This is an important time when chaos in the kitchen just means you are having a good time. You might be busy when your family gets home from school or work, and they might want to talk about something, so use this shared time in the kitchen to talk and enjoy each other as you work together preparing dinner.

On your busiest days, when you don't even have time to think about what you might cook, let alone prepare it, the easiest way to get food on the table is to order pizza delivered. You can probably get by with this once each week, or you might order a bucket of fried chicken, or something from the corner deli for a little variety.

To ease the after dinner chores, establish a routine that each person carries his or her own dishes to the kitchen. You may have noticed that many of the suggestions offered in this chapter encourage family members to practice self-maintenance — remove THEIR dishes, pick up THEIR clothes, fix THEIR lunches, make THEIR bed. If you can establish this behavior pattern, your work will be greatly reduced and the family members will become more responsible people.

A lot of families eat out on weekends, but when you run your own business it's helpful to eat out after a particularly long and exhausting day. And it's a good way to wind down. Since you probably won't be as involved in your business on weekends, you might want to use the extra time to prepare more elaborate meals for your family.

Laundering

According to a comment on Barbara and Jim Dale's memo pads: "Behind every working woman is an enormous pile of

unwashed laundry." It's not really that bad. If you keep two baskets, one for dark clothing and the other for light, it won't be necessary to sort washing, and also, you'll know when enough dark or light things have accumulated for a load. Never "do the wash" per se, but throw in a load whenever you're doing something else. Some people still think doing the wash is a big job and make an issue of it, but with modern washers and dryers, it takes just a few minutes to run through a load of wash. After the load comes out of the dryer, the children can take over, folding or hanging their own clothing and retrieving their sheets and towels.

I guess some people still iron but in our household, if it has to be ironed, either the owner irons it or it goes to the Goodwill. I'm well aware of an affinity for natural fibers and have heard of the wonders of cotton, but if I'm responsible for caring for it, wash and wear is the name of the game. I can't see spending valuable time flattening something that could have been made of non-wrinkle fabric in the first place.

Maintaining the Building and Grounds

There isn't any way to get around cutting the grass, short of paving the whole yard. Outside work doesn't end with cutting and trimming grass. Next comes raking leaves, then shoveling snow, and before long, fresh grass is peeking up again. You won't have the time yet the grounds need to be kept in order, especially if customers come to your home. This is a chore that can be assigned to your children, or if they aren't old enough, hire a neighborhood helper.

You might be thinking that if you follow the advice you've been given in this chapter, your kids won't have a free moment. It's true, your children will need to be more diligent in helping around the house but it has been shown that children brought up with responsibilities are much more capable, self-sufficient, and confident than children who have everything done for them. And they sure make better mates.

Errands

How often do you jump into the car and run an errand? There are bills to pay, books to return, the car needs gas, and you need some supplies. The time spent quickly adds up. Some errands can be done more efficiently. For instance, don't bank in person if you can bank by mail, pay bills by mail, and if you are needing something a little unusual, or if you want to compare prices between stores, use the telephone.

Use your least productive time to do errands. You might

be bushed by late afternoon and can't produce any more creative work. That's the time to run errands. Or, if you are a night person who can't think straight before noon, do your errands in the morning.

Make ANOTHER list. Yes, your desk can actually get cluttered with all the lists, but they are the best way to get organized and to get everything done. Don't put your errand list in your calendar, but on a separate card or note sheet — one you can take along as you make the rounds. List everything you must do and plan a sequence for doing it. If you need to pick up something at the grocery, do that later so the foods stay fresh. If you need money to do the other tasks on the list, go to the bank first. Plan a route so there is no backtracking. Number the stops on the list and be on your way, following the route that will get the jobs done in the most efficient manner.

KEEPING HOLIDAYS SPECIAL

Holidays function not only to celebrate an occasion but also as a break from day-to-day routines. It's very easy to get frustrated when you have more work than time, and then must stop to prepare, and celebrate a holiday. You might feel that if it weren't for holidays you could get something done, and may even wish you could ignore them. But they won't go away and it's just as well because we need a break. It's wise to make holidays special events that are looked forward to and remembered with pleasure because that will help to ease the feeling of separation from children and spouse that your business and daily work may cause. The problem is, holidays are imbued with tradition, and some of these traditions take time and energy to perpetuate.

Entertaining is a big part of holiday celebrations. Fortunately, holiday entertaining has changed throughout the years. The host used to make all the plans, and work for days to gather and brew up the traditional foods. But now, with our busy schedules, guests frequently share the work and bring part of the festive foods. If this pattern of sharing the cooking chores has not been started with your family or friends, why not start it? It's easier to start when you're to be a guest. Offer to bring part of the meal, and hope they will reciprocate in your home. Plan who should bring what and don't duplicate each other's efforts.

Holidays sometimes bring house guests, and house guests take time. Make every effort to contain the length of their visits. You may even do some business work when you have house guests. Many households arrange for guests to make their own breakfasts, by making available an assortment of foods. You're lucky if your guests sleep late because you can get a little work done while they sleep . Even if they are early risers, many guests enjoy private moments — to read the paper or rinse out a few things. Take advantage of their preoccupation to keep your business intact. Also, don't prepare any meals ahead when you are expecting house guests. Instead, help your guests feel at home by inviting them into the kitchen for conversation over a cup of coffee while you work on the meals.

Holidays also bring parties. Take advantage of the holiday season to entertain a lot of people at once. Entertaining a crowd takes less time than entertaining the same number of people, but just a few at a time. It takes about as much time and work to give a small dinner party as it does to have a blast. The most important part of planning a party isn't cleaning house or boiling shrimp, but working on the guest list and making sure interests and personalities are compatible. If the guest list is right, the rest is a piece of cake. Still, gathering the ingredients and preparing food takes time and work, and you might want to hire help either to cater the party or to prepare the foods.

The December holiday season is the most time consuming. Make a gift list early in the year and, as you think of an appropriate gift, write it beside the name. Buy gifts throughout the year as you see a sale or while you are shopping for other items. Your list will gradually be completed as the year wears on and you will not be caught in a last-minute shopping scramble.

Decorating the house for the holidays and making holiday goodies can take a chunk of your time if you insist on doing all the work. But why should you? Your children and spouse would probably enjoy helping so make decorating and baking a family occasion. If the decorations were carefully put away the previous year, then getting them in place will be a simple task.

Entertaining for Christmas or (C)Hanukkah is much the same as entertaining for other holidays, but it extends over a longer period. Many families spend the whole week between Christmas and New Year's Day in nonproductive activities. Unless your business is slow at that time of the year, and many are, you will probably need to work sometime during the holidays. Plan early-morning and late-night work sessions so you can spend the bulk of the day with family and friends, winding down the year.

ENTERTAINING

The previous section on holidays suggests some tips for entertaining, but entertaining does not start and stop with the holidays. There are occasions throughout the year when you and your spouse will want to see friends. Rather than invite friends for dinner, invite them for cocktails and then dine out. Or go out to eat and then invite them in for a nightcap or dessert. You will save even more time by combining dinner out with some special event such as the theater, ballet, a sports event or movie.

You will also be involved when your children entertain. You or another adult will need to be in attendance when they have overnight guests or friends in after school, so there should be a clear understanding as to when they can and cannot plan these activities. They must understand that your work precludes your overseeing a lot of gatherings. Still, entertaining is important as your children develop into social creatures. When they throw a party, encourage them to do the planning, invitations, decorations, and even prepare some of the food. This will not only save you time, but it will teach your children responsibility, and they will learn just how much work it takes to entertain.

Managing Yourself

Living with the boss can be trying. If the boss is difficult and demanding, you will feel overworked and underpaid. But wait, YOU are the boss. It's up to YOU to set standards, control the work schedule, and manage your energy. And you're responsible for establishing good work habits, creating a positive attitude, and controlling stress. Managing the boss is an important part of managing your business.

MANAGING YOUR ENERGY

After reading about the many things you must do to keep a business and a household running, you may be thinking you can't possibly keep up with all the jobs and responsibilities. In truth, not everybody can, but you will have a much greater chance of keeping up if you are in good health and learn to manage your energy.

The goal is to fine-tune your body so it can efficiently produce energy. There is no mystery about how to increase your energy level and get the most from your body. You need to eat properly to acquire fuel, exercise to enhance the fuel, sleep enough to allow the body to be replenished, and develop habits that do not inhibit any of the processes.

Eat for Energy

Food is the body's source of fuel and fuel is energy. Food is also the body's source of vitamins and minerals, and a deficiency or excess of any of the essential nutrients can cause fatigue. Mark Twain wrote, "Part of the secret of success in life is to eat what you like and let the food fight it out inside." It's not really quite that simple.

Depending on the food, eating triggers the release of chemical messages that either produce wakefulness or induce sleep. It's very common to feel sleepy shortly after eating a big meal. Your body is responding to the food by working to process it. This diverts energy from other parts of your body, leaving you feeling sluggish and tired. You will also feel weary if you go too long between meals or if you aren't taking in adequate calories.

Different foods stimulate the brain in different ways which, in turn, lead to different body responses. We can think of the brain as having two pathways and certain foods as activating one or the other pathway. One pathway acts to energize us, while the other pathway has a sedating effect and calms us down. It has been shown that a meal composed primarily of high-protein foods such as fish, fowl, eggs, meat, dairy products, and beans stimulates the high energy pathway and provides up to five hours of energy, whereas a meal consisting of high carbohydrate foods such as pasta, white bread, and rich desserts gives a surge of energy that lasts for about an hour, and then, by stimulating the sedating pathway, actually encourages sleep.

Knowing this, you can plan your meals to match your work schedule. If you have a heavy day ahead, it would be wise to eat a high protein breakfast and lunch to remain bright and alert, and save the carbohydrates for dinner to help you relax during the evening. If you anticipate an important after dinner meeting, then reverse your diet and eat proteins at dinner to keep from getting drowsy as the evening wears on.

As you know, the three food groups are carbohydrates, fat, and proteins. Of the three, carbohydrates play the most important role in STABILIZING your energy level. Carbohydrates should make up 60 percent of the calories of a healthful diet. They are absorbed through the digestive tract and can be used directly by the body for energy. The form of carbohydrate, simple or complex, is important when selecting foods to sustain a high energy level. Sugars, including white and brown sugar, honey, and syrups, give a surge of energy that quickly drops because they are rapidly absorbed. The resulting hypoglycemia makes you feel tired, irritable, weak, and hungry. More complex carbohydrates like those found in grains, cereals, potatoes, and whole-wheat bread can help you avoid these vacillating blood-sugar levels because they are broken down and absorbed more slowly, thereby providing a continuous supply of energy.

Vitamin or mineral deficiencies can lead to reduced energy and fatigue because vitamins and minerals help assimilate the energy-producing foods. Even if you follow a good diet, you might want to consider taking a vitamin and mineral supplement. Studies suggest that approximately half of all American women are deficient in some essential mineral or vitamin. Dr. Myron Winick, writing in *Columbia Magazine* (November, 1983) has identified four reasons why women are susceptible to nutritional deficiencies. First, the processes associated with reproduction — menstruation, pregnancy and lactation — take nutrients from the body. Second, women are inundated with the message that they must be slim, and many undertake unsound diets. Third, many oral contraceptives interfere with the absorption and metabolism of certain vitamins; and finally, women are consuming much more alcohol than in the past, and alcohol increases the elimination of some vitamins. Even though you should try to satisfy vitamin and mineral requirements through a good diet, it wouldn't hurt to pop a pill to assure that all the requirements have been met. Use a multiple-vitamin/mineral pill that contains all the recommended minimum daily allowances.

FOODS TO EAT TO PROMOTE HEALTH
AND PROVIDE ENERGY

Complex carbohydrates such as fresh vegetables, fruits, whole-wheat bread, corn, beans, and rice cereals.

Foods high in protein but low in fat such as poultry, fish, and nonfat dairy products.

FOODS TO LIMIT IN YOUR DIET

Foods high in sugar such as white or brown sugar, honey, syrups, and sweets made with these ingredients.

Fatty foods including red meat, whole milk, cold cuts, butter, margarine, lard, and oils.

Foods high in cholesterol including eggs, fatty meat, organ meats, and shellfish.

Exercise for Vitality

Exercising is one of the best ways to increase your energy level. It gives you more stamina and makes you feel better. Exercise uses energy to build energy, and if you don't exercise regularly you may well have some chronic fatigue.

Exercise increases energy by strengthening the energy-producing organs. It actually produces anatomical changes that allow for the production of more energy. Through regular and sustained exercise, the heart becomes larger and stronger and can pump blood with less effort, the lungs work better, and

muscle fibers and blood vessels grow. Also the energy-producing chemicals in the brain are stimulated.

Not only does exercising make your body function more efficiently, it also helps you to be in a better mood. It is thought that a change in brain chemistry brings this about. It has been shown that exercise sometimes works better than drugs at reducing anxiety and stress. It is also an effective way to fight depression, which is a common cause of chronic fatigue. The chemical norepinephrine is depleted during depression, but exercise regenerates this chemical. For this reason, running and other exercises can be used to treat depression.

You might expect to get tired earlier as you get older, yet we've all seen senior citizens who seem to defy their years. You can be sure many of these people have had a lifetime of activity. Exercising can stave off the slowing that goes with aging by stimulating the heart, lungs, muscles and brain.

So, now that you know you SHOULD exercise, the question is, WILL you? It's hard to start exercising. It's easier to think about it, but thinking about it won't get your body in shape. Just start. Don't do much, but do something every day. Do something you enjoy. If you like to ride a bicycle, then take a spin around the neighborhood. If you like to dance, then put on a beat, get into some outlandish outfit, and get those thighs moving. Or you might want to do two things at once. If you have a favorite "soap," but have been missing it because of the demands of your business, then put a stationary bicycle in front of the television and enjoy your ride. You could do this during your afternoon break. It's important to start slowly, building up your exercise program (now that ride or dance is a program!) until you have reached a sustained 30-minute ritual. This amount of exercising is needed to get your systems working sufficiently to stimulate all the processes that will ultimately increase your energy level.

I know you're busy, but you must find the time for this essential activity.

Sleep for Renewal

Sleep restores energy. After a hard day's work, we look forward to crawling between the sheets and getting a night of rest. Some people drop off so quickly they never remember going to bed, while others toss and turn, unable to sleep. You can develop a HABIT of going to sleep. Try to develop a sleeping pattern just as you have developed an eating pattern. Set regular hours for going to bed and getting up, and try to stick to them even on weekends or holidays. If you break your pattern by getting up several hours later than normal, it will be hard to resume your schedule because you will not be tired at your regular bedtime.

There are several ways to promote sleep. Let your body wind down in late evening by avoiding exercise and spending a few minutes of quiet time curled up with a book. Don't struggle with business or personal problems late into the night. You might not be able to stop thinking about them when you get into bed, and they can keep you awake. Also, be careful what you eat. A heavy late-evening snack that contains much fat can cause a bloated, uncomfortable feeling, while one containing much protein will keep you alert and prevent sleep. However, a light snack composed of carbohydrates will induce sleep. Also, be careful how much and what you drink in the evening. Caffeine causes sleeplessness in many people. Tea, coffee, and many carbonated beverages contain caffeine, so if caffeine bothers you, avoid these beverages after dinner. There is a widespread belief that alcohol induces sleep, and that is the reason for the "night cap." While a little alcohol causes drowsiness and leads to a light sleep, a larger amount interferes with the most restful kind of sleep, the periods of deep sleep, and this can result in fatigue the following day. The amount of fluids you drink in the evening and before retiring will determine if you can get through the night without having to go to the bathroom.

After having discussed all the ways to get more for your time, I suspect you will be surprised to read that I encourage naps. Napping can be a beneficial way of getting more time. I'm a "napper" and for me, that early afternoon nap will keep me alert into the night. A one-hour nap in the afternoon will allow me to work three hours longer at night, thus an extra two hours of productive time is realized. Plan your napping strategy lest you sleep your life away. Set an alarm, but use one that rings until it is shut off. And put the alarm way out of reach. This will force you to get out of bed. However, naps do not work for everyone.

Develop Healthy Habits

Your habits can give you a sense of well being. Stand tall, hang loose, laugh easily, and take care of yourself. Those little, everyday things can make the difference between feeling energetic or feeling tired. Even your posture is important. If you must sit for extended periods make sure you have a chair that properly supports your back, and that your feet rest flat on the floor.

If your work keeps you seated for many hours, use TWO chairs that are different shapes and trade back and forth between the two. This will rest your body by applying pressure at different places. If you must stand for long periods, stand on a resilient mat to reduce the stress on your legs, and stand before a bench or worktable high enough so you won't bend over and strain your back.

Protecting your body from harmful substances is another way to maintain your energy level. Smoking can leave you chronically fatigued. You will have less energy if you smoke than if you don't. People START smoking for psychological reasons, but they CONTINUE smoking because tobacco is addictive. If you are wasting energy by smoking, consider stopping and give yourself a break, a chance to do your very best as you embark on your business. Expect to feel tired as soon as you stop smoking because nicotine is a stimulant. As you work past the first few days without the stimulant you will notice a dramatic increase in energy. Your body immediately starts to cleanse itself and repair the damage the smoking has caused. Forty-eight hours after smoking your last cigarette your blood could be carrying as much as eight percent more oxygen, and although you may still crave cigarettes, by the third day you will feel an increase in energy. I am suggesting you stop smoking for the purpose of regaining your strength, but I'm sure you don't need to be reminded of the other health reasons for not smoking.

Alcohol also has an energy-reducing effect. If you "drink, for the night is young," you will wake up feeling old and weary, not in a condition to run a business. Alcohol is a drug. It is a depressant, and one of its side effects is drowsiness. Many people think alcohol is a stimulant because it makes them gregarious and excited, but a feeling of dullness, slowed thinking, and drowsiness soon follows. This dullness may last into the following day, and if much alcohol is consumed, the following day is greeted with a hangover.

If you are planning to work on your business for a couple of hours in the evening, a cocktail before dinner can ruin your plans. The drowsiness caused by the cocktail, combined with the energy spent digesting dinner, is enough to dull your thinking and make working difficult, if not impossible. A couple of drinks in the evening can even thwart your efficiency the following day. It might be interesting for you to evaluate your performance after you have had a couple of drinks. To do this, keep records (just put them in a corner on your calendar), noting when you have a drink and how you respond the following day. If you find that alcohol interferes with your work performance, you will need to decide which comes first. Ogden Nash wrote, "Candy is dandy, but liquor is quicker," to which I would add: "But neither is good for your work, mind or ticker."

Other drugs can also decrease your energy level and induce fatigue. You are probably well aware of the disorienting and dulling effect of some illegal substances, but a variety of prescription and over-the-counter drugs can also lead to lethargy. Many people spend their lives feeling tired because of their medication. Sometimes there is no choice but to take the medicine to relieve a medical problem, but in many cases a different drug could be used. Speak to your doctor if you are on medication and feel overly tired. Your medication may be causing the fatigue, and you might be able to use an alternate drug.

If your medical condition demands medication that makes you drowsy, then work around the problem. If you take the medicine in the morning and your energy level drops immediately, then do less demanding work during this time, and save your creative work for those times when you feel more energetic.

Sometimes the drugs we take can be eliminated — the ones we reach for at the slightest sniffle, sore back, or whenever too many problems come our way — drugs like aspirin, antihistamines, antidepressants, antihypertensives, and the like. Many of these drugs cause drowsiness and fatigue.

Another healthful habit is to avoid excesses and strive for moderation. Too much of anything can be bad for you; too much exercise, inactivity, work, play, sleep, sex, food, or drink. Too much is just that; too much. Overindulgence is the way some people cope with stress. Instead of reaching for a cup of yogurt or an apple, a person under stress is more inclined to reach for a cigarette, salty or sweet snacks, or an alcoholic drink, only to discover that they have set a vicious cycle in motion and they now crave more. Overindulgence, as a means of dealing with problems, can quickly become a habit.

Redress Stress by Addressing It

Nothing saps energy faster than unresolved problems that cause stress. Stress is caused by conflict. Whatever the problem might be, until it is resolved you will wage a psychological battle that might well exhaust you.

There are numerous ways to reduce stress. If the conflict

itself can be resolved, obviously that is the best solution. But sometimes, try as we may, the conflict cannot be resolved because it is something over which we have no control. The maxim, "Give me the strength to change the things that need changing, and the strength to accept the things I cannot change," is worth repeating as you struggle with a problem beyond your control. Look for ways to reduce the stress caused by the problem. Exercise is one of the best ways and engaging in a creative project is another. Also, keeping busy with productive work and looking for the good things can gradually make the conflict less of a domination and allow you to reduce its impact on your life.

DEVELOP GOOD WORK HABITS

Dress for Work

Those upwardly mobile, career-minded corporate workers "dress for success." But one of the perks people look forward to when they return home to work is spending time in casual clothing. It is important to set boundaries. Don't dress TOO casually. If you arrive at your office or shop in a robe, scuffling along in house slippers, your work will probably reflect a lackadaisical attitude. Dress for work. Dress like you are successful, and this will affect your attitude about yourself. Your apparel should not only look nice, but it should also be comfortable.

If you meet with customers or clients throughout the day, dress appropriately. Dress so your clients view you as a professional working at home, not a Haus frau trying to pick up a little pin money. While that is good advice, it's only fair to mention that some very successful people do just the opposite. I've an accountant friend who regularly starts her workday in a robe, sans makeup, hair care and breakfast. Marcie puts in several hours at her desk in this attire, and during a mid-morning break she takes a quick shower, gets dressed for the day, and has a bite of breakfast. She has found a routine that works for her. By contrast, Bobbi Haygood pulls on pantyhose and paints on a face before slipping into her very proper business suit. Completely put together, she picks up her purse and walks down the hall to her office. Within minutes after quitting work, she is in sweats and sneakers and up to her elbows in peat moss and plants.

What is the right dress for your business? If you are a truck farmer, bib overalls would be right for taking your produce to market. A caterer might greet customers in a nice crisp dress,

but deliver the foods and service dressed in a uniform. The trick is to dress in a way that reinforces your business image.

I buy honey from a bee keeper who plays his role to the hilt. When customers stop for a quart of honey, he greets them dressed in his official jumpsuit with bee veil and gloves. He probably doesn't use his veil and gloves all that much, but they help to reinforce his image, and I'm sure other customers feel as I do — we wouldn't consider buying honey from the supermarket when we can buy it from a real live beekeeper.

Professional people frequently have uniforms that help identify their profession. A nurse giving care from a home business will instill more confidence by wearing the uniform we have grown to associate with the nursing profession, and a therapist might wear a white jacket to help establish his or her professional position. Whatever you wear, keep in mind the need to project the right image to the customers you deal with in person.

Discipline Yourself to Work throughout the Day

Be on guard against bad habits that can creep into your workday. The proximity of your work to the refrigerator, television, bed, and liquor cabinet, and the lack of negative input from co-workers makes walking the straight and narrow a little difficult on an "off" day. Once you begin using an indulgence to cope with the stress of running a business, it will quickly become a habit, and then you will automatically stop for a nap, grab a snack, write a few letters, reach for a drink or take an extra 15 minutes for lunch. Especially damaging habits are the ones that lead to a dependency or craving. Drinking on the job, getting hooked on an afternoon television show, and snacking on salty foods and sweets are very common habits the homeworker must strive to avoid. A single drink, either to celebrate a nice contract or to soften the blow of a lost one could start a pattern of destructive behavior that could imperil your business. Even a small glass of wine with lunch will make your afternoon less productive. It's a good hard rule that not a single drop of booze can touch your lips during the workday.

Ignore the hum of the refrigerator. People working from home have problems battling the bulge because of the ready access to the refrigerator. One consultant with a Denver firm looked forward to working at home but returned to the office after gaining 25 pounds. He reports, "The food was laying in wait, ready to grab me each time I passed the refrigerator." This is a common complaint of homeworkers. If you know you are going to be hungry, plan your snacks to break the habit of reaching for calories every time you're within range of the kitchen. If, for instance, you schedule a 3 p.m. break and know you'll snack, you won't be as inclined to eat before or after that time. You can even control the snack content if you consciously prepare for the break by setting aside something when you aren't hungry, because in all probability, a prepared snack will be healthier for you than something you pick up in the heat of a hunger pang.

If you are already saddled with some bad habits, try breaking them by finding substitutes. If you smoke while talking with clients, find something else to occupy your hands, maybe a special pen that you set aside just for that purpose. Or, if you find yourself heading for the kitchen, go to the john instead, whether you need to or not.

You need breaks and you'll get more work done if you take a few minutes off and change your environment and activities. You might be inclined to pass up the breaks when your work is going well, but it's a good idea to take breaks even then. Normally, a mid-morning and mid-afternoon break should be adequate. Do whatever you like during your breaks, but try to spend the brief hiatus away from where you normally work.

Even while you are working, it is helpful to change your environment. Work awhile at your desk, then move to something different — file, pack shipments, pick up supplies. Look for ways to break your work into units, some mental and others physical.

Procrastination is another detriment. There are all kinds of things you might do that aren't work-related, and maybe some really need to be done, but if they aren't on your business schedule, either do them on your break or after finishing your business day.

Don't overwork. This was discussed in an earlier chapter, but it needs to be mentioned here among healthy work habits. Overworking can become a bad habit so set aside part of each day for leisure.

And finally, take care of yourself. Don't allow yourself to get so busy trying to manage your business and caring for your family that you don't look after the boss. On an especially busy day you might think no one is going to see you, and you don't take time to fix your hair or makeup. Just remember, your husband and children are the most important people you know, and they will see you. Be very careful to follow good hygiene, have dental and medical checkups, and don't let your appearance slip.

AVOIDING ISOLATION

Isolation can be depressing. You may be apprehensive about working alone at home because you fear you will become depressed and lonely, that you will miss the car pool and the office chatter. You can be sure you are not alone. A cottage industry doesn't appeal to everyone. Some people need the companionship of co-workers, yet they yearn for the freedom to work on their own projects in their own homes.

A good way to fight the debilitating force of isolation is by actively seeking and finding others involved in home-based work with whom you can network. Networking is, in "down home vernacular," getting together to jam, brainstorm and hem and haw. It has become one of the pleasant side benefits of the work-at-home movement. Networking is simply making contact with others. It is a growing phenomenon among homeworkers. Clubs, breakfast groups, and other organizations are being formed for the purpose of talking shop, exchanging ideas, sharing successes, solving problems, boosting morale, and sharing a few laughs. You will be surprised how these contacts and exchanges will help your business and reaffirm your sense of purpose. They can make the difference between sticking in there or giving up, the difference between success and failure.

The way to start networking is to contact other home business operators in your area, and plan a meeting to learn about common interests and exchange business ideas. You may want to look for companionship with homeworkers at large, or you may prefer to get together with workers who are in the same general field as yourself. Many towns already have an assortment of networking groups such as writer's guilds, artist's guilds, and clubs for lapidaries, photographers, and woodworkers, just to mention a few. There is also a group called Women In Networking, and an assortment of newsletters published for the purpose of networking contacts. Two are:

Alliance. Quarterly. National Alliance of Homebased Businesswomen, P. O. Box 306, Midland Park, NJ 07432.

National Home Business Report. Quarterly. P. O. Box 2137, Naperville, IL 60565.

You might also want to contact your local Chamber of Commerce, Kiwanis, Civitan, and Exchange Clubs. Each of these organizations is made up of professionals, many of whom run small businesses like yourself. Some of these organizations were once restricted to men, but their membership is open to both men and women these days. These organizations are invaluable; they are a source of contacts that can help as your business grows. It is necessary to apply for membership, and there is a membership fee.

Trade organizations are another way to contact people and learn what is going on in your field. These associations offer technical help and expert guidance through regional and national seminars and meetings. Guidance is offered in such areas as the latest trade developments, advertising and marketing, management, finance, government regulations, publicity and public relations, and techniques for problem-solving.

But networking doesn't need to be done through an organization. Many homeworkers gather on an informal basis just to talk about business and share experiences. Russell Humbert, a programmer with Rising Star of Redondo Beach, California, fights isolation by meeting other programmers for lunch. Jessie Mayes gives viola lessons in her home, and she and three other string instrument teachers have formed a string quartet meeting each week to talk and practice. Another group of homeworkers I've known for years gathers once a week for breakfast. We've shared the good times and bad, have lived through each other's financial crises, and celebrated when one of us has hired a helper or seen the red ink turn to black. We have helped each other by being available and by sharing interests and concerns, we are refueled for the week ahead.

Resource: *Networking,* by Mary Scott Welch. 1981. Warner Books, New York.

Part II

Managing Your Home Business

Choosing
the Right
Business

It's decision making time. The basic types of businesses and your options for working at home were presented in Chapter 2 so you would have the opportunity to think about them as you proceed through the book. I assume by now you have begun to make a mental commitment to some type of work. The following chapters will deal with how to set up and run a business. It would be to your advantage to have a specific occupation in mind before you read beyond this chapter. This will allow you to watch for information and tips that will facilitate your plans and help them become a reality.

Choosing the right business takes introspection and honesty. You need to evaluate your capabilities and limitations, consider your financial situation, your determination, courage, and personality traits as you decide on the kind of business to undertake. You need to find an occupation that will fit into your life, one that will take into account your personal goals, the things you do best, and the kind of work you enjoy.

Choosing the right business will be influenced by many variables including these:

- Your goals
- The amount of money you have to invest
- Your past work experience
- Your special skills, talents, interests
- Your attitude, personality
- Your other responsibilities
- The space you can use for business purposes
- The market for your product or service
- The potential for profit

As mentioned earlier, the types of home businesses fall into four main categories — manufacturing, service, creative work, or working for another business. A few comments about each is given here to help you make this very important decision.

MANUFACTURING

Some manufacturing processes require expensive equipment, but the kind of manufacturing applicable to a home business usually demands a high input of labor and personal involvement, but little equipment and a comparatively small investment of funds. Your customers may be wholesalers, retailers, industries, the general public, or governmental agencies. The most popular home-manufacturing businesses make baked goods, specialty foods and mass-produced handcrafted items.

SERVICE BUSINESSES

The largest number of home businesses are service oriented because they fit well into a domestic setting. Some can be started with little money while others require a significant investment in equipment. Some are based on brains, others on brawn.

PERSONAL services one might offer include laundry service, photography with photo processing and printing, beauty and barber services, house cleaning, catering, lawn care, tutoring, overnight lodging, child care, a singles meeting service, sewing and alterations, and delivery.

BUSINESS services include advertising, printing and copying, cleaning and maintenance, consulting, public relations, equipment rental, wholesaling and retailing, accounting, secretarial.

REPAIR services one might offer include automobile repair, automotive parts repair, shoe repair, reupholstering and furniture repair, machinery and equipment repair, appliance repair, and building repair.

PROFESSIONAL services are based on a special background or education and include legal services, medical and dental care, psychological testing and treatment, tutoring, and consulting services.

CREATIVE WORK

Working at home appeals to those interested in creative

endeavors because creativity can require solitude, and can demand so much time and energy that it becomes economically unfeasible in a commercial setting. Many creative careers are especially suited to a home business, for example, writing, arts and crafts, and research and development.

The number of written words published in this country is awesome, and each story, book or article is generated by a writer, many of whom are sitting at home in front of their word processor or typewriter. These writers pour out articles for magazines, books of fiction and nonfiction, newsletters, newspaper columns, music, manuals for businesses and civic organizations, and greeting cards. Some authors not only write the material, but in the case of newsletters, they may also print and distribute it. Other home entrepreneurs write and print their own greeting cards, while others write and publish small books, usually on specialty topics aimed at a specific audience.

Arts and crafts workers make nonfunctional art as well as functional items such as furniture, pottery, fabrics, leather goods and needlework. Some sell their own work while others sell through outlet shops and sales agents. Freelance commercial artwork is another outlet for artists. Businesses need artwork for advertising copy, brochures and book covers, logos, and other purposes.

A business can also be built around research and development. You might create inventions, make improvements on old ones, and explore unknowns. Some successful young companies such as Apple Computer are based on technological advances that started in a garage or basement where an inventor put together the right components or figured out the right formula for success. New inventions and permutations of old ones are sought by industry, private manufacturers, governmental agencies and research institutes. This field requires a keen awareness of the latest technologies and an affinity for scholarly activity.

WORKING FOR SOMEONE ELSE

You can work for someone else in your own home. A variety of information-based jobs can be done at home just as easily as in an office. There are several advantages of working for someone else rather than starting your own business. You have security — a regular paycheck — you don't have to invest your personal savings, and there is less likelihood of your evenings and weekends being interrupted with work. The disadvantages are that you aren't your own boss and must take orders from somebody else, you probably can't do the work that most appeals to you, there isn't much opportunity to accumulate wealth, there is less recognition and prestige, and you don't have the exhilarating challenge of making a business succeed.

If you are still searching for a trade, I direct you to the Appendix, which is a listing of possible home businesses with a brief descriptive statement about each. The decision you make about the kind of business you will start could affect the rest of your life. Think about it carefully. As you read the following chapters and make a market analysis and feasibility study, you may find your initial business plans will need to be changed, but go ahead and make a decision so you can get started. Yes, throw your hat into the ring and let's get down to business.

Determining the Feasibility of Your Business Plans

Now that you have decided what you'd LIKE to do, it's time to determine if it's practical and if there is a reasonable chance for success. To solidify your ideas, put them on paper. Briefly describe the business you plan to create, list the products and/or services you want to sell, and describe your potential customers.

THINK ABOUT THE WORK YOU WILL BE DOING

Think through the process of doing the work your business would entail, and make certain the *work itself* appeals to you, not just the notion that you are going to have this or that kind of business. Sometimes we get so taken in by an idea that we fail to realize what it really means. My husband runs into this every day. He counsels pre-med students, many of whom have been brought up with the idea they will be "Doctors" with a big D. He is responsible for making these young people understand that they will be dealing with sickness, with a high percentage of the elderly, with blood and guts, with healing and with death. If they can handle that, they may be pre-med material. Some are startled when they realize what a doctor does each day, and they move on to a different field. Others understand what lies ahead and anxiously pursue their goal. It is a good idea to take a mental stroll through the day-to-day routine of what you think will make up the workday of your business.

As you think about the possible procedures and events of your business day, you should realize that all work has its good and bad features. There is repetition and drudgery in every field, but there are also the good moments. An organist practices that difficult passage over and over again, but the hours of practice are eclipsed by the moment when the piece is performed. Or, a baker stands in a hot kitchen beating, pouring, and baking, yet the iced perfection makes the hard work worth the effort. A carpet and floor cleaner can stand tall when surveying the results of a day of hard work, and a repairman has to be pleased when a repaired motor purrs like a kitten.

DEFINE YOUR MARKET

After concluding that, yes, you'd like to do the work your business requires, start thinking about who your customers might be. Write down the kinds of people you expect to use your service or product and add this to your business description. Define the geographical areas from which you can expect to draw customers, and determine the population of these areas. What financial and age segment of the population will you appeal to? Is the target population stable or growing? Answers to these and related questions will help you estimate the number of potential customers. For instance, if you plan to be a chimney sweep, you need to know the approximate number of homes with fireplaces or stoves in your target area. If you plan to cater wedding receptions, then the number of weddings per year in your area would be a valuable piece of information. If you intend to write resumes, you must learn if there is a large pool of job seekers. In other words, you need to know if there are enough potential customers for your product or service to sustain your business and provide the kind of income and profit you expect. All this will help determine if yours will be a feasible business venture.

IDENTIFY YOUR COMPETITION

Having identified your potential customers, you then should learn if their needs are already being met. Just because the potential customers are out there doesn't mean they will be knocking on your door or paying for your services. Somebody may have beaten you to the market. To learn who your competitors will be: look in the Yellow Pages of the telephone directory, talk to friends and neighbors, call the Chamber of Commerce. Act as if you are a customer trying to find a business that can meet your needs. Learn who your major competitors are, and look for their strengths and weaknesses. Try to discover as much as you can about them. Become familiar with their prices, product lines, and promotional activities. Are they planning to expand? Are their profits expanding or decreasing? Have any firms of that type gone out of business lately, and if so, why? And finally, is there reason to believe you can compete successfully?

Just because you find other businesses providing the same product or service doesn't mean that the market is full. You may still do well by appealing to a different market with a slightly different product or different quality of product. You might reach a different market altogether through a new advertising approach, or become more competitive through pricing (which a home business might well do because of lower overhead costs).

As you survey your competition, these are some questions you need to ask:

- Will your business cater to a presently unserved need?
- Will your business serve an existing market whose demand is greater than the supply?
- Do you have reason to believe you can create enough competitive advantages to successfully compete with existing businesses and get a share of the market?
- Will your market share be sufficient to support your venture?

DETERMINE THE MINIMUM BUSINESS NEEDED

Plan the financial aspect of your business very carefully. Calculate how much money you will need to set up your business and the working capital needed to keep it and your family functioning until you start to realize a profit. Next, equate the minimum amount of money you can get by with to how much business activity will be required to earn that same amount. Then, calculate how much business it will take to provide a sufficient income. Is it possible, probable?

When figuring the money you will need, remember to include expenses for both the business and the family — money for equipment, supplies, insurance, utilities, advertising, interest, selling, shipping, rent or mortgage payments, food, clothing — then add a bunch more for items ranging from kid's school books to Christmas presents.

Spend a little time trying to think of any major risks associated with your products, service, or business operations. If the risks are significant, is there any way to minimize them? If there are risks beyond your control, how serious are they? Can they cause you to go bankrupt or make your business fail?

I don't intend to be negative, but you should be aware of the statistic indicating less than a 50-50 chance you will be in business five years from now. The probability improves in your favor the more thoroughly you plan, so keep asking questions and looking for the answers that can give your business that winning edge.

Selecting
a Legal Form
of Ownership

What type of organizational structure is best for you? This chapter will help you select the legal structure best suited for your home business. Each type of organization has advantages and disadvantages, and it is important to understand how the legal organization of your cottage industry can influence your business opportunities.

There are three ways your business might be organized – the sole proprietorship, partnership, and corporation. Most home business operators prefer the sole proprietorship because they are seeking independence; they need relatively little capital to get started; and the chance of liability claims are minimal. Partnerships are formed when more money or extra workers are needed or when enthusiastic cohorts share a common dream but liability is not considered a threat. Home-based businesses are incorporated when several people are interested in working together; when larger amounts of capital are needed; when the company intends to grow into a larger firm, and/or when the threat of liability (as with lawsuits or business debts) is intimidating.

THE SOLE PROPRIETORSHIP

The sole proprietorship is a business owned and operated by one person. It is the most common type of business organization, and at least 85 percent of the home businesses operating in this country are sole proprietorships. It is the easiest kind of business to start and stop. A sole proprietor can start a business by putting out a shingle and getting to work, and stop business by not going to work. The advantages of the sole proprietorship are: 1) its ease of formation; 2) the profits are

not shared; and 3) there is no one looking over your shoulder telling you how it should be done or berating you when something goes awry. Since there are no co-owners or partners to consult, decisions can be made quickly in response to changing circumstances. Also, there is little governmental control or special taxation. In fact, you and the business you run as a sole proprietorship are treated as one in the eyes of the IRS. This is especially helpful for those working another job while trying to start a business. Generally, a business loses money for awhile, and these losses can be deducted from earned income before taxes are figured.

The biggest disadvantage of a sole proprietorship is the liability the owner must assume for all business debts, taxes, and lawsuits that might be filed against the business. You can plan for taxes because you expect them, but business debts and lawsuits can hit when least expected. When you are in business, you pay your debts or quickly discover your credit rating destroyed, and that is tantamount to committing business suicide. The liability of business debts becomes a problem if the business fails. If you borrow heavily to start a business, and the business fails, you will be responsible for all debts that have been incurred. Fortunately, most home business operators don't borrow great sums of money to get started, so this is not an overwhelming problem. The possibility of a lawsuit is much more worrisome. In our society, liability can threaten not only the business investment, but also all the proprietor's personal holdings, including cars, house, livestock, and other possessions. Every effort to protect oneself against this eventuality should be taken (See Insurance, Chapter 21).

Another disadvantage of the sole proprietorship is the limited viewpoint, since one person, rather that several or many people, is contributing ideas. (However, the main reason many businesses operate from home is that it gives the owner an opportunity to test ideas without the limitations conferred by a boss or other less intrepid souls.) Another disadvantage is that less capital is available to a sole proprietor than multiple owners, but again, this may not be an important factor because home businesses don't require much capital to get underway.

All in all, the ease of formation and the flexible nature of the sole proprietorship make this the most widespread of home-run business organizations.

PARTNERSHIP

A partnership is an arrangement between two or more people for the purpose of conducting business to make a profit. The roles of the partners are usually defined in an Articles of Partnership document, and include the contribution of each partner to the business. A partnership should never be based on a handshake. The contribution of the partners might be financial, material, or managerial. Home businesses are not usually looking for managerial help, but some of them need financial backing, especially to get started. If you select this type of organization for your business, you must be very careful because partners can influence business decisions you might feel should be under your control. That is the reason it is important to retain at least 51 percent interest in the business or you may find yourself working for somebody else.

Many kinds of partnerships can be established. Some partners are active and share in the day-to-day responsibilities of running the business, while others are limited partners and their role is only to financially subsidize the business, and they do not become involved in its operation. The association may or may not be known to the public. A limited partner who does not participate in the management or conduct of the business is usually not subject to the same liability as a general partner, and risks only the agreed investment in the business.

It is very easy to form a partnership, and there is little governmental control or special taxation. However, profits must be shared and there is less freedom because authority and decisions are also shared. But again, the biggest disadvantage is the liability problem. Partners who operate the business will be burdened with the same unlimited liability as a sole proprietor. Also, like sole proprietors, it remains difficult to acquire much capital for long-term financing, although pooling resources yields more working capital than a single person might have. That is usually the reason partnerships are formed.

A partnership is not a common organization for home-based businesses simply because most people who work at home try to avoid sharing business decisions with someone else. There are numerous exceptions to this, such as good friends who brew up a business while chatting over a different sort of brew. I'm reminded of several women teams who are happily working together – their businesses grew out of friendship and shared interests. Of course, there are informal partnerships, as when parents subsidize a business venture of their offspring, whether the offspring is still a child trying to set up a lemonade stand or an adult trying to find a niche in the business world. This type of partnership should be entered into with an awareness of how the business partnership might affect the family relationship and vice versa.

CORPORATION

A corporation is surely the most complicated of the three business structures. It is a legal entity, distinct from the individuals or the personal worth of the people who own it. The term "legal entity" is enough to scare away those unfamiliar with this type of jargon, but at least take a look at the advantages and disadvantages of incorporating since this may be just the organization you need for your home business.

A corporation must have a minimum of three officers who form the board of directors, but the "board" can be much larger than three members. (Some states require only one director to start a corporation.) The board of directors for a small home business might consist of Mom, Dad and their child; or a couple and one of their parents; a couple and a friend, or other combinations.

There are several big advantages to being incorporated. In the first place, and perhaps most importantly, it is much easier to secure capital in large amounts and from numerous investors if a business is incorporated rather than unincorporated. The two main sources of capital are through the issuance of stock and long term bonds. A home business that is incorporated can offer shares of stock for sale and use the money received from the stock to finance the business. The stock sale can be limited to family members until money is needed for expansion, when shares can be offered to others. Also, it is easier to obtain long-term financing from lending institutions by taking advantage of corporate assets and the personal assets of stockholders.

Another important advantage of corporate organization is that liability is limited to the assets of the corporation, and personal funds are not threatened in the event of liability claims or bankruptcy.

Another advantage (or disadvantage, depending on your point of view) is that incorporated businesses usually delegate authority and rely on more than one person for ideas, skill and expertise, although this is not always the case. Many home businesses are incorporated to put structure into the organization, acquire capital, and protect the operator from unlimited liability, but the business is actually operated by one person.

The biggest disadvantage of being incorporated is the government regulations and reports that must be filed. Also, it costs more to form a corporation, especially if you must hire a lawyer. You can do your own legal work, (see **Resource** below). Another disadvantage of incorporating is that the earnings are taxed twice — the business profit is taxed, and a tax is paid on the individual salaries and dividends. However, a corporation can elect to be classified as an S corporation if it meets certain qualifications. This status allows taxes to be paid as if the stockholders are partners. It is important to beginning businesses because it allows shareholders to offset business losses incurred by the corporation, against their personal income. An incorporated business qualifies for S status if: (1) There are no more than ten employees, (2) There is only one class of stock, and (3) There are no nonresident alien shareholders. The size of the corporation's income and assets is irrelevant.

So, the question is, should you or should you not incorporate? If you plan a small home business and do not foresee it growing into a large operation, and the probability of overwhelming liability is very slight, then you probably would not gain much by incorporating. However, if you are planning a cottage industry but expect it to grow into a larger operation, maybe even move to a larger location eventually, it might be wise to incorporate early to take advantage of the more readily available financing, the limited liability, and the input of funds, expertise and ideas from members of the board and the stockholders. Of course, you don't need to start as a corporation. You could begin as a sole proprietorship or partnership and change to a corporation as your business grows and its needs are better met by incorporating.

Resource: *How to Incorporate in Any State Without a Lawyer.* Laurence Pino, 1991. University of Florida, Gainesville, FL 32611.

Creating a Business Image

The image you project can make or break your business. There is a skill to creating image, but first you must decide what you want the public to think about your business. Do you want them to view it as unique, or solid, or maybe that you do quality work, or that your products or service are reliable? If you could select a single adjective or phrase to describe your product or service, what would it be — the best, trustworthy, creative, useful, dependable, a class act, convenient — what?

You're probably aware of businesses that produce very similar products, but one is successful while the other just barely hangs on. Sometimes the only significant difference between the two is how the public views them. An image problem can plague small businesses as well as large companies. In the last few years J. C. Penney has been trying to the shake the "dime store" image. Although they now carry better quality products and even designer clothing (Halston and others), they are still considered by many to carry modestly priced merchandise, and consequently, are regularly passed by as shoppers go to "pricier" stores down the street.

Cosmetics can also illustrate the point. Many cosmetic companies get their products from the same manufacturer who packages the same product under different labels. The labels are designed to fit the image each company wishes to convey. Some of these companies hike the price and spend the extra bucks on elaborate advertising campaigns, while others keep prices low, spend little on advertising, but pick up sales because they are modestly priced. The image projected by these companies determines who will buy their products and how much they will pay.

As your business gets underway, you will not have a background of proven sales and satisfied customers, so you will need to become an illusionist — to create an illusion of success and reliability. Strive to give the impression that you are established on the first day you open shop. Let your confidence show you are in complete control, quite capable, and up to the tasks at hand, even when working with your first or second customer. This in turn will inspire confidence in your new customers, and they will view you as a serious contender in the marketplace.

To continue the illusion of having been around for awhile, number purchase order forms and invoices with a high number, starting with something like 2036, for example, rather than the telltale "Number 1." Who's to know you haven't been filling orders for years? (This is more effective when dealing with customers through the mail or phone, but is a little difficult to pull off when customers visit and the new paint still smells wet.) Of course, any impression you give must be backed up by a good product or service, and then the illusion melds into reality.

NAME YOUR BUSINESS

What's in a name? The name you select and the logo that accompanies it will be the signal to the world that you are functioning as a specific business. It is important to select a name that will best convey the business image you want to establish. It should have several characteristics. Select a name that is descriptive but at the same time is somewhat general or flexible so it will accommodate a diversified and changing product or service. If possible, it should have a ring of familiarity, it should inspire confidence and elude to desirable traits. That's a tall order to fill, but let's look at some examples.

Select a name with a positive image. If you were to look in the telephone directory for a florist and had to select between "Brown's Flower Shop" or "Green and Growing," there is little doubt which one you would call first. Those names weren't made up for the purpose of illustration. Ted Brown didn't realize the name of his business sent a subliminal message, but he knew he had problems when he didn't attract enough business. One day Ted needed a certain type of flower and didn't have time to order it from his supplier. He turned to the telephone directory to find another florist when it hit him. He had seen it before, but this time, seeing his business listing, he knew immediately what his problem was. People don't call for brown flowers. He changed the name to "Green and Growing" and his business is now flourishing.

A name with a familiar ring will make a customer think they have heard it before, and that alone can be what causes them to dial one number rather than another. In a basketball-crazy town where the local university's mascot is called the 'Aces,' it is not surprising that Ace's Sportswear is more successful than Miller's Sport Shop.

A substantial name, one that suggests stability, evokes a feeling of security. A family name might be used if it is well known and has been associated with good works in the community. Vance Hartke used to be the mayor of my hometown, but he has long since left the area for the environs of Washington. His brother has used the Hartke name in his local business because it is familiar and people vividly remember the 'Hartke era.' In some curious way people confer the success of one Hartke brother onto the other and willingly take their business to him.

A name with celebrity status also sells. Paul Newman's dressings may not taste one bit better than Brook's or Henri's, but the name will make us pay a few cents more as we recall those vivid blue eyes. However, you can't use a celebrity's name for your products, but you CAN use something similar. If, for instance, your name is Sarah Neuman, you could have your own line of Neuman's dressings.

When a business is just getting underway, it's difficult to know how it might change to meet the market, and for that reason it is wise to select a name that is a little ambiguous, one that could have several meanings. If you recall, the name of my family's home business is "Printed Tree, Inc." We selected this name because it alludes to various paper products, and leaves us with several options. We could make greeting cards, publish, write newsletters, or for that matter, even manufacture decorated paper plates. Also, our business stationery can be used for my business letters to editors for freelance writing.

Be clever but not "klever" when naming your business because this might suggest a small, less serious operation, and this can cause problems when dealing with suppliers. Some companies will deal only with established businesses, and if your name suggests a small home operation, they may be reluctant to sell to you or even respond to your inquiries. Also, avoid starting your business name with "the" because it might confuse customers trying to find your business name in directories. If, for instance, a business is named "The Red Sled," some people would not know if they should look under "T" for "The" or "R" for "Red."

And finally, the name of your business should be short, one that will "fall off the tongue," — not something that is lumbering and difficult to remember or say. Keep all these things in mind as you try to create the best name possible for your business.

Having decided upon a name, telephone the office of your Secretary of State in your state capital for a name search. The office personnel will punch the name you have selected into their computer, and you will learn if the name is already in use. Unincorporated businesses are not listed, but at least you will know if an incorporated company is already using the name, in which case you will be prohibited from using it. You might also register your company's name with the city or county clerk. This isn't absolutely necessary but is a protection against another business using it. This could become important if another business selects the same name and it becomes necessary to settle a dispute in court.

DESIGN A LOGO

Design a logo that visually defines what you do. It should be pleasing to the eye and should demand a lingering look or tickle the imagination. If you have a flair for art, make your own logo, but hire help if you can't make it look professional. This symbol will be the way your business is identified and, like the name, it must convey the right message. Many businesses use stylized initials of the owner for their logo, but initials don't suggest anything and are ineffective. You can lose a powerful advertising tool if your logo does not make an impression or provoke a thought. A design that incorporates the name of the business into the logo can be very effective. An example is the Whirlpool Corporation, whose logo is a huge whirlpool-like configuration cutting across the company name.

A "one-liner" might be your logo instead of a design. You may be familiar with the chain of Hale's Auto Parts, whose owner's name is Hale. The one-liner on the company trucks and on all advertising is the play on words, "Go to Hale." I'm not sure the connotation is exactly right, but this logo popped into my mind as I tried to think of an example, and that is what logos are all about — making potential customers remember your business. By the way, designing logos for private and public organizations and businesses is a very nice cottage industry, one that can operate from a drawing board tucked somewhere within the household.

After designing a logo, make it work for you. Use it on everything that goes out of your shop or office. Put it on stationery, calling cards, and advertising, and on all signs and vehicles you use for business purposes. If you manufacture a product, be sure your logo appears on each and every item. This is a good way to advertise and reinforce your business image without spending much money.

STATIONERY AND OTHER PAPER PRODUCTS

How do you look on paper? With your business name and logo in place, it's time to get some stationery printed. You can get stationery printed on 20-pound paper and it doesn't cost much — but it looks like it doesn't cost much. Go ahead and spend the few extra dollars for 24-pound paper. This will give the impression that your business is alive and well. Have envelopes printed at the same time. You'll be surprised at how much stationery you will use, especially as you get started, because during this period you will be writing to companies to locate supplies and to make your presence and services known. You might as well start with a printing of 500 sheets of letterhead and 500 envelopes.

You can save quite a lot of money if you do the pasteup for your stationery and other business forms. Pasteup means designing the letterhead and making it ready for the printer. If you don't know how to do this, you might want to learn because you will probably need a variety of printed forms for your business, and each form will need to be designed or pasted up. It's quite easy to learn to do pasteups and, with a little practice, they can be made to look very professional. Use rub-on letters (available at art or office supply shops), a ruler, and a black-inked pen. Never use a pencil to draw lines or write on the original because the lines will appear light and irregular when they are printed. Everything must be exact, but you can make corrections or cover mistakes with white liquid paper because the printing process only picks up solid black marks. If you can't do this type of work and aren't interested in learning how, your printer can do it for you.

After your stationery is printed, ask the printer for the original and keep it on file. You will need the original for each subsequent printing. Some printers offer to keep it in their files, but it is your property since you made it or paid to have it made, and it is wise to keep it in your possession just in case you want to change printers. Also, the printer might lose or damage the original, and you will need to have another made. I learned this through the "get smart too late club." The printer lost the original for our home business stationery and we were forced to redraw the entire logo and letterhead.

Fancy paper isn't enough to convince potential customers you mean business. Everything that goes out of your office or shop should be accurate and look good. Obviously, some kinds of businesses don't need to look as "uptown" as others. For instance, messages sent from a small motor repair business don't demand the sophisticated look that law office messages would. Yet each must reinforce the image the business person wishes to convey to clients, and this is accomplished through both the character of the stationery and the way the messages are written. Whether or not the message sent from your business is a formal letter typed on business stationery or a memo, the message should be accurate, tidy, and to the point.

(The use of advertising to establish your business image is discussed in Chapter 18.)

Resource: *How to Do Your Own Pasteup for Printing.* Edmund J. Gross, 1979. Halls of Ivy, 3445 Leora Ave., Simi Valley, CA 93063.

Financial Management and Record-Keeping Systems

Financial management and record-keeping systems are combined in this chapter because one depends on the other. A bookkeeping system that clearly identifies business transactions is necessary to interpret financial records. This interpretation is a prerequisite to successful financial management.

You, the readers of this book, are coming from different financial backgrounds, and what is important to one will be of little value to another. Some of you are planning to operate a part-time business from your home and what you earn will supplement another income; it probably won't be a calamity if your business doesn't yield the profits you anticipate. But others intend a home business as the sole source of income. Some are planning a business that will require very little money to get started; others will need a sizable sum. Perhaps some of you have been diligently saving money to start your business, while others are barely making ends meet and have no savings put aside. I have tried to provide the guidance for a diversity of financial situations in the following pages.

DON'T BURN BRIDGES

If you have a job, keep it, unless your spouse is working and can support the family while you start a business. If you haven't a job, and have little money, property or valuables, get one. You may think that's strange advice to give someone who wants to run their own business, but this advice is based on the reality that a new business will not yield a profit immediately, and you will need another source of income. Also, it takes money to start a business — much more than you might suspect. It is premature for you to consider starting a business if you haven't any money to invest in the venture. You will need to earn money by working for someone else before you can hope to work for yourself. But, but, but... you might protest — but that's just how it works. Perhaps you think you can borrow the money you need. You can only borrow money if you have something of value, (collateral) to provide as security to the lending institution. The bank will claim the collateral in the event you can't repay the loan.

If you have a job and need an income while your business gets underway, it would be a good idea to lay the groundwork and get the business started on a part-time basis while you are still working. This will allow you to get well into or even through the unprofitable phase before leaving your paying job. I suspect many of you are planning to convert a hobby into a business. In that case, you have already mastered the necessary skills and know where to get supplies, but you will still need to set the merchandising wheels in motion before letting loose the security of a regular paycheck.

It's difficult to decide exactly when to let go of a job and go for broke. A colleague of mine found herself caught in the when-to-stop dilemma. She taught school, and her income was needed to cover the family bills. But she loved to write and spent her evenings and weekends writing articles for confession magazines. She discovered she could consistently sell her work but was caught in a bind. While teaching school she couldn't write enough to earn much, but she thought if she could write full time, her income would equal her teaching income — IF she continued to sell the work — and that was a big IF. She took the gamble, stopped teaching and, as planned, started a full schedule of writing, only to find the plots that had always been brewing in her head were no longer churning about. What Linda hadn't realized was the value of those half-heard conversations in the teacher's lounge — they were the basis of her steaming true confessions. Linda has returned to substitute teaching and seems to have found the combination that works for her. She doesn't have to sell THAT many articles because she is making a little money teaching, and the contacts she makes at school provide the characters and plots for the articles she writes. (Very few people can make a living writing articles for magazines. See FREELANCE WRITING in the Appendix.)

Whatever your situation, don't burn the financial bridges that can carry you from where you are now, to a business that yields enough profit for your needs.

DETERMINE YOUR FINANCIAL NEEDS

Most home businesses are rather small so the financial demands are modest. Nonetheless, these needs must be adequately met before the business has much of a chance. Thoroughly plan your business and evaluate its assets before approaching possible sources of capital. A potential investor will be looking for the same degree of professionalism in your small home business as shown by larger firms, and you should be aware that you will be competing for the same dollars.

How much money will you need? The following discussion will help you figure how much money it will take to cover start-up costs, the operating funds necessary to keep the business functioning until it's profitable, and the amount of money required to meet your personal and family needs.

Cost-of-Living Budget

What does it cost to meet your monthly financial obligations and sustain your home and family? (It is assumed that during this lean period you will spend no more than is absolutely necessary.) Your budget should include the following items:

1. Household expenses including utilities, telephone, repairs and maintenance.

2. Food

3. Personal expenses such as clothing, laundry, medical care and medication, auto repair and gas, education, entertainment, gifts, contributions, and spending money.

4. Monthly payments for rent or mortgage, car and car insurance, loans, health plan, and insurance premiums.

5. Federal and state income taxes and property taxes, particularly those not withheld from your paycheck.

Carefully calculate expenses for each of the above for a single month, then add them together. Since it is unreasonable to expect to earn a profit for a minimum of three months, and more likely five or six months, multiply the monthly amount accordingly. The resulting figure is the amount of money you will need to have available for cost-of-living expenses.

Start-Up Expenses

The cost of starting a business will vary for each kind of enterprise, but can include any or all of the following items:

1. Legal, accounting, and secretarial fees.
2. Licenses, if needed.

3. Office supplies: stationery and envelopes, purchase orders, file folders, rubber stamps, and miscellaneous office items.

4. Office equipment: desk, chair, filing cabinet, shelving, lights, typewriter or computer.

5. Equipment and supplies needed to manufacture products.

6. Equipment and parts needed for repair work.

7. Product or parts-related equipment such as storage cabinets and bins.

8. Shipping supplies including boxes, tape, scales.

9. Postage stamps, long distance phone calls, shipping.

10. Initial banking expenses.

11. Car expenses for business-related errands.

12. Signs and advertisement.

13. Research and development of product(s).

14. Dues and subscriptions.

15. Petty cash and miscellaneous expenses.

Add together the start-up costs to determine how much money you'll need to get underway. You can be sure you can't anticipate many of the expenses you will have so be very liberal in your estimates. Now add a goodly amount to circumvent a cash-flow crisis. It's difficult to calculate how much cash will be needed to keep the wolves from your back, but figure high rather than low, maybe even one-third to one-half of starting costs. The total is the amount of money required to start and sustain your business until it starts to earn a profit.

A few things need to be mentioned about cash flow because new business managers are sometimes surprised to find themselves in a cash flow bind. You can expect to run into this problem in the early stages of a new business. Cash flow is the manner in which cash comes in from sales and goes out as expenses. When a serious cash-flow problem arises, you might feel as if you have bought a new toy (your business) but haven't the money to buy a battery to make it work. A business can grind to a halt without the cash that's needed for day-to-day expenses. There are many reasons this problem develops, but the most common one is that customers owe you money, but fail to pay promptly, while you need the money for more supplies and for operating expenses. A cash flow crisis might strike when you are trying to establish a good credit rating, and you will feel compelled to pay your bills on time. It may be necessary to obtain a short-term loan to get through a cash shortage, although encouraging your customers to pay their debts is the more direct way to alleviate the problem.

Controlling your cash flow is vital if you are to pay your bills when they come due, and plan promotions, and cover unexpected expenses. There are ways to control the movement of cash. Make a chart showing WHEN your various bills are due each month (loan payments, utilities, etc.). If a lot of money is needed early in the month, wait to pay yourself until later in the month. Also, in anticipation of cash needs, send invoices well enough ahead so your customers will pay their bills. If you are really strapped for money, you can offer a discount for early payment. Go after overdue bills aggressively, as described below.

WAYS TO FUND YOUR BUSINESS

Funds to get started are the most difficult to find because the business is only marks on paper and a vision in your mind. You have nothing tangible to show that the planned business can succeed. The problem is, you can't make it work without the money, but you can't get money until you show it can be successful. It's another "Catch 22" situation, but others have overcome it and so can you. After you have demonstrated your ability to make a profit, money is much easier to acquire.

The sources of capital used by most businesses (banks and various other lending institutions) are not the most likely places to find support for a home business. The following discussion explores the various fundraising avenues open to you. As you look for the funds you need, remember the old German proverb, "He who borrows sells his freedom," so make certain you know what you are "selling" as you gather money for your business.

Personal Funds

You will need some personal funds to get started. Business consultants advise that at least 50 percent of your business investment should come from your own funds, and most lending organizations insist that you have a 50 percent minimal investment before they will even consider granting a loan. This is the reason you were advised earlier to get a job if you don't have money to invest in your business. Using an inheritance or your savings is obviously the easiest and best way to get started. Even so, it is important to make detailed business plans lest you waste your nest egg on a poorly conceived project. When the money is available, there is sometimes a tendency to jump ahead and start with inadequate planning. Resist this temptation. After your business is established and showing a good profit, you may want to return your personal investment money to your personal savings. Since this is a return of capital and not income, this money is not taxable.

If you have no money saved and no collateral, you might think you can just buy a few things, get started and keep putting everything back into the business. This might work for a very small business that can grow slowly or for a business that is more a hobby than a meal ticket, but it certainly won't work for more ambitious ventures. Generally, it's unwise to "just start," unless of course, you have no financial obligations and your business will have few expenses.

Private Investors

Family or friends may be interested in getting in on the action and contributing some money to help finance your business. It's very common for people about to embark on a new business to talk about it so much that their friends get tired of hearing about it, but sometimes their enthusiasm sparks an interest in friends or family, and they become willing to loan some money. Remember that anyone who loans you money is expecting something in return. They might want "equity" or part ownership, or they might expect to earn an attractive rate of interest. Even though it is not required, it is wise to prepare a detailed statement of your business plans, a budget, and a realistic repayment plan. Have everything on paper, and be sure your investors understand the arrangement and particularly the risks which you have accepted and are now sharing with them.

One word of caution. People who invest money in your business might feel they can influence the course it takes. It is important to have an understanding that you are in complete control. Also, be especially diligent, and repay as planned so as not to jeopardize relationships. John D. Rockefeller said, "A friendship founded on business is better than a business founded on friendship." Keep that little jewel in mind as you look for investors in your circle of friends.

Lending Institutions

Lending money is big business. Banks are in the business of loaning money, but they are looking for established enterprises and aren't especially keen on making LONG-TERM loans to unproven ones. Their decision on whether or not to loan money is based on the borrower's personal credit history, the ability to repay, and the borrower's experience and potential in the proposed business. When you are starting a home business, you may not have the required qualifications to garner a loan. However, after your business is established you may return to the bank for operating capital or SHORT-TERM loans.

Another option for obtaining money is the savings and loan associations. These institutions usually offer a mortgage on your personal property but many charge a rather high rate of interest, and that could make your financial position rather precarious. Life insurance companies also offer loans on certain types of policies that have accumulated a cash value over the years. The advantage of this kind of loan is that the interest can be deferred as long as the premiums are paid. If the loan is not repaid, the policy value will be reduced by the amount of the loan and the accrued interest.

Government Loans

The Small Business Administration has funds available to loan, but the competition is stiff and the waiting period seems interminable, though its only three to eight months. SBA loans are available only to people who have been turned down by two banks, and they usually go to those with special circumstances such as minorities, the handicapped, and Vietnam vets. Beyond the difficulty of getting an SBA loan is an interest rate that is one to one-and-a-half percentage points more than bank loans because of the increased risk. Also, some SBA loans require the borrower to put up 50 percent of the total capital needed. As you can see, it is very difficult to borrow money if you haven't some personal seed money to begin with.

APPLYING FOR A LOAN

Before trying to find funding, prepare a detailed business plan using the format found in loan application forms. It is helpful to go through the steps of preparing a bank loan application even if you don't need to borrow money because this will force you to be realistic and thorough. You can use a form from a bank or you can put together one of your own. In either case the following subjects should be addressed:

1. Cover letter. Use a cover letter to introduce yourself and set the stage for the loan application.

2. Business description. Start your application by describing the business you are planning, giving its name, location, and an explanation of what you will do or make. And put it right

up front — state how much money you need. The business will be explained in detail in the following sections.

3. Product or service. Describe your product line or service and show how it compares to competitors' products or services.

4. Market analysis. Describe the market, industry trends, your target market, and the competition.

5. Manufacturing procedure. The bank will want to know what it is you will be making (if applicable) and how you plan to make it. Describe the materials to be used, your suppliers, and explain your production methods.

6. Marketing strategy. How will you distribute and sell your products or service?

7. Organization. Define the business organization, and name the Board of Directors if the business is incorporated. Include your personal resume since you will be running the business, and explain why you have the background to make the business succeed.

8. Financial information. Show how much money it will take to start the business and state how much you have and how much more is needed. Make financial projections, and explain how you arrived at the figures. Clearly relate the money requested to your financial needs. And finally, lay out a plan for repaying the loan.

Writing a loan proposal is a demanding task, but it's worth the effort to develop a package that a lending organization can't refuse. Do your homework and make the plan sound feasible and, through your presentation, show you are capable of running the business and confident of its success. Also, make the application look professional. If you can't put it into final form, hire a typist because the application's appearance will influence the decision-makers.

Resource: *How to Borrow Money from a Banker: A Business Owner's Guide.* Roger Bel Air, 1988. AMACOM, Trudeau Rd., Saranac Lake, NY 12983.

BOOKKEEPING AND FINANCIAL RECORDS

Financial records are the heart of a business and it is imperative that you keep accurate and organized records as a part of your daily activities. You might think you will know how things are going just by watching the daily operation, but that can be misleading. Only when you get the numbers on paper and are confronted with the cold numerical facts, can you evaluate the financial condition of your business. Also, records are needed to validate business transactions when you prepare tax returns or if you are audited or subjected to an investigation.

When To Use An Accountant

It would be wise to consult an accountant for help in setting up your books and learning what kinds of records to keep for tax purposes. You will also need to use an accountant's services at least once each year to help prepare tax returns, prepare an annual statement, and to analyze the financial condition of your business. The analysis will inform you of strengths of the business that can be built on and weaknesses that should be corrected.

Hiring an accountant will be an expense but will probably save money in the long run because this expertise can be used to help organize your financial activities to take advantage of tax breaks. An accountant is also helpful when you are confronted with contracts. The fine print and the terminology in contracts causes trouble for some small business owners who discover too late what they have signed. Advice at the appropriate time can help circumvent a disaster by allowing you to understand the full scope of the contractual obligations you are considering. Then you can make decisions based on the facts rather than on assumptions. Also, it probably will be necessary to furnish a financial statement prepared by a certified public accountant if you intend to apply for a bank loan.

Don't pick an accountant at random, but ask business friends for a recommendation. Make sure the person you hire is experienced with small business accounting. Also, your accountant must be someone you can bare your soul to and trust without reservation because he or she will know more about your financial condition than anybody else. Before hiring an accountant, discuss charges and fees so you aren't surprised by a larger bill than you expect.

Other financial advice is also available to you. Two good sources of free help are the Small Business Administration and SCORE, an acronym for "Service Corps of Retired Executives." SCORE is sponsored by the Small Business Administration and, as the name implies, is made up of retired business executives who share their expertise with beginning and struggling business people. Also, if you borrow money to get your business started, the bank loan officer can offer some no-nonsense advice. If all else fails, read a book on the financial management of a small business. There are many on this subject in nearly every library.

Bookkeeping Made Easy

Your bookkeeping system does not need to be elaborate, only thorough enough to let you and the IRS see what you are doing with your money. Your system should be easy to use and understand, consistent, and it must be kept up to date. It should allow you to see at a glance where money is coming from and where it is being spent.

The term "single entry" refers to a bookkeeping and accounting method in which all transactions are recorded in one set of books. It is the easiest form of bookkeeping and is quite adequate for a small business. A journal is used to record every receipt and expenditure, and a ledger is used to distribute expenditures and receipts to accounts that indicate their use. Your home business might have accounts for raw materials, utilities, office supplies, tools, and the like.

The journal of receipts and expenditures is maintained daily, while the ledger of accounts is usually brought up to date monthly or quarterly. It will be up to you to keep the daily records, but you may want your accountant to work with individual accounts to analyze expenditures and receipts.

The following chart lists the various activities you should perform so you can evaluate your financial position.

FINANCIAL CHECKLIST

Daily

1. Determine the cash on hand.
2. Summarize sales and cash receipts.
3. Record monies paid out.

Weekly

1. Accounts receivable — send out notices for late accounts.
2. Accounts payable — pay your own bills to take advantage of discounts.
3. Payroll and taxes, if you have employees.

Monthly or Quarterly

1. Prepare a Profit and Loss statement. This statement lists the total income from sales and the cost of producing the product or rendering the service. The difference is the gross profit or loss. Taxes are then deducted from the gross profit to show

the net profit or loss. Use this information to evaluate progress and to make changes as needed.

2. Prepare a Balance Sheet showing assets, liabilities, and your investment.

3. Check that the Bank Statement of your checking account agrees with your books.

4. Check that the Petty Cash Account is correct, with receipts and expenditures equaling the amount of cash deducted from the account.

5. Make sure tax payments are made.

6. Arrange accounts receivable in the order they are due, and send notices to late accounts.

7. Bring the inventory records up to date, and use the information to adjust the inventory to optimum levels by marking down product prices to reduce inventory or ordering goods to increase it.

Expense Records

You will need to record all expenses related to the products you make or the services you perform. This will include the cost of supplies and materials and any leased or purchased equipment. You will also need to record all expenses that are not product or service related but are needed to maintain the business.

No doubt your car will be used for business errands, and the cost of using it is a justified expense for tax purposes. However, you will need to keep a careful record because the IRS requires that you record the mileage of each business trip. The easiest way to do this is to keep a notebook in the car and record the mileage at the beginning and end of each business-related outing. Make this notation a habit, just like turning on the key to start the motor. You will be surprised how quickly those miles add up.

Keep all receipts, noting on the back of each the reason for the expenditure. You probably will buy many things too small and too numerous to pay for by check (a bottle of glue, a package of paper clips.) Collect the receipts for these small purchases and once each week or month reimburse yourself for these purchases from the checking account or petty cash. You may wonder what you should do with that pile of receipts that keeps growing throughout the month. Stash them in a large manila envelope and on the outside of the envelope note the month, along with a running total of the receipts and any

unusual purchases. Seal the envelope at the end of the month and tuck it away in case it is needed to verify an expense.

When Do YOU Get Paid?

One of the reasons you want a business is to earn money, remember? When and how do you pay yourself? The kind of business you undertake will determine when you can start taking money from the till. If your business is giving piano lessons, there would be no need to save money for supplies and to cover other expenses, so you can immediately use the money to pay yourself. But if you have a small manufacturing business, the income from sales will probably be paid out almost immediately for more supplies and maybe for additional equipment. Don't upset the delicate financial situation of your fledgling business by taking a salary prematurely. That is why, when you're in the planning stage, you need to ensure that living expenses are covered until your business starts to turn a profit.

Base your salary on the money received. Your salary may not be as large as you want or need, but if you overdraw money, the financial health of your business can be threatened. Be patient. If the business is as good as you expect it to be, the time will come when you will be able to take a larger salary.

To pay yourself, transfer funds from your business checking account to your personal checking account, clearly identifying the transfer in an appropriate account in your business records.

THE IMPORTANCE OF TWO CHECKING ACCOUNTS

It is wise to maintain a clear separation of your personal and business finances. One of the best ways to do this is to have two checking accounts, one for your personal use and the other for business purposes. This is important for three main reasons. First, the IRS may want to look over your books. An audit by the IRS is no fun, but it is usually confined to specific parts of a tax return, and the investigating agent is not interested is reviewing every item. The investigator will not inadvertently single out expenses unrelated to your business if the two accounts are clearly separated. Secondly, separate accounts will allow you to have both business checks and personal checks. Part of establishing your business image is having specially designed checks with your business name and logo imprinted on them. This costs a little more, but is worth the extra expense. When you have your business checks printed, start with a high serial number so it isn't obvious you are just getting started. The third reason for separate accounts is to avoid confusing business and personal finances. Also, determining profit and loss becomes much easier. At any moment you can look at the checkbooks and know exactly how much money is available, and by studying the check stubs you can quickly recall the expenses.

For convenience, keep both accounts at one bank, and if the services offered by the banks in your community are nearly equal, then do your banking at the closest or most easily accessible location. However, not all financial institutions handle business accounts, so you will need to locate one that will meet your needs. Full service banks carry business accounts, but the service charges vary significantly between the banks. Some have a service charge on every deposit and some charge for each check within a deposit. Most charge a fee of several cents for each check written, but they pay a small percent of interest on the average daily or monthly balance. You should try to figure which combination of charges and interest results in the best deal, but that is no easy task. Some savings and loans will open business accounts, and their service charges are often lower than full service banks. A credit union is another banking possibility. Some of these now open business accounts to meet the needs of their clients. A teacher's credit union, for example, will probably have business accounts because a large number of teachers operate a business during the summer months.

TERMS OF SALE, CREDIT AND COLLECTIONS

The profit your business makes isn't based on the merchandise you distribute or the work you do, but rather, on the money you are paid for your products or services. There are ways to increase the probability of being paid, and they involve the triad: terms of sale, credit, and collections.

Terms Of Sale

Making a sale to a retail or wholesale customer usually requires a detailed but brief set of specifications known as "Sales Terms and Conditions." These specifications define how and when you will be paid for your services or product and are important factors in both the financial management of your company and your relationship with customers. There are several options open to you.

COD or Cash On Delivery is used most often when selling by mail to new customers for whom you are unable to get a credit rating or whose credit rating is poor. (In the latter case, you may even want the COD to be paid in cash.) United Parcel Service allows you to specify either form of payment for the packages they deliver. We at Printed Tree, (our family business) learned that checks used to pay for COD shipments don't always clear. In one case we realized a shop owner was stocking his shelves with merchandise ordered COD, and paid for with bad checks. We discovered most of the merchandise came from small businesses, many of which, I suspect, were just trying to survive. It made us angry enough to pursue the matter. We contacted the police department and the Chamber Of Commerce in the small town where the shop was located, and as a result of an investigation, the shop was put out of business. These kinds of operators can only cause trouble for unsuspecting small (or large) businesses, usually in the form of an inordinate amount of time spent trying to collect the overdue bill, not to mention the lost merchandise. Be careful with your credit and shipping terms, but if you do get stuck don't be afraid to contact the appropriate authorities.

Prepayment is another term of sale, and as the name implies, the merchandise isn't shipped until it has been paid for. This eliminates the possibility the merchandise will be refused if it is shipped COD. Like COD sales, this form of payment is usually used with new or unreliable customers. An additional precaution is to make sure the check is good before sending the merchandise.

"Net 30" is a very common term of sale, and it means that you, in a sense, extend credit to the customer for 30 days in the amount of the purchase, and that the merchandise should be paid for within 30 days of delivery. A discount is sometimes offered to encourage early payment, and this is commonly net 30 less 2 percent in 10, which means payment is due in 30 days, but if you pay within 10 days, you can deduct 2 percent from the bill. It is written 2%/10-net 30.

Terms of sale customarily noted on the bottom of the invoice, should specify 1) who will pay packing and shipping charges, 2) minimum order and if there is a charge for less than a minimum order and 3) returns and claims policy, stating to whom claims should be made, the time limit for making them, and if you will accept returns without prior authorization.

Credit Ratings

Credit ratings are assigned to businesses based on their record of paying bills. A good credit rating indicates the business can be trusted to pay bills within the established time. Extending credit to new customers without first checking their credit history is risky. A credit history can be checked by calling (expensive, if long distance) or writing (slow) several of the new customer's past creditors. Of course, the customer supplies the names of references, and they surely wouldn't give names of businesses they have failed to pay, but still, you at least have a clue as to their trustworthiness. You may want to investigate one of the credit-checking services operated in many cities.

While you check credit references of your CUSTOMERS, your SUPPLIERS will be checking YOUR references. Establishing a good credit rating is important because it allows goods to be purchased with money that is, essentially, loaned for 30 days. Those 30 days of credit are often needed to ease cash flow problems. You will discover that establishing a credit rating can be a challenge as you get underway. Your first few purchases will probably need to be COD or prepaid simply because you will have no history of purchases. But how can you get a reputation for paying bills on time if businesses won't sell to you on credit or net 30? We solved the problem by listing as credit references, the businesses owned by friends. Of course, the suppliers checking our references didn't know of this relationship. It took only a few businesses who would sell to us on credit for us to establish a list of legitimate credit references located in several distant cities, not just in our hometown.

Collecting Can Be a Problem

After a service is rendered or a product delivered, the sale is not complete until the service or product is paid for. Collecting the money due you can try your patience, but you will be amused and amazed at some of the ingenious explanations for overdue bills. Collection problems usually fall into two categories: bad checks and slow payers.

BAD CHECKS

You might think you have a good sale, but if payment is by check, you can't be sure you have truly been paid until the check clears the bank. If you get stuck with a bad check, the loss comes out of your profit, and finally out of your pocket. You can protect yourself by being alert to a few simple rules.

1. Accept a check for only the amount of purchase.

2. Don't accept third party checks.

3. Before accepting any check in person, ask to see at least two ID's including a major credit card and a driver's license. If there is a photo on the driver's license, compare it with the person before you. Don't be casual or cavalier. Double-check the signature.

If a check bounces, it could be that the customer's deposit has not yet been credited to their account, and the problem there could be one of timing. Call the customer and tell them the check was returned but you will be sending it to the bank again. Wait a day so the customer has a chance to make a deposit. Most banks usually accept a check a second time, and it will usually clear the second time through. If it is returned again, take legal action or contact a collection agency if the check is for a significant sum, otherwise it may not be worth the trouble and expense. However, if a suit is filed in a small claims court, the usual practice is to award the plaintiff three times the amount of the check, if they win the case. (The person bringing the complaint is the plaintiff.)

SLOW PAYMENT

This is a big problem for small businesses, and it can be the main contributor to a cash flow problem. The customer who does not pay on time is, in effect, borrowing your money without paying interest, and that's not fair.

Of course, you should have checked the credit references before selling, but even a business or individual with good references and a solid and responsible payment record can hold up payments when they are short on cash. It should go without saying that you are asking for trouble if you extend credit (net 30) to a customer with a poor credit history.

When a bill is not paid on or near the due date (allow a few days for slow mail delivery) get on it right away. There is a truism worth heeding — "the older the bill, the harder it is to collect." You will need to get your money before the next batch of overdue notices start inundating your slow paying customers. Pursuing unpaid bills is vitally important to your business. Just keep in mind the customer has your profit in his or her pocket, and it belongs to YOU!

Be prepared for unpaid bills. You might prepare a series of letters with one going out every few days until you collect your money. The first letter should politely remind the slow-payer of the unpaid balance. Each letter should be progressively more insistent. Another method is to make copies of the original invoice and write messages on them. To start your collecting campaign you could write, "Just a reminder this bill is past due," with the next notation reading, "Please remit promptly on this past-due bill." It sometimes helps to send along a pre-addressed envelope with your notice. If you don't get a response in a reasonable time, it might be a good idea to phone and inquire what the problem is. There could be special circumstances, and you could arrange a payment schedule. Remember, the goal is to collect the money owed and, if possible, retain a good relationship that will keep the door open for possible future business. But if only one of the two can be attained, opt for getting your money. Who needs customers who don't pay their bills?

In our home business we have been extremely successful in collecting overdue bills while maintaining a cordial relationship with our customers. I believe it's because of our "secret weapon." Our daughter is responsible for collections. One day I realized we weren't having the problem many businesses have in collecting — virtually everybody pays us. I asked my daughter why she thought we were so fortunate, whereupon she whipped out her secret weapon — a series of guided missives. Janet has a series of letters in which she lays it on the line, explaining that we are a small operation and will be forced out of business if we aren't paid the money owed us (which, of course, is true if a lot of people don't pay). The third letter in the series is a real tear jerker, but it works!

Of course, while you are pursuing overdue payments you are spending money on stamps, phone calls, and perhaps wasting valuable time and, who knows, you may be sending good money after bad, so always keep this in mind as you try to collect. If the bill remains unpaid after sixty to ninety days, inform the customer you plan to take further action if the bill is not paid immediately. What kind of "further action" is at your disposal?

COLLECTION AGENCIES

Uncollected bills can be turned over to a collection agency. Many small business owners are intimidated by the notion of hiring a collection agency, but it is a simple matter and you will have the opportunity to regain at least some of your money, besides having the satisfaction of knowing your customer didn't succeed in cheating you out of the money due. Collection agencies keep a percentage of the money they collect. They can be found in the Yellow Pages of your telephone directory. One of the better collection agencies is Dun and Bradstreet, which operates throughout the country and is tied to local credit bureaus. They have an annual service charge, and for this fee will provide you with forms and stickers to use as you privately pursue unpaid bills. These forms and stickers alone are often enough to scare a customer into paying because some authority is associated with a Dun and Bradstreet sticker, and customers don't want to lose their good credit rating. If this approach does not work, your next choice is to give the bill to a collection agency. Most agencies do not charge if the bill is paid within ten days after they send a notice, but as they become more involved in the collection proceedings, they claim a larger portion of the recovered money. If they must locate the debtor, involve a lawyer, or invoke other types of persuasive tactics, then the charge is around 15 percent on bills over $6500, 25 percent on bills under $1000, and 50 percent on bills less than $100.

THINK PROFIT!

Profit — that's what business is all about. It's been said that profit is a way to keep score. It's what's left over after all expenses, including taxes, are deducted from income, so any change in either expenses or income affects the amount of profit.

Profit can be increased in several ways:

1. Sales increase but costs rise at a slower rate,
2. Sales remain constant but costs are cut, or
3. Sales increase while costs decrease.

The question is, how can you make one of these happen (preferably number 3), and the answer is in making accurate observations about your business and reacting in positive ways. It is vital that you periodically analyze your operations to find ways to increase the difference between what comes in and what goes out. Watch for unprofitable products or services, and discontinue or modify them to earn more profit. Can you find a better price for raw materials; is there a cheaper way to ship; should you have minimum orders; do you spend money too freely; do you have too many outstanding bills; are your credit checks adequate; is too much money tied up in inventory; is your product or service competitive; is there a better way to market your business — what questions are appropriate for your business?

There is a misconception that increased production will increase profits. That is not necessarily the case, and giant companies across our land, bending under the high cost of materials and labor, will testify to that fact. If costs keep up with increased production, there is no net gain in profit, so growth for growth's sake leads to more work but no more profit.

What happens after, having been in business for awhile, you look at the books and realize there isn't much money in the bank? If you can't make a profit from all your effort, is it worth it? Well, maybe it is. One of your business expenses is your salary. Even though you may not be making much profit, you ARE making a living. Your business will not grow if you don't make a profit, but earning a salary may be enough for you, because, as Christopher Morley has said, "There is only one success — to spend your life in your own way." If you are doing what you want to do, then growth may not be an important factor. Only you can decide.

Setting-up Shop

The time has come to stop talking and planning and put those dreams into action. It's time to set up shop. Space to house your business was discussed in Chapter 6, and now that space will be filled with the trappings of your new venture. You will need to buy furniture and equipment as well as the supplies and raw materials you need to develop your enterprise.

CREATE AN APPROPRIATE WORKSPACE

Furniture and Equipment

The accouterments you buy will depend upon the type of business you will operate and of course, upon what you already have on hand. If you are setting up an office, you will need the basic office furniture and equipment. You can start with less than an official desk — maybe even a card table if you haven't budgeted much for office furniture — but try to find a comfortable chair, especially if your work requires sitting for an extended time. A chair with rollers is ideal because you can roll rather than get up each time you need to move a little. A filing cabinet and a typing or computer table should complete the basic furnishings.

Office equipment is more important than office furniture. A typewriter or personal computer is a must for most businesses. If you still haven't gotten around to trying a personal computer, now may be the time. A personal computer with a word processor can be bought for just a little more than a fancy typewriter, and it will make the typewriter obsolete. It takes some effort to learn to use a personal computer, but after the initial learning period, it will save time and make writing and keeping books much easier than "the old way." Visit the computer stores in

your area if you are interested in buying a personal computer. Tell the sales people your needs and learn what they recommend. Also, talk to friends who own computers and ask their opinions on the best piece of equipment to fill your needs. If the computer choices appear about equal and if you don't know ANYTHING about them, I would recommend buying the same kind a friend has (if they are happy with theirs,) because they can give you invaluable help in learning to use it. Along with your computer, you will also need a printer. A printer with a "daisy wheel" yields printed material that looks like typewritten pages and is of much better print quality than that produced by most "dot matrix" printers.

You will also need a few other items for your office — surely a telephone and maybe a phone answering machine. And you might need a calculator (inexpensive) and a paper copier (we're talking big bucks if you buy one, but leased equipment is available).

Many office supplies you'll need are typical household items such as scissors, pliers, and even a coffee pot. These things can be pirated from the household, but it's a good idea to buy a duplicate of each to prevent a groundswell of discontent from the family as they look for articles they expect to find in the living area of the house.

As you gather the various furnishings and equipment, arrange them for efficiency but also so they are visually pleasing. Keep the arrangement flexible, and change the pieces around as new procedures or more equipment is added.

There are a variety of ways to acquire the furniture and equipment needed to start your business. Don't spend a disproportionate amount of money on fancy office furnishings or new equipment if used furniture and equipment will do the job. Shop discount stores, yard sales, estate sales, business moving and liquidation sales, second-hand stores, unclaimed freight stores, and especially newspaper classified ad sections such as "Business Equipment" and "Articles For Sale." Whenever buying business items, ask for a commercial discount and also a cash discount if you are buying from an established business. Also, have friends and family members watch for items you need.

If you buy new furnishings or equipment, don't accept a box that has already been opened because there is a good probability something will be missing or damaged. The item was probably returned by somebody else, and if it wasn't good enough for them, it's not good enough for you. I can't remember the number of times I have returned something because of a missing part. One incident sticks in my mind, and although it isn't about office furniture, it illustrates the point. I was vacationing in the Smokies with my family. We had rented a chateau high in the mountains and just when the weather turned unbearably hot, the air conditioner coughed and died. Dripping with sweat (no, it wasn't perspiration) and desperate, my sister went down the mountain to buy an electric fan. There wasn't a fan to be found in town, so she went to the next town, and the next, and finally, after several hours and many miles, she returned to the chateau with her prize. The family gathered around to witness the unwrapping, only to break into uncontrollable laughter when she retrieved the fan from the box and discovered it didn't have any blades.

If you need expensive pieces of equipment, you might consider renting or leasing, instead of buying, to avoid tying up so much capital. Generally, it is more economical to rent a piece of equipment that is used infrequently, but a leasing arrangement might be better if the equipment is an integral part of your day-to-day operation and requires frequent servicing. There are distinct differences between renting and leasing. Renting is an ordinary business expense, and the rented item is returned to the owner after use. Leasing is, for all practical purposes, a way to finance the purchase of equipment. The equipment remains the property of the leasing company during the term of the lease, but at the end of the lease it can usually be purchased for a nominal portion of the original price. There is either no down payment or a very small down payment for leased equipment compared to a credit purchase, which usually requires a down payment of about one third of the purchase price.

There are several disadvantages to leasing. In the first place, it's expensive because the leasing company charges enough to cover the cost of the equipment, and also enough to cover their overhead and make a profit. Also, many of the leased items, such as copiers and computers, are rapidly becoming less expensive as design technology continues to evolve and automated production becomes more cost-efficient. By the end of a leasing term, you may be left with obsolete equipment that can be replaced for less than you have invested. The same is true of equipment you buy on time. Of course, you have had the use of the equipment during the leasing or purchase period. If you decide to rent or lease, read the fine print on your contract, and be sure you are dealing with a reputable company because the contracts are binding. You can find yourself in an untenable position if you aren't careful.

Environmental Control

Make your workspace pleasant as well as efficient. If your office, studio or shop is in a huge room and you want to create a warmer, more intimate feeling, use large pieces of furniture, area rugs, bold contrasting colors and incandescent lights. You can make a tiny room appear larger by using sparse simple furnishings and a light color on the walls. Avoid drapes, but use light-colored mini blinds if a window treatment is needed. Wall mirrors and fluorescent lighting will also give the illusion of space.

Your office or business should impress your customers as a site of business activity, not household happenings. Keep it tidy and organized. A client shouldn't stumble over children's toys or need to move a newspaper to find a place to sit.

Also pay attention to the lighting, temperature, and sounds in your workspace, because these can influence the amount of work you produce and the impression you make on clients and customers.

Bright lights make bright people. It has recently been demonstrated that light can influence mood and light is even being used to control depression. When exposed to bright light for an extended period every day, depressed people become less depressed. When the light intensity is lowered, they regress back into depression. Bright lights seem to "keep their batteries charged." Most of us don't depend on light to escape depression but, nonetheless, our work efficiency is influenced by light. Incandescent lighting is more relaxing but less brilliant, while fluorescent lighting is brighter but seems harsh or cold to some people.

You will also be more efficient and productive if the temperature in your work area is carefully controlled for maximum comfort. Rely on a furnace for warmth during business hours rather than a fireplace. While fireplaces are a delight, they take time to tend, and you will be distracted from your work each time a new log is needed. Your real loss will be the time it takes to retrieve your thoughts and get on with your work. Save the crackling fireplace for those times when the family is at home and you are not involved with business activities.

Colors too can carry subtle messages and can make you feel warmer or cooler. By using the correct color scheme your workplace can be made more comfortable. If you work in a chilly basement, warm colors like rusts and oranges on the walls and in the furnishings will convey a feeling of warmth. On the other hand, cool colors like blue or green might counter the higher temperature of a sunny south-facing room.

Humidity will also influence how warm or cool you feel. A high humidity during the winter months will make you feel warmer, while a low humidity during the summer will make you feel cooler. A dehumidifier might be needed if you work in a basement. This will make the air more comfortable and protect your furnishings against mold and moisture damage.

If your work produces dust or offensive odors, an exhaust fan will help make your work area cleaner and more comfortable.

Another environmental factor that can influence your work is sound. It can either promote or inhibit productive work. Loud, unpleasant noises can quickly lower your efficiency and cause headaches and tension, while soothing sounds will likely increase your work efficiency. Soft music, a ticking clock, or the sound of bubbling water can sooth and actually delay the onset of fatigue. If you must work around loud noises and soundproofing is not feasible, then by all means wear ear plugs or similar ear protection to reduce tension and prevent long-term hearing loss.

The sounds produced by children are a totally different phenomenon. They evoke a range of emotional feelings such as apprehension, contentment, anger, anxiety, or pleasure. The sound of children playing in the next room, maybe serving tea to their dolls, might produce a feeling of contentment (or maybe a little anxiety as you wonder where the tea is being poured), but the sound of kids chasing through the house while you're trying to concentrate may make you angry. These sounds, and the feelings they elicit, will influence your work, and if the sounds can't be controlled, it may be necessary to schedule your work during quieter times of the day.

Storage Places and Storage Systems

The best way to keep your workspace tidy is to have a place for everything. What isn't in use should be in storage; otherwise things are out of place.

What you think will be enough storage space is never enough, or so it seems. No doubt your initial plans will include storage space appropriate to your type of business, but I predict within a few months you'll need more space as you accumulate supplies, finished products, and business records. As your storage needs become acute, you must look for more ingenious areas, using perhaps the space beneath a staircase, under a bed, drawers, and kitchen cabinets. Even a wall can be "paneled" with pegboard to increase your storage space. You can easily forget where rarely used things are stored, so keep a list of business-related materials, indicating where they are in the household.

Clearly identify stored material. For example, boxes holding your old business records should have a list of the enclosed materials on the outside. Magazines, newsletters, and business pamphlets should only be kept if you expect to refer to them again. Printed material is more easily retrieved if stored in chronological order.

Business debris will quickly accumulate so it is essential to keep culling files and discarding material you no longer need. If you fail to do this, you will find yourself surrounded by trivia that, while once important, has since become little more than clutter that can get in your way and consume precious space.

Finding Supplies

Supplies needed to keep an office functioning are easy to find. Most can be bought at a department store or even at convenience markets, and the rest can be picked up at an office supply store. However, locating the suppliers of raw materials needed for your specific business may be more difficult, and if the supplies are unusual, it may take persistence and patience.

When looking for supplies, first try to find a local source. A local supplier saves transportation costs, and you will usually be able to get the goods faster than if they must be ordered and shipped. If the materials are not available locally, go to retail shops that carry the kinds of things you need; check labels and boxes, noting the companies that sell merchandise to the shops. For instance, if you are trying to locate a supplier of lace, go to a fabric shop and look on the lace bolts for the names, addresses and telephone numbers of the companies they buy from. (You want a better price than the fabric shop can offer you.) If a name is on the item, but no address or number is listed, either ask the personnel in the store for this information, or call the information line at your local library and ask if they can find the address and telephone number for you. Research librarians are God's gift to small business people; they can find the most remote bits of data.

You might also look for suppliers in the *Thomas Register*, which is a multi-volume reference work found in even modestly appointed libraries. The Thomas Register lists practically all major manufacturers and suppliers of raw and finished products in this country. Make a list of the companies that might have the supplies you are interested in, and phone the ones who have an 800 number. Write the others, explaining what you need, and ask for a catalog and price list. It's not a bad idea to start gathering catalogs for future reference.

Locating suppliers is a never-ending job. Even after you find a steady source for each supply you need, you should continue your search and look for a source that will give you a better price or better terms. This is just one of the many ways to increase profit by reducing costs. Also, some supply sources dry up, and for this reason you should line up alternate sources.

Resources: *Directory of Wholesale Printing and Office Supply Sources.* Joe Soukup, 1991. Premier Publishers, P.O. Box 330309, Ft. Worth, TX 76163.

Directory of Office Supply Companies. Success Publications, 2812 Bayonne Dr., Palm Beach Gardens, FL 33420.

The following are examples of companies that offer office products.

Office Depot offers low prices on products and services (copying, printing, custom rubber stamps, etc.), and twenty-four-hour ordering by phone or fax. Call 1-800-685-8800 for a free catalog of the products and services offered.

Penny Wise Office Products offers low prices, free delivery. Call 1-800-942-3311 for a free catalog, and ask for free software that lets you shop on-line, twenty-four hours a day.

Inventory

Your inventory is every tangible item in your business that has value, including your desk and the paper in your desk drawer. For the purposes of this chapter, "inventory" will mean 1) products on hand that are for sale, 2) raw materials that will be used to make products for sale, or 3) parts used in repair work. Another term for inventory is "stock." Inventory represents an investment of money in raw materials or parts, and an investment of time and labor to convert the raw materials into finished products. This investment can be converted into income and profit only by selling or "turning over" the inventory.

The importance of inventory management cannot be overemphasized; it is essential to making a profit. The goal is to strike a balance between raw materials, finished products, money supply, production capacity, and projected sales.

One question every business person must deal with is, — what is the right amount of inventory? There must be enough stock on hand to fill orders, or if you sell at retail, enough to have a good selection for your customers. If you do repair work, you need enough parts in your stock room to make the repairs. However, every item in inventory has to be bought, and as long as it remains a part of inventory, it is costing money, especially if you are paying interest on the money used to buy it. The question you must ask is, what is the minimum stock needed to take advantage of business opportunities?

TURNOVER

The time interval between the stocking of an item, its sale, and restocking it is called "turnover time" and may range from less than a day to many weeks or months. Turnover time will

197

affect the rate of return on your investment. The more rapid the turnover of stock, the more your investment works for you and the higher the return on your investment, (unless the stock is sold at a loss). For instance, let's say you produce an item for $5.00 and after a week sell it for $10.00. The turnover time is a week and in this time your original $5.00 has generated $10.00 in income or $5.00 in gross profit. If the item had remained in stock for a month before it was sold, your $5.00 investment would have been idle for four weeks rather than one, and during this time the money would not be available for the generation of further income. Obviously, the shorter the turnover time, the more efficiently your money can work for you and the more profit you can be make. This is a particularly important concept to understand because of its significant positive or negative effect on profitability.

Inventory, or stock, is not always sold at a profit. Your products may have to be sold below cost if they lose their market appeal or if they are up against a more successful competitor. It may be better to lower the price and move the items than to maintain them in your inventory because some money can be recovered even if the product is sold at a loss, whereas no income is realized if it remains a part of inventory. Also, unsold merchandise appears on the books as an asset and increases your tax liability (see below). For these reasons, it is important to be sensitive to market trends and carefully control your inventory. If you are caught with something showing slow sales or no sales, try to find a way to cut your losses. If the item can be converted into something else, make the change quickly and get the product to market. Or, it may be better to lower prices and run a special to get the merchandise out of inventory. Another way to reduce inventory is to donate an overstocked or slow-moving line to charity and take the tax advantage.

JUST-IN-TIME

The "just-in-time" inventory concept was developed by the Japanese in an effort to get more out of their business dollar. The principle of just-in-time is having just enough inventory to cover orders, without investing more until more merchandise is needed. The reasoning behind this approach to inventory control is to keep money working rather than tying it up in merchandise stockpiled in bins or warehouses.

In order for "just-in-time" to be effective, you have to know EXACTLY how long it takes to get materials after they have been ordered from your suppliers, and how long it takes to make those materials into finished products. Careful record-keeping can give you the information. For instance, if you use ten different supplies to manufacture or craft something, it will be necessary to know how long it takes for each of the supplies to reach you after they have been ordered. Some materials may come from suppliers who keep a large inventory and ship the day an order is received, while others may come from suppliers who keep a low inventory and must first gather the goods before shipping. Whatever the case, determine the time needed to collect materials by noting the time between placing an order and its receipt.

Next, your manufacturing or crafting time must be known. How long does it take to make, say, fifty items? Can you make then as needed or should they be made ahead? Usually a small manufacturer will see a pattern of orders developing and will work to maintain the necessary output to meet the demand. Whatever you do, don't get too far ahead on any given item because overstocking can seriously affect your cash flow. Also, you can't be sure an item that has sold well in the past will continue to sell well.

INVENTORY CONTROL

Maintaining inventory at the proper level is an important key to profitability, and this can be accomplished only by keeping careful records. One of the best ways to gather information about stock movement is to keep a running or perpetual inventory record, recording everything that is added to or taken from the stock. This takes dedication and consistent (but easy) record-keeping. (This type of inventory record is especially important if you keep a large number of different items in stock.) With this information you can make informed decisions on sales tactics, product acceptance, and the level of production needed to meet demand.

Inventory records can be kept in a notebook with a page devoted to each item, in a card file with a separate card for each item, or in a computer. Whatever method you use, note the date on which an item is added to or taken out of stock and also keep a record of the balance on hand. It is very important to get into the habit of showing the new balance. Make a notation on the records indicating the standard reorder or remake quantity per time interval. By comparing that number with the balance on hand you will know when to add to the inventory.

These running records allow you to evaluate your business and help you make timely adjustments. They show sales patterns for the finished products, usage patterns for raw materials and parts, and the sales success of each product. These records should show clearly which products are winners and which might be candidates for the scrap heap.

INVENTORY AND TAXES

The inventory you maintain affects not only your money supply and return on investment, it also bears on the taxes you must pay. It is in your best interest to have a low inventory at the end of each year because inventory is considered an asset and, therefore, is taxed that way. You can decrease your tax liability by reducing your inventory at the end of the year. The following example illustrates how adjusting inventory affects gross profit.

If the total receipts for the year are,		$15,000
and the inventory at the beginning of the year was	$ 1,500	
and the year's expenses (including overhead and cost of production) were	6,000	
The total cost of the inventory is	$ 7,500	
But if you have inventory at the end of the year that is worth	2,000	
that inventory is considered an asset and is deducted from the total cost, leaving the net cost at	$ 5,500	
Deduct the net cost from the net receipts to determine the gross profit		−5,500
		$ 9,500

Now let's see what happens if the amount of inventory is reduced at the end of the year.

Starting again with total annual receipts of		$15,000
And a beginning year inventory worth	$ 1,500	
Year expenses	6,000	
Total	$ 7,500	
Less year-end inventory of (instead of $2,000)	500	
Yields a net cost of	$ 7,000	-7,000
And a gross profit of		$ 8,000

As you can see, just by reducing the inventory at the end of the year you can reduce the profits upon which you will be taxed. In the first example taxes would be paid on a gross profit of $9,500, but in the second example, just by reducing the amount of year-end inventory, taxes would be paid on a gross profit of $8,000.

Although you keep a running inventory record throughout the year, it is necessary to make a thorough and complete inventory count at year's end. That includes everything — all parts and raw materials, products in production, and finished goods. This is a good time to discard damaged and shopworn goods. The dollar value of inventory items is the purchase price of raw materials and the cost of production, not the selling price of the finished products.

ANOTHER KIND OF INVENTORY

There is another, intangible kind of inventory that is just as valuable and one that cannot be taxed. That is an inventory of ideas. A backlog of ideas is especially valuable to people involved in creative work — writers for example — but they are also valuable to the business person looking for a better product, service, or a better way to do business. By all means keep a notebook and build an inventory of your ideas and thoughts.

Do You Need Employees

Wait, don't skip this chapter. Maybe you'll need an employee or two to watch the store while you soak up sun in the Caribbean, spending some of the fortune you made with your home business!

The couplet that appeared with the discussion about hiring help for home or family responsibilities can also be applied to business tasks and responsibilities.

> Do the things you do best,
> Hire someone else to do the rest.

When considering whether or not to hire help, it comes down to deciding whether you CAN, SHOULD, or WANT to do all the work yourself. You may regard yourself as independent and self-sufficient, quite capable of doing all the work for your business — but why should you? Why not hire someone to relieve you of what keeps you away from "the things you do best." There are several reasons why it might be wise to hire an employee: (1) You lack the skill or expertise to do a particular job, (2) It costs more to do a job yourself than to hire someone else to do it, (3) Two people are needed to do a job, or (4) There are certain tasks you simply don't want to do.

It's valuable to learn how the U. S. Department of Labor legally defines an employer and an employee:

"Generally the relationship of employer and employee exists when the person for whom services are performed has the right to control and direct the individual who performs the services, not only as to the result to be accomplished by the work, but also as to the details and means by which the result is accomplished. That is, an employee is subject to the will and control of the employer not only as to what shall be done but how it shall be done. In this connection, it is not necessary that the employer actually direct or control the manner in which the services are performed; it is sufficient if he has the right to do so.

The right to discharge is also an important factor indicating that the person possessing that right is an employer. Other factors characteristic of an employer, but not necessarily present in every case, are the furnishing of tools and a place to work to the individual who performs the services.

In general, if an individual is subject to the control or direction of another merely as to the result to be accomplished and not as to the means and methods for accomplishing the result he is not an employee."

A couple of examples will illustrate what that means: If you hire someone to cut out wooden letters, and you buy the wood, provide the saw and the work area; and then if you show them what to do, and have a work schedule that defines work hours, lunch breaks, etc., there is little doubt that you have an employee. Whether the person cuts wood full-time or parttime is immaterial.

That person would NOT be an employee in the legal sense if you provide the wood and saw, and show him or her how to do the work, BUT THE WORK IS DONE WHEN AND WHERE THEY WISH. The helper would probably work from home and according to his or her own time schedule. Many home business operators use this kind of help because it frees them from the detailed record-keeping and paperwork normally associated with regular on-the-premises employees. Instead, the only required paperwork is to inform the government at the end of the year how much you paid each individual during the year (if they made over $600.) The helpers are responsible for reporting and paying taxes on their income. In a sense, these helpers are independent contractors who have their own cottage industry, and you are their customer since you pay them for their finished products.

WHAT KIND OF HELP WILL YOU NEED?

As your business gets underway you will probably do nearly everything yourself, both to save money and to get things started like you want them. At first you will probably be able to handle all the business you can generate, but after you become established, a burst of orders can leave you in dire need of help, and it might be necessary to hire someone.

What kind and how much help will you need? Will a little support from the kids or your spouse be enough, or will you need more than they can give? Here are some options you might consider if you need help in your business.

You could hire a regular employee to work either part-time or full-time in your business. But do you want someone coming into your home each day, and is there enough room for another worker in your home? One of the reasons people work at home is to keep overhead low. Adding an employee will surely increase your overhead, and you will have to meet their salary requirement before you can meet yours. Another problem with regular help is that they report for work even when there isn't much to do and you could be forced to "make work" to keep your employee busy during the slow periods. Several part-time employees may fit better into your business than a full-time employee. If special skills are needed, you might hire several people, each capable of different tasks. For instance, you might hire a part-time accountant, cleaner, secretary, and delivery person — and still not spend as much as you would for a single full-time employee.

Another possibility is "farming out" some work to independent contractors. This type of helper was described earlier. You might think of these workers as "freelancers." They usually work in their homes and perform specific tasks that you pay for individually. This kind of arrangement is handy because the workers don't take up valuable space in your work area, and they can be called upon whenever help is needed, yet they are not considered employees, and therefore you're not responsible for all the myriad paperwork.

Another source of help is temporary-help agencies that provide short-term assistance, especially secretarial and office management personnel. These agencies generally charge more for their services than you would normally pay, but they can provide quick, efficient help, which spares you the trouble of locating and selecting employees. Also, you pay the agency and they pay the workers; you are relieved of that record-keeping chore.

Before you become too serious about hiring an employee, you should know just what that means in these days of rules, regulations, and taxes. Long gone is the day when you could hire someone to help out occasionally and pay them in cash at the end of the day. When you hire an employee to work on your premises, you must subscribe to a whole array of rules and regulations. You will be responsible for meeting a payroll, filling out numerous forms, and making payments into Social Security, workmen's compensation, and unemployment insurance accounts. You must also withhold taxes from the employee's earnings and forward them to the state and federal governments, and you may be expected to pay for holiday and vacation time. And of course, you must spend time and money hiring and training an employee only to start over again should the person quit.

This investment of time and added expense is worth it if the employee can produce enough to significantly increase your profit. You will surely have to hire helpers if you want to make your business grow into a large enterprise, but growth and a large profit may not be among your goals. You may be perfectly content to do what you alone can do and enjoy the freedom from hiring and managing employees.

HIRING AN EMPLOYEE

If you decide to hire an employee, you should first obtain a federal employer identification number (EIN) from the Internal Revenue Service. At the same time you should get the most recent federal publication regarding employees, which is IRS Circular E, Employer's Tax Guide. This covers the federal regulations that apply to the employer-employee relationship. (Your state tax agency can inform you of state guidelines pertaining to employees.) The Employer Identification Number should be placed on all documents you file concerning your employee. There is a lot of paperwork indeed when you employ an in-house worker, and you might want to periodically consult an accountant to make sure the required documentation is in place. The first time you must cope with the procedure is the worst; after that it's just a matter of repeating the process with each additional employee. If you really need and want employees, don't let the paperwork intimidate you.

FINDING THE RIGHT EMPLOYEE

If you are looking for help, hiring SOMEONE isn't your goal, but hiring the RIGHT one is. Before you can hire the right person, you have to decide what it is you want that person to do, what experience and skills are needed, how much they will work and what you will pay them. If the person will work in your home, you'll want to consider such things as attitude and disposition, which, if not compatible with your personality, could create tension. Writing a job description is a very important part of hiring. It makes you think about how the employee will fit into your operation and helps you define the characteristics you hope to find.

With the job description in hand, you are now ready to look for that right person. The most obvious way is to place an ad in the classified section of your local newspaper. DON'T put your address in the ad, only a telephone number or a box number provided by the newspaper. This way you can screen applicants by phone and check out references before telling them where you are. Agree to personally interview only those individuals you consider to be possible employees.

Another place to look for help is a college placement office. You will surely be able to find young helpers if you live in a college town because there is usually a long list of students looking for part-time work. Help can also be found at the other end of the age spectrum. Generally, retired people make excellent employees because they have had a lifetime of work experience. A recent business trend in America has been to hire older or retired people who can offer experience and stability to the workplace.

Ask friends, networking buddies, and business acquaintances if they know someone who is looking for the kind of work you need done. These are usually good sources because the worker comes with the recommendation of someone you know.

Finding the right person is a blend of logic, chemistry, study and plain luck. There are several tools to help you select the right employee from a group of applicants. Ask the applicants to fill out an application form. This does not need to be long and detailed but quite brief and to the point. Ask that resumes be submitted with the application form, and as you study these, try to read between the lines. Check references and former employers by calling them. This is quicker than writing a letter, and you can listen for any hesitation that might suggest a negative feeling. If you detect something, probe into the matter in a diplomatic fashion. If the applicant checks out, set up a personal interview.

A personal interview will allow you to study the appearance, behavior, and personality of the applicants, and you can find out if you would enjoy working with them. As you talk with each applicant, observe how they respond to various business situations and duties you describe. Your best way to get information is to avoid asking them yes-no type questions, but rather frame your questions so the job-seeker must talk. This allows you to size up the person relative to the job, and in most cases, the person will either talk themselves into or out of a job. Be alert to any factors that might exclude them from further consideration such as job-hopping, excessive indebtedness, poor communicative skills, poor emotional control, too high a standard of living, and unexplained gaps in their employment record.

It is impossible to know how a person will perform on a day-to-day basis, even after a thorough interview. For this reason, you should hire new employees for a trial or probationary period. A six-week or two-month trial should be long enough to evaluate their personal characteristics and work. During this time keep close watch over what and how they are doing, but don't expect new help to know what you want done without your telling them. The time you spend teaching and helping a new employee is time well spent. Make sure they understand what is expected, how much must be done, and treat them like you would want to be treated. Praise good work, pay on time and, with rare exceptions, you will find your employees trying to fulfill your expectations.

HELP FROM FAMILY

Many of the rules that apply to regular employees do not apply to your spouse, children or grandchildren. For instance, both federal and state legislation make it unlawful to employ children under 14 and regulate the employment of children to 18 in some occupations. However, minor children CAN work in their family's business, and there is no need to pay Social Security or unemployment taxes on minor children. Also, a child pays no income tax on the first $3,400 of income, and their salary is a deductible business expense.

Be diplomatic if you are thinking of asking family members for free help. Don't try to pressure them or make them feel guilty if they prefer not to be involved. If you really need their help, and they are reluctant to volunteer, either offer wages or find help elsewhere. You will surely want to avoid the ill feelings that could result if family members are coerced into working.

Pricing
for Profit

Setting the right price for your service or product will be among the most important business decisions you will make. When you set a price, you not only determine if you can make a profit or operate at a loss, but you make a statement about the quality of your product or service. You can do everything else right, but if your price is wrong, your business will fail. If it's too high, customers will look elsewhere for a better buy. If you have priced too low, they may beat a path to your door but leave you with a tattered doormat and little else, and might equate inexpensive with "cheap". As you can see, you will need to study the market, make some careful calculations, and try to "psych out" your customers and competition before setting prices.

Four major elements need to be considered when establishing prices. These include:

1. The **DIRECT** costs to produce a product or perform a service
2. The overhead or **INDIRECT** costs of maintaining the business
3. A reasonable amount of profit, and
4. The amount the customer will pay for a service or product.

The first three elements are rather straight forward. The costs of production and overhead can be determined by keeping records (some of these will be estimated as you get started), and a reasonable amount of profit can be calculated and put into the pricing formula. It's a little harder to put the customer into the formula and arrive at a price, because the motivation to buy is a complex issue that often escapes even the most sophisticated marketing analyses. Many factors influence buying patterns, including competition, status seeking, need, usefulness, desire, and self-image to name a few. All of these factors must be taken into account as you set prices, but most of them are elusive, except competition, which will probably be one of your first considerations in establishing price. Even after you have determined direct and indirect costs through careful record-keeping and relate these costs to price, competition will surely continue to influence what you charge for your services or products.

There will always be a pressure to arrive at a "good" or low price, but Thomas Paine observed that "what we obtain too cheap, we esteem too lightly." A low price tends to undervalue your effort and should be weighed against the alternative of setting a higher price that establishes an image of quality. Generally, lower prices bring more sales, while higher prices result in fewer sales. But remember, your goal is not increased sales if they do not bring increased profit. It's quite possible to lower prices by five or ten percent and significantly increase the sales volume but not the profit.

COST/PRICE RATIO

Before setting a price, you need an accurate accounting of the costs involved in delivering a service or manufacturing a product, including both direct and indirect costs. At first, you will probably know the cost of such items as materials, labor, shipping containers, and sales commission, but you may not have an accurate figure for indirect costs such as utilities, promotions and product development or refinement. A general rule of thumb is to at least DOUBLE THE DIRECT COSTS FOR A MINIMUM WHOLESALE PRICE. Later, after you have been in operation for awhile and have a backlog of expense records, you can change the price to reflect costs more accurately. However, when setting the initial price, keep in mind that customers will more readily accept a price reduction than a price increase.

Another factor that should enter into your price structure is the difference between development and production. It takes a lot of money to get a project underway, and if your price is based on the cost of developing the early samples it will surely be too high. Instead, after you design what you feel will be a salable product, try to calculate what it will cost to make it in quantity, and base the price on that figure.

In general, retailers normally sell products for double the wholesale price. Yes, that seems like a huge markup, and you may think it is out of line. Why should retailers double the price of an item when all they do is sell it in their store and you do all the work of designing and producing it? If you consider the overhead expenses and the risk-taking of retailing, then doubling the wholesale price seems a reasonable markup.

Retail stores have many expenses associated with sales. They attract customers by offering a wide variety of attractively displayed merchandise; they advertise, extend credit, maintain a building or space, hire workers, and may even provide off-street customer parking. It is estimated that 50 cents of each gross dollar pays for merchandise and 45 cents goes toward overhead. That leaves the retailer with a 5 cent profit from each dollar in the cash register.

If you make products and sell them, don't sell them to customers for the price you would charge retailers but for the price a retailer would charge customers. In other words, you are functioning as both manufacturer and salesperson, and you can increase the price accordingly. If your wares are sold by retailers, it is very important that you sell at the same price the retailers ask. You will have problems if you sell for less because this will leave the retailers with overpriced goods, and they will be reluctant to continue carrying your products. It can also cause hard feelings among customers who have paid the higher price. Craftspeople sometimes underprice their products at fairs. They might reason that their only overhead is booth rental, so they sell their work for less than it is sold in retail shops. Sure, they make a quick profit, but they reduce chances for future sales to shop owners.

Just to reiterate the pricing formula for manufactured or crafted products when you are starting out and do not have accurate indirect cost figures:

1. Double the direct costs to get the wholesale price, and
2. Double the wholesale price to get the retail price.

A different formula is needed to calculate service charges. The largest cost in a service business is labor, although materials can be an important factor. While mass manufacturing can bring down the cost of producing goods through volume discounts and assembly-line production methods, the cost of labor used to perform services remains nearly constant. For instance, it takes a given number of minutes to type a page, whether you have 10 or 100 pages to type. However, overhead becomes a smaller percent of the operating costs of a service business as the amount of service grows or the cost of the service increases.

The price of the service you perform will reflect the price you put on your time. Will you work for minimum wage, or do you expect to make $10 or $20 per hour? How can you decide the value of your time? We all think our time is valuable (and it is), but the question is, how much will people pay for a service, and how much time and effort has it taken to prepare yourself to deliver the service?

Creative talent or skills that require more training to master usually command a higher price than services that demand less training or talent. Thus, a doctor can charge more than a nurse; a baker can charge more than the person who delivers the baked goods; an artist who designs business logos can charge more than the printer who copies them; and an accountant can charge more than a typist. This is clearly another kind of pecking order our society recognizes and willingly perpetuates because of the value we place on talent, skill, and services.

COMPETITION

Henry Ford II said, "Competition is the keen cutting edge of business, always shaving away at costs." Of course, competition can also whittle away your profit. Still, it keeps us trying harder and looking for better and more inexpensive ways of doing things, and consequently, competition plays a major role in raising our standard of living.

You can be sure someone will be competing for your customer's business and money. It is important to study the competition before embarking on a business venture, but after concluding that there is room for your business, then approach the competition head on and claim your corner of the market. If competitor's prices are so low that you cannot make a profit if you compete with them, then change your product or image, or appeal to a different segment of the population where competition will allow prices that will yield a profit.

I have watched and admired a young man who found himself in a glutted market when he started his business. When he realized the competition could keep him poor, he changed the image of his service and now operates a quality carpet and furniture cleaning service. It's incredible, but this young man has established a cleaning service that is recognized as a status symbol! He apparently does what the other cleaning services do, but he does it better, dresses in a clean white uniform, has good equipment that he keeps immaculate, and he knows how to put people at ease when he handles fragile and treasured possessions. He charges considerably more than the other cleaning services in town, yet he has a waiting list of customers, all of whom are word-of-mouth referrals. All his clients are in the upper income bracket, quite capable of paying his high prices.

PRICE CUTTING

Random price cutting can undermine the financial well-being of your business. It is not the same as a clearance sale, which is used to get rid of end-runs, discontinued items, and seconds. Price cutting is reducing the price of your service or merchandise, either across-the-board or on selected items. It is sometimes used to combat competition or it may be a response to a lingering customer interested in the work but reluctant to pay the asking price. If your price was arrived at by calculating costs and incorporating a reasonable profit, then price cutting can be very costly and can even cause the financial breakdown of your business. You might think you are giving a one-time price cut to a particular customer, but customers talk and you can expect others to ask for the reduced price. If you cut prices as a result of competition, you may be able to sell more, but if the profit is slight, it may not be worth it. It reminds me of the old fella who said, "We lose a nickel on every sale, but we make it up in volume." Profit, not sales, is your goal. It is the PROFIT on each product sold or service rendered, multiplied by the number of sales, that will determine your earnings, not the sales volume alone.

Instead of cutting prices in the face of competition, it may be more valuable to ask why competitors can make a profit with prices that would make you go broke. Do they have better suppliers or more efficient methods? Maybe you are offering a better product or service than your competitors, but potential customers opt for the competitor's product because you have failed to demonstrate the value of your goods. This then, becomes a matter of creating the right image, and you will need to review your marketing plan, not reduce your prices.

Resource: *How to Set Your Fees and Get Them.* Kate Kelly, 1989. Visibility Enterprises, 11 Rockwood Dr., Larchmont, NY 10538.

Marketing Methods

Marketing includes all activities undertaken in an effort to convert your products or service into money. It includes publicity and advertising, image, timing, pricing, and finally, selling.

ADVERTISING AND PUBLICITY

Attracting attention to your business to create an image and promote sales is the goal of advertising and publicity. There are many ways to promote your business and bring it to public attention. Some of these methods involve only a small expenditure, but you may quickly discover, vast amounts of your resources can go into advertising.

Signs

If it doesn't move, paint a sign on it. (Actually, it's a good idea to paint a sign on things that move too.) Signs are a splendid way to advertise.

Just recently I was driving behind a pizza delivery truck that had a "Stop" sign painted on its side with the message, "Stop me and I'll sell you a pizza." In the brief period while I travelled behind this truck, a car whipped up, honked, and as I drove past, a sale was in progress. Apparently, this is a new wrinkle in the advertising and sale of pizza.

It's only good business sense to have an advertisement on your business car, truck, or van. The message should include your business name, telephone number, and logo. A hint about the business, whether it's a phrase or picture, would make the sign a more powerful advertising tool. Since your goal is to reach the maximum number of people with your advertisement, paint a sign on the sides and back of the vehicle. Instead of rolling into the garage when you return home, park at the curb or in the driveway near the street so the message can be seen by passersby.

A sign on your property can direct customers to your business and serve as a reminder that you are in business. A discreet sign in your frontyard is appropriate for a home business and is surely necessary if customers or clients come to your home, if for no other reason than to reassure them that they're at the right place. If people don't come to your home but phone for orders, then the yard sign in your yard should display your telephone number in big clear numbers. Signs can be a maximum of two square feet in size in most residential areas.

Free Publicity

You can create a media blitz and get publicity without spending any more than the postage to mail a few letters when you start a new business. Unless you live in a large city, the local papers will probably be glad to write a story about your new venture, and they might even publish a picture or two with the story. No amount of money can buy this type of coverage. Don't contact the media without first having something that will capture the attention of the reporters and the public. You might think your business is a lot like the next guy's, but if you look hard enough you can find an interesting angle for even the most mundane enterprise. Make the initial contact by writing a brief letter, listing a few succinct points, and close by saying you will call in a few days to make an appointment to discuss the idea. (Be sure your telephone number is on the stationery in case they want to contact you.) Then, as promised, call and see what kind of story you can get. Remember, media people are always in need of new material, and you are offering them something they can use. If your business is based on the arts or creative work, address the letter to the arts reporters. If it is sports-related, contact the sportswriters. If it doesn't seem to fit any special section, send your information to the business editor.

Television coverage is also a possibility. I have seen some remarkable free television publicity about new businesses under the guise that they are newsworthy. The trick is to find an angle to attract the newspeople. For example, Christmas tree or poinsettia growers can invite the camera crew out for a seasonal viewing, or an artist can invite them to an opening of a new show. This can yield valuable publicity and attract customers.

Still, of the two, newspaper coverage is more valuable because it seems to make a more lasting impression, and the reader can reread the piece if it stimulates a special interest. In this regard, I have written many articles that have appeared in regional and national magazines, about people and their work, and invariably these articles have brought them customers and widespread recognition.

Another source of free publicity is trade journals. These magazines cater to a particular industry or occupation such as construction, engineering, retailing, and decorating to mention a few examples. Many of these journals carry information about new businesses and print photos of new products. Every time we introduce a new product in our home business we submit it as a "press release" to the appropriate journals and get free publicity. Some journals even have postcard inserts that allow readers to checkmark those items that interest them. These responses are then forwarded to the companies that have been checked and the interested readers can be contacted by phone or descriptive literature can be mailed to them. These responses can bring in a lot of new business — and all of this is a result of a free press release! It is amazing that magazines can offer this kind of free service, but since they do, by all means take advantage of it.

Resource: *How to Write and Use Simple Press Releases that Work* by Kate Kelly. Visibility Enterprises, 450 West End Avenue, New York, NY 10024 ($7 ppd). This book contains guidelines for writing press releases and contains a media resource directory.

Paid Advertisement

The number of ways you can advertise is limited only by the amount of money you have to spend. Newspapers, classified ads, handbills, direct mailings, billboards, radio, magazines, television — the list goes on.

As you plan your advertising campaign, keep in mind that your goal is to bring in customers for the least amount of money. Advertising can become very expensive, so you will need to watch the cost versus the benefits and evaluate the advertising's effectiveness.

You must first determine what media can carry the message to the right market for the right price. For instance, if your product appeals to older or perhaps retired people, you have the age and occupational group targeted. Next, ask yourself, what do they read, and what advertisements might come to their attention? How can they be reached? There are literally scores of weeklies and magazines directed to the older population. Many of them are locals published in retirement communities such as those in parts of Florida and Arizona. Their names can be found in library reference books that list the periodicals, weeklies, and newspapers published throughout the country. Publications directed to the older population will be listed under "retirement" and will include weeklies such as *Golden Years* and *After Sixty*. Your librarian can help you find the material you need. The next step is to write to each publication to learn their circulation and cost for a classified or column ad. Dividing the cost of an ad by the circulation will tell you the cost to reach one reader of the publication — this will usually range from a few cents to less than half a penny. A small ad in a limited circulation weekly will cost from 15 to 20 dollars, but a small ad in a magazine with a national circulation will cost hundreds of dollars.

This example gives me the opportunity to suggest that if you are still trying to decide on a type of business, you might want to consider the potential offered by our aging population. Demographics show our population's average age is increasing, and this trend will continue because good nutrition and medical advancements are keeping people alive longer. Every one of these senior citizens is a potential customer. They need hearing aids, support shoes, lift chairs, beauty aids, help with home maintenance, nursing care, help with food preparation, entertainment, delivery services, and a host of other articles and services. Maybe you can create a business that meets a need of these people.

If you have a service business, consider advertising with handbills stuffed in mailboxes or on car windshields. Again, the goal is to aim your advertising toward the right audience. If the service you offer is performing as a magician or clown at children's parties, then the handbills would be more effective if placed on cars parked at a zoo or outside a circus than a hospital parking lot. However, if your service is renting hospital beds and equipment used during convalescence, then the cars in the hospital lot would be the right place for your handbills.

One of the simplest, yet most effective, advertising methods is sending mailings to past customers. Of course, you need to have customers in order to do this, and when you are just getting started this is not feasible, but as you start gathering a list of customers, send them mailings or reminders. Just a few examples illustrate the effectiveness of this approach. If you repair furnaces and air conditioners, just prior to the heating or cooling season, send a reminder to your customers to get their appliance cleaned and checked. A dentist might send a reminder six months after the last visit that it's time for a checkup, and a veterinarian could send "checkup and inoculation notices." The reminders can range from a simple printed post card to a color-printed brochure.

The owner of a Chinese restaurant I know used targeted mailings to win back his diners. He had enjoyed a steady stream of customers but noticed a sharp decline in business when two more Chinese restaurants opened in the area. The owner consulted with me, hoping I could advise him how to bring back his customers. We devised a plan. He would offer two free dinners each week to the person whose name is drawn from a box near the cash register. Diners would print their name and address on the back of their dinner check and, after paying their bill, drop it into the box. This enticement of free dinners is being used to build a mailing list of people who enjoy Chinese food. One month after eating at the restaurant, customers receive a miniature of the restaurant menu in the mail. This targeted advertising has proven to be exceptionally successful and the restaurant is bustling with activity again.

If you do not have a list of prospective customers, you can purchase a mailing list for a specific market. There are lists of art patrons, doctors, plumbers, society matrons, jewelry connoisseurs, teenagers, sport enthusiasts, religious activists and many more. Companies that sell such lists can be found in the Yellow Pages of the telephone directory under the heading "Mailing Lists." The lists sell for 30 to 50 dollars per thousand and include a set of mailing labels. Usually you buy a one-time use of the list.

Assessing Advertising Success

Whatever type of advertising you use, it is important to evaluate the results. You will most likely want to continue some form of advertising, and you must know which approaches are the most productive. If you simultaneously place ads in various media, use a slightly different return address by adding a different "Department" to the address in each ad. This will tell you which advertisement yields the most responses. For instance, in the ad in one magazine, include "Dept. A" in the address; in another add "Dept B" to the address, and so on. Obviously, this is going to take some record keeping, but it's very straight forward. As replies are received, record the department letter that tells where your respondent saw your ad. You will soon learn *which* publications are reaching the *most* prospective customers. Use this same technique on all mailings and fliers so you can identify the source of the response. This information will be invaluable as you continue to develop your advertising strategy.

The cost effectiveness of advertising can be determined in different ways, but you will probably want to calculate: (1) cost per customer response, and/or (2) cost per dollar of sale generated. There are other ways of determining advertising effectiveness, but these calculations should give you a fairly good handle on your advertising strategy.

SELLING MERCHANDISE

The approach you use to sell your products will be determined by what you are trying to sell. Mass-produced articles are handled differently than one-of-a-kind arts and crafts pieces and other original works.

Direct Sales

Many artists and crafts people find direct sales are quite adequate for selling their work. Direct sales include selling to friends and neighbors, to customers who visit your home, at fairs and shows, and selling by mail order. I suspect many of you reading this book operate (or are considering) a home business based on handwork, and for that reason I will explain in some detail several ways to sell your products.

FAIRS AND SHOWS

The country is alive with craft fairs and shows. Many are held throughout the spring, summer, and fall; and there is another spate of them in late November to pick up the Christmas market. Some who do handwork follow art and craft fairs and sell all they can produce.

When you were an amateur working on your art or craft in the evenings and on weekends, it was probably all you could do to get together enough pieces for one or two fairs each year. What you earned at fairs probably supplemented another income. Now, having made the commitment to use your hobby as a business, the focus is on volume, and you'll have to make and sell many pieces if your business is to flourish.

Fortunately, you are riding a wave of interest in original arts and crafts. The fascination with handwork has been revived in recent years, and people are buying handcrafted items and original art like never before. This may be a rebellion against the mass-produced, machine-stamped, robot-assembled goods that clutter our lives and homes.

When looking for places to sell your work, look first in your immediate area. Because of the growing interest in this kind of work and because fairs can be a community "happening," many towns, cities, organizations, neighborhoods, churches and schools sponsor art and craft fairs. Every one of them wants real live artists and craftspersons to show their wares. Some fairs will draw huge crowds intent on seeing and buying the artwork, while others bring in a few browsers who wander around aimlessly, barely focusing on the art. I live in a city of 150,000, and in the immediate area, we have perhaps a dozen fairs throughout the year that attract an estimated 300,000 people. There are repeaters — some go to every fair — but still, a large number of people attend the fairs, and many are looking for that special item to add to their collection or give as a gift.

If you intend to "do" shows and fairs outside your immediate area, you should get a show listing and learn what you can before selecting the ones you will attend. You should know:

1. Is the show/fair held indoors or outdoors? This can be very important for some types of art/craft work. Wind, rain, and sun can damage merchandise. If it is outdoors, is there a rain date?

2. What is the fee, and how much space do you get to display your work?

3. How long has the show/fair been in existence, and what kind of attendance has it had in the past? If the show is in a mall, the attendance numbers cited might include all the shoppers then in the mall.

4. Are there special restrictions or requirements on the exhibitors? Must the work be original and shown by the artist, or can it be made from a kit or sold by a distributor? This is an important clue as to whether impostors or importers will be selling right next to you.

5. What are the physical arrangements? Is security provided, and can the display be covered and left overnight? Are electricity, tables, and chairs provided?

A list of nearby fairs and shows can be obtained by writing your state arts commission or the local Chamber of Commerce. They may be able to list dates and past attendance, fees, and other pertinent information.

You may be interested in traveling to shows farther away

from home. Lists of shows throughout the country can be obtained by writing *Craft Horizons,* American Crafts Council, 44 West 53rd Street, New York, NY 10019, and *National Calendar of Indoor-Outdoor Art Fairs* published by Henry Niles, 5423 New Haven Avenue, Ft. Wayne, IN 46803.

The cost of attending shows must be considered. Booth and entrance fees usually run between $15 and $50, but the cost of travel, lodging, and food can make it a rather expensive outing. Of course, most of these are business expenses and tax deductible, and the expense of attending is money well spent if you sell a goodly amount of merchandise. Also, frequent fair-goers travel in vans and either camp out or sleep in the vans, thereby reducing their expenses considerably. Many become close friends, seeing each other year after year at the main events. Besides selling goods and making money, the camaraderie and camp atmosphere are an important part of the affairs.

Keep careful records of your expenses — including all vehicle costs, meal receipts, road tolls, phone calls, and lodging — in case you need documentation for tax purposes, and also to determine how cost-effective the show has been.

If you intend to use fairs and shows as the major outlet for your work, then design compositions for that purpose. Very expensive, heavy, or abstract art is rarely bought at these events, while inexpensive to moderately-priced items that appeal to less sophisticated tastes do sell. It may cramp your style to crank out less inspired pots and sell them for $50, but if you intend to make a living selling crafts, they must appeal to the wide spectrum of people who attend the shows.

Many fine artists and craftspeople arrive at these shows totally unprepared and disorganized and expect a table piled with their work to bring in the crowds. You can increase your chance of sales with an appealing display booth. Design a booth that is sturdy and attractive and one that can be easily assembled. Arrange your crafts so they can be viewed and also protected. Put fragile items away from main traffic lanes, and secure small, easily picked-up items under glass.

Crowds will more readily gather at your booth if you can demonstrate your artistry or your crafting skills. If you can throw pots, work with stained glass, or paint, it will surely attract people to your work. However, you can't do two things at once, and you will need a helper to watch over the booth and to transact sales. If demonstrating your art or craft is inappropriate, then engage in light conversation with prospective customers to keep them at your booth, looking at your wares. Crowds attract people so make an effort to induce fair attendees to linger at your booth. Have printed brochures or calling cards available for those who are not ready to buy then but might contact you later.

It's a major chore to get ready for these events. Every single item you take must be properly wrapped and packed, and haste can only result in damaged goods. When the show is closing, there is a tendency to pack away the leftovers as quickly as possible and get out because you're hot, tired, and want to go home. This is when you must slow down and methodically repack the wares so nothing is damaged.

One last suggestion. Avoid flea markets. They can be a disaster for artists and craftspeople because they attract cheap imported goods, and you will feel as if you are caught in a circus. Flea markets convey the feeling that everyone is looking for a bargain, and this takes away from the atmosphere you need to attract those interested in nice pieces of original work.

RETAIL STORES OR SHOPS

Instead of attending shows and fairs, you may choose to sell the goods that you or others have crafted or manufactured from your studio or home. In other words, your home business will be a retail shop, boutique, country store or the like. If you sell your own goods, then you needn't look further for suppliers of finished products. However, if your business is selling other people's goods, then the quality and type of products in your inventory will have a great deal to do with your business success. When selecting product lines, be very sensitive to your location and the character of the clientele you intend to attract. An awareness of your customers — their interests, desires, needs — is essential to your success.

Although most of the information in this book can be applied to a home retailing operation, there are many additional details you may want to know and they would fill another book. If you are planning a retail shop as your home business, I suggest you consult publications dealing specifically with retailing. The Small Business Administration has published several concise and worthwhile pamphlets on the subject. Copies can be obtained from your local SBA office or by writing to SBA, P.O. Box 15434, Ft. Worth, TX 76119. Also consult your local library for books on retailing.

CONSIGNMENT

Selling on consignment means the shop stocking your product does not pay you for it until it's sold. Arts and crafts are the type of items most frequently sold on consignment. You will receive from 60 to 70 percent of the selling price, instead of the 50 percent usually paid when shops buy the merchandise outright. The advantages to the shopowner is that no money is being tied up in merchandise, and they are taking no risks. You should realize that since the store has no financial commitment to stock your goods, their profit margin is less, and they may push your merchandise with less zeal than their other inventory.

Another disadvantage of selling on consignment is you must wait for your money and will get it only if the articles are sold. If they aren't sold, you will get them back after six months or so, and they may be tattered or soiled, and you will have lost your investment in materials and labor.

Still, many artists and craftspeople sell their work on consignment because the shopowners will not purchase it outright, and at least it's a way to get their work seen by possible buyers. This is particularly true for unknowns trying to become established. After demonstrating that the work sells, it's only fair for the shop to buy your goods wholesale and pay up front instead of continuing the consignment arrangement.

If a store agrees to take your products on consignment, it is advisable to take a few steps to protect yourself and your products. The most direct way is to have a consignment agreement that takes into account each of the five issues listed below. The agreement should be signed by both you and the merchant with whom you are dealing.

1. Make a list of each item and describe it clearly.

2. Specify how long the merchandise will remain in the store before it will be returned to you.

3. Settle on the price you will receive for each item. (You can either set the price, and receive a percentage or the shop personnel can set the price, but you will be paid an agreed-upon dollar amount.) If you are selling very expensive art or craft work, you might give a price range, which allows the shop to negotiate with the customer. But remember, the shop wants to sell the goods for whatever they can get and take their commission, so you must be adamant about the minimum amount you will accept.

4. The agreement should include the method of payment. If, for instance, the shop has many small items, then you might expect monthly payment, while one very expensive piece should be paid for immediately.

5. Who is responsible for consigned items if they are damaged, stolen, or destroyed by fire? Either the consignee can carry inventory insurance, or the store or gallery can carry insurance to cover the consigned goods. It should be clearly understood who is responsible.

SELLING ON MEMO

"On Memo" refers to a quasi-consignment type of selling arrangement. Merchandise is shipped or taken to shops and left with a 30- or 60-day return privilege, or sometimes even a 10-day return privilege, for new items that you are anxious for the merchant to see and handle. The unsold items are returned after this period along with the payment for the sold pieces, or they are purchased by the store. This, again, is used mainly by artists and craftspeople. However, manufacturers also use the 10-day return privilege when a new item is being introduced, and they are anxious to market them. New items might be included along with an order shipped to an already established customer, with the privilege pre-paid postage for returning.

MAIL-ORDER SALES

Mail-order sales can be initiated either by advertisements in newspapers and magazines or by mailings of brochures or catalogs to selected individuals. Mail-order marketing is considered by some to be the ultimate form of retailing, while others believe there are hidden costs and pitfalls. Bob Stone, chairman of Stone and Adler, a direct-mail advertising agency observes: "Catalog marketing is an attractive business because there is no high rent to pay, you operate from a warehouse instead of prime real estate, and you do not have any of the costs of salesclerks and bulging inventories." However, he has not taken into account the cost of advertising and the cost of preparing and mailing brochures or catalogs, and these costs can be considerable.

The fact is, mail-order selling is riskier than selling through standard retail channels. It has been estimated that around half of all new catalog ventures fail within two years, and that is a higher rate of failure than other retail outlets. Still, some kinds of merchandise sell well through the mail. Generally, mail-order merchandise should NOT be readily available through retail stores, it *should* be instantly recognizable, and modestly priced. It is difficult to sell expensive goods via mail-order unless it is through a well established and reputable firm. An example of extraordinary success with mail-order sales is Betty Bearden, who sold needlepoint from a couple of shops in Atlanta. When she opened her first shop, she simultaneously put out a catalog, Papillon, in which she advertised needlepoint and related products. The catalog sales resulted in over 50 times the amount of sales as her shops, and this year she expects to sell nearly $9 million worth of needlepoint and other merchandise through her catalogs. She has closed her shops and sells exclusively through the mail. She said: "There's just a limit to what you are going to sell in two needlepoint shops in a year."

Generally, mail-order merchandising is either very successful, or it fails miserably. Administrative problems can sabotage a mail-order operation. If a product sells quickly, you could be left with numerous unfilled orders, but even worse, if the merchandise does not move, you could be left with a large inventory of goods and no way to discount it. Whether selling through ads or mailing lists, you must assume you will get orders, and you will need to build an inventory to fill them before you even know if the public is going to respond to your ads or mailings. Many novice business persons have lost a great deal of money as a result of both the cost of the advertisements or mailings, and the cost of stocking up on something few people seem to want. Still, if you find the right combination of merchandise, can create a compelling catalog with snappy copy and photos, and can target your market, then mail-order sales may be your best form of merchandising. If you use this method of marketing, be cautious, and keep careful records so you can determine where you are getting your best response.

Resources: *National Mailing List House.* A free bibliography from the SBA, (P. O. Box 15434, Ft. Worth, TX 76119) listing names and addresses of major "list houses" throughout the U.S.

Successful Direct Marketing Methods. Robert Stone, 4th ed. NTC Publishing Group, 4255 W. Touhy Ave., Lincolnwood, IL 60646. (This is an excellent book on direct marketing. Keep in mind that it was written by a man involved in promoting direct mail sales through his advertising agency and may not reflect the negative aspects of this type of merchandising.)

Wholesaling through Sales Representatives

If your home business manufactures mass-produced goods, or if you import merchandise, you will need to find a way to distribute and sell the merchandise to outlets. Who will sell the goods, and to whom?

You will have little time to either wholesale or retail your products because frankly, it takes one heck of a lot of time and energy just to oversee production. You may want to visit a few stores and try to initiate sales because it is of value to observe how buyers for the stores react to your products. However, you probably won't be able to spend day after day selling, but that is exactly what is needed to keep orders coming in. Also, if you are manufacturing or importing a lot of goods, the local shops won't be able to sell enough and you will need to find markets outside of your immediate area. So the question remains: Who can sell your goods and how do you find them?

Sales representatives are the link between the manufacturer or importer and the marketplace. I never noticed sales reps before I started hiring them, but they are everywhere — in groceries, gift shops, office supply stores. They can be found in literally every business, identifiable by their telltale satchel and somewhat weary look. When I see them I am reminded of the proverb by Confucius: "Cow who stands on hill has two legs short, two legs long." Sales reps may well have one arm longer than the other — stretched from carrying the heavy sales kit that contains samples, brochures, and ordering materials.

Large businesses have sales representatives that carry only their product. The reps are paid a salary plus a commission on the dollar amount of goods they sell (and some make a VERY good income) or they are paid a salary only or a commission only. Independent sales representatives are not employed by any particular business, but are self-employed and sell merchandise for many manufacturers. You might hire this kind of sales rep to sell your goods. You will want to hire several or many sales reps, each covering a defined geographical area, such as a portion of your city or state or several entire states. Most sales reps want "exclusive territory," which means they are the sole representative of your merchandise in that area. This arrangement is fine if the rep aggressively sells your product. The best part of hiring a sales rep is that your only costs are for samples and purchase orders. You don't pay them anything until they sell something, and then you pay an agreed-upon percentage of the sale.

The whole idea of hiring a group of sales reps to carry your merchandise might boggle your mind, but it is a very effective way of selling manufactured and crafted goods. During the first year of our home business, we hired 53 sales reps, and that's why our sales took off so dramatically and our business grew so rapidly.

Locating sales reps to carry your goods is a simple process.

For a small fee ($15 to $30) trade journals carry advertisements of people looking for sales reps and the ads of sales reps looking for lines to add to their portfolio. You would, of course, advertise in a journal appropriate for your merchandise.

There are several things to consider when hiring a sales rep. Do they work alone, or are they with a rep organization? It is easier to hire an organization with multiple sales reps because you need to send only a single mailing of each notice or update and write one check each month to cover several commissions.

The location and the area the reps work is an important consideration. If you hire numerous sales reps it would be wise to keep a large map and color in areas that are "taken." In this way, you can tell at a glance which areas are not served by reps. You can also avoid a territory overlap this way. You should ask to see a list of the other lines the rep carries to see how your merchandise fits into their portfolio. Obviously, it will be to your advantage to have your goods carried by reps who call on stores where your merchandise will "fit."

To each sales rep you hire, you'll need to provide samples of your products, brochures showing your merchandise, and also some orders forms which they may or may not use. Some prefer to use their own. The samples and brochures are sent at your expense, but these are tax deductible so note the value of everything you send.

Some sales representative companies rent space in showrooms in larger cities. It is here that buyers for shops and stores come several times each year to order merchandise to replenish their shelves. Sales organizations with showroom space have access to a large market of potential buyers, and they are generally quite aggressive in seeking out new accounts. If you hire them, you will need to supply samples for the showroom.

You'll quickly discover which of your sales reps are effective by the orders they send to you; some send an abundance of orders while others only make only an occasional sale. If other reps are asking for the territory taken by an unproductive rep, you can inform the poor salesperson the territory is being reclaimed, and then reissue it to another rep.

Sales commissions are paid monthly, and usually are 15 to 20 percent of the total sales. You realize, of course, that you must include this expense in the cost of the product when you are setting prices. It's great to write big commission checks because that means a lot of merchandise is being sold. Some businesses pay commissions only after they receive payment for the merchandise, while others pay at the end of the month the sale was made. I prefer paying the reps, whether or not the payment for the merchandise has been received because that keeps them motivated to sell your goods.

Besides selling to stores and shops, catalogs are also fair game. Either you or your sales reps can initiate these sales. There is a very specific procedure required when submitting goods to be considered for inclusion in a catalog. Find the appropriate catalogs for your products and write for submission dates and procedures (the addresses are on the catalogs.) It's a waste of time and money trying to introduce products at different times and without following the correct format.

Resources: *Directory of Wholesale Reps for Artisans and Craft Professionals,* available from Northwoods Trading Co., 200 Sunnyvale Lane, Minnetonka, MN 55343 ($5 ppd). This directory lists over 35 sales rep organizations that sell nationwide to a variety of outlets.

Profitable Crafts Marketing by Brian T. Jefferson, 1985. Timber Press, P. O. Box 1631, Beaverton, OR 97075.

The Secrets of Practical Marketing for Small Business by Herman R. Holtz, 1982. Prentice Hall, Inc. Sylvan Ave., Englewood Cliffs, NJ 07632 ($7.95).

MARKETING A SERVICE

Contracting for a service involves an act of faith on the part of the customer. How does a customer know the work will be done well, and what can they do if it isn't? Well, the best way to increase your business volume is to offer good service. That way, subsequent business will come through recommendations.

Workers who do an especially good job or have exceptionally competitive prices will get more jobs as a result of recommendations, while those who deliver poor service will need to keep attracting new customers through advertising. Their business grows only as a result of advertising, which of course, takes money, and this can force the ones delivering poor service to charge more than those who deliver good service.

If pleased customers readily recommend a worker, and that worker receives two new jobs as a result of each pleased customer, the number of new jobs will grow exponentially. At this point the person delivering the service will be unable to do all the work and will need to make a choice. He or she can elect to keep operating on the same level and turn down some of the jobs when they become too numerous, or, since more service is being sought than can be delivered, the business can continue the small-scale operation and increase the price. Those customers willing to pay the increased prices will get the service, and the business will generate a higher profit. The other alternative is to hire additional help to meet the growing demand. It then becomes necessary to closely monitor the employees to make sure the service continues to fulfill the customer's expectations.

SELLING WRITTEN WORK

This section is just for you pencil pushers and key punchers. Many home workers are writers, and some do a pretty good job of it, but a very low percentage of the people writing books, poems, and articles will ever see their work in print. The reasons are twofold. First, the writing is inadequate or the subject is of little interest. But the second reason is that writers are notoriously bad business people, and many stop just short of carrying their project to completion. They question their ability and lack enough confidence to keep pursuing a publisher until one is found. Consequently, their work remains unread in a drawer.

Many fine pieces have never been read because the writer didn't know the pathway to publication. In truth, it's a pathway beset with obstacles, and as a result, very few people can actually make a living and support a family with the money they earn by writing. On the other hand, many writers handsomely supplement a spouse's income by selling their work.

If you intend to earn money writing, then you should write the kind of material that has a better chance of selling. Fact: nine times more nonfiction than fiction is bought and published. The purpose of nonfiction is to convey information, so it follows that in order to write nonfiction you must have some information to pass along, and that takes study, experience, and work. What about novels and poetry? Unless you happen to have a rare special talent, forget about writing novels, and poetry might be fun to write but it is difficult to sell, and poets are paid very poorly (supply and demand at work).

Still, if you are determined to write, then how and where can you get your work published? You will need to market your written material just as manufacturers market their products. Become familiar with the market. If you are writing magazine articles, study the magazines you hope to publish in and observe the kinds of material they use. If your interest is books, then keep a list of publishers who print books on subjects you intend to write about. This book is a good example. I have a good working relationship with another publisher, but when I decided to write about home businesses, I contacted Betterway Publications, Inc. because they publish books about small businesses and have marketing outlets and an established reputation.

The basic selling tools for writers are *The Writer's Market* and *Literary Market Place*. These books are updated and published annually, and both can be found in libraries or book stores. They list almost every American publisher along with information on how to submit material. Both books categorize the publishers according to types of works or subjects they publish and give a brief statement about each company.

Most writers write a book and then try to find a publisher. That sequence might be necessary as you get started, but it is much more efficient to write an outline, a couple of chapters, and then locate a publisher. This allows you to shape the book to the expectations of the publisher and then less rewriting will be needed to complete it. Some publishing contracts will include a monetary advance to the author to cover expenses incurred in the writing. The advance is of value in that it keeps both the writer and publisher committed to the project.

If you intend to sell a lot of material, it is essential to submit your work to multiple publishers simultaneously, informing them of the simultaneous submissions, and also informing them when the manuscript is sold. It is necessary to keep records of where and when an article is submitted and any response you get from the publisher. Upon acceptance, the publisher will make you a monetary offer. Unless you sign a contract that specifies otherwise, you are selling only the article's "first rights," which means you are free to resell the article to another publisher at a later time.

There are times when self publishing is the answer, but you must be careful as this can be very expensive. Let's say you write a piece about your family or some poems that are very personal but that you want to share with family and friends. Obviously, this would not be suitable material for a regular publisher because of the limited market, but you might want to see the work in print and be willing to pay for the printing and binding. This is one reason for self printing, but under these conditions, it would cost rather than earn money.

Other situations can allow you to earn money through self publishing. An acquaintance of mine, Brad Chaffin, suffers from multiple sclerosis. This is a man of remarkable will and goodwill. Among his other accomplishments is the book, *Creative Living with MS*. Rather than spend the considerable time and energy needed to find a publisher, Brad self-published his book. He has been very active in the National Multiple Sclerosis Society and knows many people suffering with MS. As a result of his work with the society, he had access to their mailing list, and he could make contacts through the society's newsletter. This was a natural vehicle for marketing his book. He found a printer, did his own layout, and published a fine book, and one that fills a need. The book has sold well to the group for whom it was written.

Resource: *Writer's Market,* from Writer's Digest Books, 1507 Dana Ave., Cincinnati, OH 45207. Annual edition. This book lists several thousands of publications, names of editors, and the kinds of material they print, their pay scale, and other valuable information.

Packing
and Shipping

Packing and shipping can be as important as the careful crafting of your product. It is needed to get your product to market.

PACKING

Rest assured that every box you pack will be subjected to some shock in transit. It may be tossed, squashed, or dropped even though the box labels cry out the messages "Handle With Care," "This Side Up," or "Do Not Stack." The container and packing material must absorb this abuse, not the contents of the container.

The nature of your merchandise will influence packing procedures. Unbreakable articles, like plush animals, can be protected from moisture and dirt by bagging them in plastic and, since they won't break, they can be literally stuffed in a box, sealed, and shipped. Fragile items will need to be surrounded with an abundance of shock-absorbing material. Particularly fragile items are better protected if they are wrapped in bubble-cushion plastic, placed in a box, and then packed in a larger box, with packing material between the two boxes.

A variety of packing materials are available; price, weight, and convenience should be taken into consideration when deciding which to use. Wadded newspaper is lightweight, absorbs shock and costs nothing. Styrene "mushroom caps" or "peanuts" are ideal for fragile items because they absorb shock, resist crushing, and add hardly any weight to a package, and plastic bubble paper is perfect for wrapping fragile items before placing them into cushioning material. Heavy articles can be protected with sturdy corrugated cardboard.

Will your product arrive at its destination in good condition? Test your packing procedure by trying various combinations of materials and box sizes and putting the boxes through stress and shock tests just as you expect them to experience in shipment. Then unpack them and examine the contents to learn which packing method leaves the contents in the best condition.

It is very important to master the packing process. Not only can products be destroyed if the packing is inadequate, but customers may become annoyed if they must file a damage claim and wait for another shipment. You certainly don't want them looking elsewhere for suppliers.

Prepare an itemized packing slip and make a duplicate copy for your records as you fill each box for shipping. (It's easiest to use carbon copies of the invoice with the prices blocked out.) The packing slip can be enclosed in the package (put it on *top* of the goods rather than at the bottom), but better still is attaching it to the outside of the shipping box in an envelope marked "Packing Slip Enclosed." The packing slip is used to verify that the entire order has been received, and you'll need a copy if you have a breakage claim. Claims should be initiated as soon as possible after the damaged shipment arrives at its destination. You can hope that the recipient will take care of the claim, but if not, you will need to do it.

You'll be surprised what you need just for the packing and shipping part of your operation. Businesses that sell shipping supplies can be found in the Yellow Pages under "Packaging Materials." Also, check the surplus and damaged freight stores in your area for shipping supplies since they frequently have some on hand.

Shipping cartons can be purchased much cheaper in large lots than small lots. Inquire about the shipping charges because several hundred cardboard cartons are quite heavy, and shipping can add a significant amount to the cost. Try to locate a supplier in your vicinity so you can get the boxes faster (and therefore won't need a big inventory) and with less transportation costs. If you can use all kinds and shapes of boxes, you might be able to get what you need among the discards BEHIND stores. Many stores restock their shelves on certain days, and you'll quickly learn when to pick up a supply of boxes.

You will also need: shipping tape, a tape dispenser for sealing the boxes, rubber stamps for special instructions (Fragile, This End Up), mailing labels, packing material, and a UPS/

Parcel Post scale with a capacity greater than the maximum weight of what you'll be shipping.

The cost of the carton, tape, and packing material can add several dollars to the cost of a shipment and should be added either to the price of your product or passed on to the customer as a separate charge. You can save a few dollars by recycling the boxes and packing materials from shipments you receive, but don't try to save money on shipping supplies if it puts your products at risk.

SHIPPING

Most of your merchandise will probably be shipped by "common carrier" — companies that transport goods for a fee by rail, air, ship, bus, or truck. They are regulated by government agencies and must charge all customers the same fee for the same service. Local truckers are called private carriers who aren't bound by a fee structure. They charge what the market will bear.

Trucks are the usual shipping method used by small manufacturers because they're faster and deliver to more destinations than other forms of shipping.

Locate truckers in the *Yellow Pages* under "Trucking-Local Cartage" for local delivery and "Trucking-Motor Freight" for long distance delivery. The 800 number for United Parcel Service can also be found in the Yellow Pages of your directory.

The United Parcel Service (UPS) has earned praise from a multitude of businesses because of their fast delivery and careful handling. They are less expensive than the U. S. Postal Service, and for a small weekly fee a truck will stop at your home every day to pick up shipments. UPS does not accept boxes that measure over 108 inches in girth and length combined, or boxes that weigh more than 50 pounds. But for most shipments, UPS can't be beat.

You can use either a motor carrier or a freight forwarder to ship very large or heavy boxes. Motor carriers cost more but are faster than freight forwarders. Everything is carried by truck and is picked up and delivered. Freight forwarders take shipments to a central destination where they are consolidated and forwarded whenever a load is gathered. It might be shipped by truck, rail, air, or water. Each package is taken to a terminal near its destination and then transferred to a local truck for final delivery.

Business Taxes

Taxes! If we didn't have taxes we'd be RICH!
We wouldn't need to keep careful records,
And we'd be driving long cars — on dirt roads.

Taxes are the glue that holds our society together. Ralph Waldo Emerson observed, "For every benefit you receive, a tax is levied," and that homily also defines the connection between cost and benefit. Various taxes and the ways to deal with them are discussed in the following chapter, but more detailed instructions are given in the free booklet, *Tax Guide for Small Business*, IRS Publication 334, which can be obtained by writing SBA, P.O. Box 15434, Fort Worth, TX 76119.

KEEPING RECORDS FOR TAX PURPOSES

No specific record, document, or bookkeeping system is required by the Internal Revenue Service. However, you must be able to somehow substantiate claims or prove statements made on your tax return. You are required to maintain permanent books that identify your business income, expenses, and deductions. Unlike a court of law where you are innocent until proven guilty, the burden of proof lies with the taxpayer when he or she is confronted by the IRS. For this reason, your records must reflect all your income and expenses since the IRS may disallow any deductions you cannot substantiate.

The records discussed in Chapter 13 are adequate for tax purposes, and consist of checkbook stubs and canceled checks, a cash receipts and cash disbursements journal, and petty-cash fund receipts and records. You will also need a record of fixed assets such as equipment, buildings, and vehicles so you can note their depreciation and gain the maximum tax advantages. Depreciation schedules and records must be kept for at least as long as the replacement cycle of the assets.

If you hire employees, you will need to keep additional more extensive records, including the amounts and dates of all employee wage payments subject to withholding taxes.

HELP CAN HELP

You will probably need expert help when preparing tax returns to use the tax laws to your best advantage. The obvious person to enlist for this is your accountant, who will know what records to keep and will show you how to manage your finances so you don't pay unnecessary taxes. Consider hiring a tax consultant if you don't have an accountant. Tax consultants usually save their clients more than the cost of they're services because they are familiar with the latest regulations and can develop a financial strategy in their client's best interests. You can get free help and advice from the IRS, but the IRS's main concern is filling out forms, and they will rarely share with you their knowledge of how to turn the tax laws to your advantage. They are, after all, in the business of collecting money for the government.

BUSINESS TAX FORMS

You are required to fill out various federal and state forms as you start and operate your business. The federal tax forms required for a proprietorship, partnership, or corporation that has Subchapter S status (see Chapter 11) are listed below. Tax requirements for a regular corporation are not discussed in this book since very few home businesses are organized in this fashion. You are advised to seek the guidance of a tax consultant if your business is a regular corporation.

The tax forms you will need if you have NO EMPLOYEES:

1040 Individual Income Tax Return.

1040C Profit or Loss from Business or Profession.
   This form is used to itemize your business deductions. You will need to determine your end-of-year inventory to complete this form. (See the IRS *Tax Guide for Small Business* for procedures on taking an inventory.)

1040ES Estimated Tax for Individuals, paid quarterly.
>   You are responsible for making advance payment of your estimated federal income tax. These payments are due by the 15th of January, April, July, and October. You must pay at least 90 percent of the tax you owe or you will be charged a penalty.

1040SE Computation of Social Security Self-Employment Tax.
>   Your estimated tax payments will also include payment into your Social Security fund. Since you are self-employed, you will need to pay the full amount, unlike employees who pay half the amount; the employer paying the other half.

4562 Depreciation and Amortization.
>   Discussed below.

If you HAVE EMPLOYEES, you will need these forms:

All of the above, plus

SS-4 with Circular E. This is the application for the Employer Identification Number (EIN).
>   Circular E, The Employer's Tax Guide, explains the Federal income and Social Security tax withholding requirements.

940 Employer's Annual Federal Unemployment Tax Return.
>   This is used to report and pay the Federal Unemployment Compensation Tax.

941 Employer's Quarterly Federal Tax Return.
>   Use this form to report income tax and Social Security tax withheld from employees pay during the previous calendar quarter, and matched by you, the employer.

W-2 Employer's Wage and Tax Statement.
>   Used to report to the IRS the taxes withheld and compensation paid to each employee.

W-3 Reconciliation/Transmittal of Income and Tax Statements.
>   Used to total information from the W-2, and sent to the Social Security Administration.

The IRS conducts periodic workshops to teach you how to use their tax forms. You can learn when and where the workshops are held by calling your local IRS office.

DEDUCTIBLE EXPENSES

Business expenses are tax deductible. Knowing and using legitimate deductions will significantly affect your profit and thus the amount of taxes you must pay. Any money spent to make your business work is a legitimate business expense and includes among other things, rent, supplies, wages, utilities, sales costs, traveling expenses, shipping, and raw materials.

Home Business Deductibles

Home business deductibles were discussed in Chapter 6, but a few additional details need to be mentioned. First, your home/business deduction can be no larger than the gross income from your home business. Secondly, capital gains tax must be paid on that portion of your home you claim as a business deduction when you sell your property. As you know, you can defer the capital gains tax when you sell your home by reinvesting the money in a new home, but if you have been taking a business deduction you cannot defer the tax, but must pay it immediately. This can amount to a sizable tax bite. However, if you anticipate selling your home and do not claim the home/business deduction for *one year prior* to selling it, then you do not need to pay the capital gains tax. Thus, planning ahead is the key to taking advantage of this tax break.

Regular Business Deductibles

Regular business expenses include those that are needed to keep your business in operation, but are not a part of the home/business deduction. Some are obvious; others less so, but in any case you should be able to justify the deduction and show evidence of the expense. Always be alert to expenses that are unique to your type of work or your way of doing business, and therefore are not among the items normally listed, yet are legitimate expenses.

Legitimate business expense deductions:

Accounting and tax preparation
Advertising expenses
Bank service charges
Books, magazines, newspapers, and periodicals related to
  your business
Car expenses
Commissions paid to agents and sales representatives
Consulting services
Dues for trade organizations

Employee wages and expenses
Eighty percent of entertainment cost (be careful, as this
    raises an audit flag)
Equipment (discussed below)
Insurance premiums
Interest on business loans
Legal fees
License fees
Office furniture
Office supplies
Printing and duplicating
Promotional items such as gifts
Seminars and conferences on business matters
Taxes
Telephone
Travel that is directly business-related

To Deduct or to Depreciate?

The cost of large pieces of business equipment can either
be used as a deduction (expensed) or it can be depreciated. If
the cost is depreciated over the life of the equipment, a tax
credit can be taken. A credit is more valuable than a deduction
because it is subtracted directly from the taxes you owe, whereas
a deduction is subtracted from your taxable income. Still, it
is sometimes to your advantage to deduct the entire cost of a
new piece of equipment in a single year, if for instance, you
have an especially profitable year and want to use the deduction
to show lower profits. The maximum amount eligible for a
capital-expense deduction is $10,000, and the excess amount can
be depreciated. Deciding on whether it is better to deduct or
depreciate equipment costs is one area where planning and
strategy play an important role, and you will probably need
the help of an accountant to work out the best plan for you.

STATE AND LOCAL TAXES

Sales tax is a state tax. It is collected when a product is
sold at retail to the final consumer. A manufacturer does not
pay sales tax on supplies and raw materials that will be converted
into products for sale. Neither does a service business pay sales
tax on repair parts, or a builder on construction materials.
However, taxes must be paid on an article which is used directly
for the business, but isn't resold. For instance, a manufacturer
of dolls would NOT pay tax on the material, doll faces, stuffing,

thread, and buttons used to make the dolls, but WOULD pay tax on the sewing machine used to sew the dolls together.

If you live in a state that has a sales tax (most states do) you will probably need a sales tax number, and you should apply for it before buying supplies for your business. When supplies are purchased and sales tax won't be collected, the merchant must mark the tax exemption number on the invoice. If taxable goods are bought, but the tax is not paid, the buyer and merchant are subject to fines.

If yours is a retail business in a state having a sales tax, then you must collect the sales tax on your sales, keep a record of the tax collected, and remit the collected tax to the appropriate state office each calendar quarter. The state may allow you to keep a small percentage of the collected tax to cover your collection costs. Procedural matters will vary among the states, so contact your State Information Center (in the Government section of the telephone directory) for information about a sales tax account number (also called your sales tax exemption number) and other details. In most states the number is good for the life of the business.

The tax rate and kinds of taxes vary from one location to another, but you might be subject to, besides a sales tax, a tax on gross income, often levied by state governments. Local governments frequently levy property or real estate taxes.

SURVIVING AN AUDIT

Most people hope to slip past the watchful eyes of the IRS, but the chance always exists that you will be selected for a closer look. Still, there are several ways to make your tax return less conspicuous and reduce the probability of an audit. Most of the following tips are little more than common sense, but if I were limited to just two words of advice they would be either "DON'T EXAGGERATE" or "BE HONEST."

Using a home office as a tax deduction, in itself, attracts the attention of the IRS. Still, it's a legitimate claim, and one you should surely take. But make sure you meet the criteria outlined in Chapter 6, and be prepared to substantiate your claims. If the deduction seems too far-fetched, you might be audited. The agent might actually measure the area you claim as business space, but if you DON'T EXAGGERATE, you have nothing to fear.

The IRS is alerted when family members are employed in a home business because this is a way to reduce profit and thus lower taxes. The collection agency is well aware of the fact that sometimes family members are paid but do not work in the business, so keep careful records of the hours worked and the type of work done to verify the family involvement. And don't pay them more than you would pay a non-family employee.

Be sensitive to possible audit flags as you prepare your tax return. Don't claim ridiculous business deductions; however, if you have a curious deduction or unusual claim, provide adequate documentation, canceled checks, and even add a letter of explanation to satisfy the tax examiner.

If you receive an audit notice, calm down and get help from your accountant. The IRS will indicate specific areas of interest. Thoroughly organize the information the IRS wants to see, and make it available to them. But do not lay out all of your books for the auditor to pour over. Both you and your accountant should be involved in an audit. You will be responsible for the records you provided to your accountant, and your accountant will be responsible for the way the records were interpreted and used to prepare your tax return.

Records are your best defense when confronted with an audit. Ordinarily, the statute of limitations for records expires three years after the return is filed, and the IRS does not investigate older cases except where the taxpayer omitted over 25 percent of the gross income or a false or fraudulent return was filed. Still, it's wise to save for seven years records that show accounts payable and receivable, canceled checks, inventory schedules, payroll records, sales vouchers, and invoice details. Checkbooks, depreciation schedules, the ledger or accounts, journals, and all financial statements and audit reports should be kept considerably longer. Also, copies of income tax returns should be saved, not only as records, but also because you can use them in subsequent years to help prepare the new returns.

Resource: *Guide to Year-Round Tax Savings* by Julian Block, Dow Jones-Irwin. This book covers personal income taxes with information on tax breaks for the self-employed. It is revised annually. Available in many bookstores.

Being Insured is a Good Policy

Early in this book you were given the odds for succeeding at your own business — and they weren't very good — but you have persisted in reading, probably with every intention of going ahead with your plans. Has it occurred to you that you are a gambler — that you are willing to take risks? Theodore Roosevelt said, "It is impossible to win the great prizes of life without running risks," and that surely applies to starting a new business. When you decide to start a business you are taking a "speculative risk": you may or may not succeed. Speculative risks cannot be insured.

"Pure risks" are different in that they are not risks you choose to take, but instead, are inherent in human activity, and they may result in a loss. Examples of pure risk are fire, a fall from a banana peel, an auto accident, a ladder breaking. Pure risks can be insured. There are special kinds of pure risks associated with operating a business, and because of these risks, insurance becomes necessary. An insurance policy is a way to transfer some of the risk from yourself to the insurance company for a fee, or a premium as it is called.

Priorities must be established to determine what to insure. The question you must answer when you develop an insurance package is, what are you willing to risk? A good rule of thumb is: You should insure what you can't afford to lose.

PERSONAL LIABILITY INSURANCE

Generally, you are financially responsible for injuries that occur on your property. The standard homeowner's policy protects you when a visitor is injured in your home, but it does not apply to people who visit your home for business purposes. For very little extra money, a rider can be added to your homeowner's policy to provide personal liability coverage for business visitors, although a larger amount is required for child-care or other people-care businesses. This will not cover claims for injuries or damages that result from the products you sell or the services you render. For instance, a baker would be covered if a customer slips on a waxed floor and breaks a tooth in the fall, but would not be covered if the tooth is broken when the customer bites down on a pit in a cherry pie. The latter would be covered by a *product liability* insurance policy discussed below.

You might need general liability insurance if your business operates from your home, but you actually do the work in the customer's home. This would protect their property in the event of accidental damage. If you hang draperies, for instance, and you break an antique vase while working, a general liability policy would pay to replace the vase. Another example demonstrates a different need for general liability. Let's say you are teaching aerobic dancing in a church activity room, and a student trips over the cord to your stereo equipment and fractures an arm. The injured student might sue and name you as the defendant in the case. General liability would come to your rescue. The policy should be written to cover attorney fees and other costs of defending yourself, besides payment to the injured party.

PRODUCT OR SERVICE LIABILITY

Product or service liability insurance is needed to protect yourself against claims for damages or injury that results from the services or products you offer. Product liability coverage can be purchased for as little as $100 a year if the products aren't considered hazardous, but that rate can rise astronomically if there is even a hint they might be hazardous. Services or products concerned with body care or treatment usually carry a high-risk factor and protection is very expensive. The type of liability best suited for your particular service or product might be product liability insurance, malpractice insurance (for professional services), commercial liability, or others. Your insurance agent can help you determine what coverage you need. By the way, an insurance agent is heavily insured in the event they are sued when a client discovers he or she was poorly advised and has inadequate insurance to cover a claim.

PROPERTY INSURANCE

You probably have a homeowner's policy that covers your property should damage or loss occur. Make a point to check that the policy is valid when a business is operated on the property because some policies are void under these circumstances. As you add business equipment, furnishings, and inventory, it would be wise to increase your coverage to include the additions. Insurance agents can issue a binder that will insure the additional items from the moment you contact them. Also, periodically review your insurance to keep it current, and have an automatic inflation adjustment built into the policy. It is easier to validate insurance claims if you have photographs of the insured property. Photograph each room in your home, and also take an outdoor view of the front and back of your property. Keep the photographs in a safe deposit box or some other safe place away from the insured property.

You probably have some basic health and disability insurance. There are many other kinds of insurance you can buy, but you must be careful not to become "insurance poor" — your insurance costs so much that you have little left. On the other hand, it is dangerous to be underinsured.

Consult an independent insurance agent, and choose one who represents numerous companies, to help you put together a cost-efficient insurance package that will fill your needs. These agents can pick and choose from various company offerings, unlike an agent who represents a single company only.

Insurance is a way to manage pure risk, and with your home, life, and business insured, you can proceed with the assurance that you are protected from some of life's uncertainties.

Resource: *Insurance Checklist for Small Business.* Free management aid from the SBA, P.O. Box 15434, Ft. Worth, TX 76119.

Evaluating Your Business

The most effective way to review and evaluate your business is to make evaluation a continuous process. Most businesses have a quarterly or semi-annual review, but this isn't nearly as effective as a continuous evaluation. As you go about your daily activities, keep your eyes and mind open for clues that indicate an especially good feature or a potentially troublesome one. By constantly monitoring your business you can capitalize on good directions and intercept problems before they get out of hand.

FINANCIAL EVALUATION

GOOD MONEY MANAGEMENT WON'T MAKE YOUR BUSINESS GROW, BUT IT WILL ALLOW IT TO GROW. Your ideas, work, service, and reliability need to be fertilized by responsible fiscal management in order to give rise to a healthy, viable business. One without the other will result in failure. Money will be wasted if it is spent to support poor ideas, slovenly work, and unreliable service, while good ideas and service will flounder if financial management fails.

To evaluate the financial condition of your business you need information, and this information can be obtained only with an adequate record-keeping system. Evaluating your financial records means deciding if you are spending enough but not too much, and if you are spending it in the right places. If you detect a leak in your financial dam, take action right away. Watch for ways to reduce expenses, but don't reduce them if you'd significantly reduce the quality of the work you deliver. The old adage, "A penny saved is a penny earned," doesn't always apply when operating a business. You need to spend money in order to make it. Your job is to figure out how best to use your finite supply of money to get the best results.

DON'T FORGET YOUR CUSTOMERS

Remember who pays the bills. It's not your supplier, delivery boy, or hairdresser — customers pay your bills by bringing you business, and it is through them that you can stay in business. If you aren't careful, you can become so involved with the intricacies of running your operation that you lose sight of the fact that it is your customers who make your business grow. Focus on them and seek their feedback. Make a habit of carefully listening to what they have to say and use their suggestions to help shape your business plans.

Attracting customers for "repeat business" is an ideal way to make your business grow. Four elements keep customers coming back. The initial sale sets the process in motion, but then you must (1) deliver exceptional quality, (2) provide outstanding service, and (3) establish a reputation of reliability.

The fourth element that brings customers back is recognition — not their recognition of your business but *your* recognition of your customers. Customers respond to attention and recognition. I have trouble remembering the names of my best friends, let alone customers, but I'm working on it simply because it's so valuable. If you can remember not only customer names but also some facts about them — something that makes them feel special, they will return with more business. I have a hairdresser friend who keeps a file on each of her customers. She records the names of each customer's husband and children along with tidbits of information the customer passes along while sitting under the dryer. The kinds of information she records isn't earth-shaking — maybe Johnny won a music contest, the husband repairs mantle clocks — these kinds of things. Each morning before her first appointment, she quickly scans her files and refreshes her memory of names and incidences that will help in the "small talk" that goes with hair care. She also clips articles from the newspaper about her customers or their families so they can have an extra copy. It's no wonder that this gal's business is flourishing. She is making the extra effort that draws people to her. Of course, this same principle applies to private relationships — people pursue relationships with those who recognize their individuality.

KEEP WATCHING FOR
THE WEAK LINK

A business that has the potential for success might well fail if there is a serious problem, a single weak link. The following list suggests the types of problems you should watch for besides financial management and customer relations.

A wrong business decision might be a weak link. Many decisions must be made, and the ramifications of these decisions are usually unknown at the time, so it is not surprising that some of them will be wrong and must be corrected. Also, a good decision might not continue to be good as conditions change, and therefore it's important to continue an ongoing review of your operation and correct problems as they arise.

Another weak link could be with one of your suppliers. If you need many supplies, a single supplier who fails to deliver on time or cannot deliver quality materials, can interrupt the flow of your business. Late delivery can halt manufacturing and cause a backup of orders, or leave you unable to provide a service. Thus, it is imperative to know of an alternate source of supplies even if they cost more than you normally pay.

Could the problem be advertising? A business that offers a good product or service will survive only if enough people are convinced they need or want it. Use your advertising dollar to define clearly what makes your business unique. It might be worth skimping in other areas so you can increase your advertising budget. Then blow your bundle where it will attract the most attention and make the biggest difference in your business. The potential customer needs to be reminded over and over again about your business, reinforcing the message that you can deliver the goods or service.

Could it be that you're spending too much on advertising? Is your advertising cost-effective; does it bring in more business than it costs? The appearance of prosperity can be misleading and may not be a true reflection of your business health. A colleague of mine felt his business was booming, yet he never had enough money to pay his bills. When he finally had his books analyzed, he discovered he wasn't attracting enough business to cover his huge advertising budget. Don't let a rush of sales lull you into a sense of well-being and keep you from carefully analyzing the Profit and Loss statement.

Pricing might be the problem. Suppose you have a good product or service, a lot of business, good suppliers, and everything seems to be going beautifully, but you still aren't making a profit. Maybe you aren't charging enough. Or, suppose you have a good product or service, good suppliers, but not enough business, and that's why you aren't making a profit. This suggests that you're charging too much, and people are taking their business where the prices are better. The guideline is, determine what the market will bear, and adjust your prices accordingly. If you can't make a profit using this guideline, then you must change your business so a profit can be realized.

The weak link could even be your product or service. Just because something sold well last year doesn't mean it will be in demand next year. If there is a unifying principle of the marketplace, it is the CONSTANCY OF CHANGE. But changing conditions present different opportunities that you might turn to your advantage. Also, be aware of demographics, particularly the changing age make-up of your market, and respond to these changes.

One of the big advantages a small business has over a large one is its ability to respond quickly to a changing market. Just as the lumbering dinosaur was felled by changing conditions, so can huge companies be vulnerable to change. On the other hand, a small business can evolve with our evolving society because it's not burdened with many levels of decision making and can quickly react to changing styles, values, and laws. The key to being responsive is to stay flexible so that new ideas are spawned and new products can be created. If you manufacture a product, watch for product obsolescence and keep working on plans for new products that can be substituted if the old ones become obsolete. Don't get too comfortable with a product.

The same principle applies to service businesses. Let's suppose you live in a quiet area on the edge of town and operate a day care center for children of working parents. A new highway is being planned, and it will pass directly in front of your home. You may be disheartened at the prospect of a highway near your home and worry about caring for children so close to fast-moving traffic. Look for an alternative — for a way to turn the changing roadway to your advantage. Perhaps you could convert the space used for child care into guest rooms, offering a "Bed and Breakfast," if the new traffic pattern would bring in overnight guests.

It's a good idea to keep an eye on your competitors and watch how they adapt to the changing market. If you catch a competitor napping, take advantage of their lapse and move to fill the niche they leave. (No, that's not unethical, that's good business.)

One disastrous weak link is an inability to collect bills owed to you. Your good product or excellent service is to no avail if it isn't paid for. Credit ratings have been established for a reason, and it is absolutely essential that you use them in your dealings. If you continue to do business with customers who don't pay their bills, you are subsidizing them at the risk of damaging your business.

What about you? Have you considered that YOU could be a weak link? It's difficult to consider yourself as the problem in your own business, but you must remain alert to that possibility. Perhaps you haven't honed the skills or acquired the expertise needed to accomplish your goals. If your goals are realistic, there are several ways to remedy your deficiency. Let's suppose you operate a woodcrafting shop. Perhaps you aren't quite good enough at your craft and aren't able to produce the unusual pieces people want to buy. You can gain these skills by taking classes or by working with someone else as an intern. Or, you could continue operating your own shop while you improve your techniques: work on less demanding pieces and charge less for your products until you become an expert craftsperson.

You might be a weak link if you are not working up to capacity. Many things can interfere with work efficiency, such as tiredness due to the overwork or stress of running a business, or depression as a result of being isolated. If you are failing to work at capacity, make the adjustments needed to revitalize your life.

You could also be a weak link if you do not have a disciplined work schedule. Maybe you have trouble getting to work in the morning and tend to linger an extra half-hour over coffee. Those 30 minutes may not be important, but could set a pattern of allowing interruptions throughout the day. It has been said that if you lose an hour in the morning, you will spend the whole day trying to find it. Make moves to strengthen your business discipline whenever you detect a faltering resolve.

Maybe the weak link is not you but one of your helpers. Whether your helpers are your children, spouse, or "outside" help, each person involved in the business has specific duties, and if one fails to perform properly, the whole business can suffer. Workers will produce more and better work if they have responsibilities and if they are rewarded for work well done. They respond to rewards both of pay and praise. Also, workers will be more enthusiastic and aggressive in their work if they have realistic goals, so think through the assignments you give them to be sure they can be accomplished. If you are having trouble with work performance, evaluate your expectations and reward system, and make corrections if you find them lacking. However, if your expectations are reasonable and the rewards are adequate, then evaluate the efficiency of your helpers and make changes as needed.

These are but a few of the problems you might encounter. Detecting and solving problems can make the difference between success and failure, or the difference between being very successful rather than moderately successful. All businesses have weak links, and I can't overemphasize the need to keep watching for them so you can make changes and strengthen your business.

STOP PLANNING AND GET ON WITH IT!

Some people know intuitively how to make things work, and the businesses they run show this in spite of what appears to be little planning and little review. Actually, intuitive people do plan and review, but it takes place at a near subconscious level. Their intuition isn't some supernatural instinct but is based on an awareness and constant observation and comparison.

Other people lack a strong intuitive sense, but they make up for it by planning carefully, trying harder, and by trying more things. Eventually, something is bound to work for them. Most of us fall into this category. We consciously think about and make plans to get from point A to point B. At this moment, point A is not owning a home business and point B is operating a home business. Reading this book is just a part of your planning process. You are already learning how to run a business. Now make plans and get on with it.

A third group of people become stymied in the planning stage. They are so hung up trying to anticipate every possible problem before they take action that the net result is inaction. To quote a phrase from Peters and Waterman's book, *In Search Of Excellence*, "Don't let analysis lead to paralysis." Don't get stuck looking at records, making charts and working and reworking plans, because you will fail to make that commitment that moves the plans into action. Just accept the fact that you will never know for sure if something is going to work until you try it. It's true, you might avoid problems through extensive planning, but even then, "the best laid plans of mice and men sometimes goes astray." If something doesn't work the way you planned — just try to learn from the plans that go astray. The important thing is to carry on, be persistent, pick up the pieces and get on with it. Do something rather than do nothing.

References and Resources

There are numerous resources available for guidance as you start your business. A few are listed below. An exhaustive list is given in another Betterway book, *Homemade Money*, by B. Brabec, 1507 Dana Ave., Cincinnati, OH 45207.

Books:

Business for Profits. Allan Smith. Success Publications, 2812 Bayonne Dr., Palm Beach Gardens, FL 33420. *How to Become Successfully Self-Employed*. Brian Smith, 1991. Adams, Inc., 260 Center St., Holbrook, MA 02343-1074. *How to Start Your Own Business While Avoiding Twenty Common Mistakes*, 1991. Gordon Press, P.O. Box 459, Bowling Green Station, New York 10004. *Small Time Operator*. Bernard Kamoroff, 1991. Bell Springs Publishing, P.O. Box 640, Bell Springs Rd., Laytonville, CA 95454. *Starting on a Shoestring*. Arnold Goldstein, 1991. Wiley, 605 Third Ave., New York, NY 10158-0012. *Working at Home: A Dream That's Becoming a Trend*. Lindsey O'Conner, 1990. Gordon Press, see above. *Working-at-Home Sourcebook*. 1992, Gordon Press, see above. *Working From Home: Everything You Need to Know About Living and Working Under the Same Roof*. Paul Edwards and Sarah Edwards, 1990. J.P. Tarcher, 5858 Wilshire Blvd., Los Angeles, CA 90036.

Periodicals:

Entrepreneur. A monthly that contains how-to tips for operating a small business. Includes success stories and offers a large selection of small business development catalogs. 2392 Morse Ave., P.O. Box 19787, Irvine, CA 92713-9787.

Home Business Monthly. Contains how-to articles for starting and operating a home-based business; includes relevant book reviews. 38 Briarcliff Rd., Rochester, NY 14617.

Home Office Opportunities. A bimonthly that provides information, tips, how-to's for the individual who operates a home business. P.O. Box 780, Lyman, WY 82937.

In Business. A monthly for small businesses based on crafts, alternate energy and a back-to-earth lifestyle. JG Press, P.O. Box 351, Emmaus, PA 18049.

Income Opportunities. A monthly that contains valuable information for the small business person. 1500 Broadway, New York, NY 10036-4015.

Mother Earth News. A bimonthly with home career ideas. Sussex Publishers, Inc., 24 E. 23rd St., New York, NY 10010.

Small Business Opportunities. A bimonthly that provides how-to information on starting and operating a small business. 1115 Broadway, New York, NY 10010. Available on newsstands.

Organizations:

AMERICAN HOME BUSINESS ASSOCIATION. P.O. Box 995, Darien, CT 06820-0995. 20,000 members. Works to assist members to operate profitable home businesses. Offers discounted prices on office supplies, health insurance plan. Monthly newsletter; annual convention.

MOTHER'S HOME BUSINESS NETWORK. P.O. Box 423, East Meadow, NY 11554. 5,000 members. For mothers who work at home while caring for children. Quarterly publication.

NATIONAL ASSOCIATION FOR THE COTTAGE INDUSTRY. P.O. Box 14850, Chicago, IL 60614. 14,000 members. For home workers. Acts as an advocacy group and provides home-business tips, methods, success stories. Conducts regional conferences; bimonthly newsletter.

NATIONAL ASSOCIATION OF HOME BASED BUSINESSES. P.O. Box 30220, Baltimore, MD 21270. Provides support and development services. Quarterly publication; annual convention.

NATIONAL ASSOCIATION FOR THE SELF-EMPLOYED. Offers many services, advice and group insurance plan. P.O. Box 612067, DFW Airport, TX 75261-2067. Bimonthly publication; annual convention.

SMALL BUSINESS ADMINISTRATION (Government Agency). Publishes an extensive list of booklets about starting and operating a home business. Many are free; others cost a nominal fee. For a free listing of all the booklets available, write: Small Business Administration Publications, P.O. Box 15434, Fort Worth, TX 76119. Or call the United States SBA Answer desk in Washington, DC (1-800-827-5722).

Appendix

OCCUPATIONS SUITABLE FOR A HOME BUSINESS

The following list of occupations will alert you to the types of businesses that work well as cottage industries. While the list is by no means complete, it can make you think about the needs of your community and the businesses that make a community function. Make a note of the ones that appeal to you as you glance through this list. Besides the numerous books devoted to the subject of home occupations (some are listed at the end of the appendix) another source of ideas is the signs planted in residential areas that silently bear testimony to the large number of homes harboring a business. Some of these occupations require a skill, while others thrive on unskilled but dependable service. Don't reject an idea because it requires preparation, such as taking a class or honing a skill. It is well worth the time and effort to prepare for an occupation you will enjoy for many years. If you are interested in an occupation but don't know much about it, find a book that explains what the job entails. Don't hesitate to call on library personnel in your search.

Many home businesses can be undertaken only with a substantial outlay of money, while others require a modest amount to get started. Keep this in mind as you study the following list. (The procedure for applying for a business loan is explained in Chapter 13.) Some home businesses work well in rural areas, while others need to be located in a city. Very specialized services demand a large population in order to generate enough business opportunities, but other businesses, such as manufacturing, can be located in remote areas, and the products are shipped to market. Combining various occupations can provide continuity of income. Work that is seasonal can be supplemented with the income from a home business. A farmer or builder who is idle in the rainy or cold seasons might turn to crafting objects at home, building up an inventory of products to sell at craft fairs or in shops.

Some home businesses aren't cottage industries in the true sense because, rather than working IN their homes, the entrepreneurs operate FROM their homes. For example, a chimney sweep would receive the calls about appointments at home, but the actual work would be done outside the chimney sweep's home. Examples of these businesses are included in the list and are identified with an * before the entry.

ACCOUNTANT. Many small businesses aren't large enough to hire a full-time accountant, but they rely on part-time help with their books. A good home business is serving as the accountant for other small businesses. Resource: *Accountant as Business Advisor*. William K. Grollman, 1986. Wiley, 605 Third Ave., New York, NY 10158-0012.

ANTIQUES. Buying and selling antiques continues to be a lucrative business that can operate from a large garage or extra room. If you have a large country home and unused rooms, you might create an appealing shop by furnishing several rooms with antiques. Resource: *Buying and Selling Antiques* by Don Cline and Sara Pitzer, 1986. Storey Publishing, Pownal, VT 05261.

APIARY. Raising bees for their honey has been a cottage industry for centuries, but it would take a huge apiary to support a family. More likely, this business would supplement other sources of income. Resource: *ABC and XYZ of Bee Culture: An Encyclopedia of Beekeeping*. Roger Morse and Kim Flottum, 1990. A.I. Root, P.O. Box 706, Medina, OH 44258-0706.

BAKER. Baking pies, cakes, and breads for restaurants and special occasions is a way to earn income at home without a large investment. A restaurant is a reliable source of business, although baking by special order can also be profitable. You can usually charge more for products if you sell directly to the consumer rather than to a restaurant. The U. S. Department of Agriculture Home Extension Agent in your area (there is one in every U.S. county) can provide practical advice on the many aspects of businesses dealing with specialty foods.

* BALLOON RIDES. Hot air balloon rides have become very popular as birthday or anniversary gifts. A hefty investment and training is needed to get started in this seasonal business.

It can become a year-round operation by selling ballooning equipment and teaching others to pilot balloons.

BEAUTICIAN. Women have been providing this service in their homes for years. Basic beautician supplies and equipment, as well as training, are needed to get started. The business can be tucked into an extra room, and appointments can be made to fit the schedule of both the beautician and the customer. Usually a small sign in the front lawn or on the mailbox and "word-of-mouth" advertising is enough to bring in neighborhood business. Resource: *Successful Salon Management.* E.J. Tezak, 1985. Milady Publishers, 2 Computer Dr. W., Albany, NY 12212.

BED AND BREAKFAST PROPRIETOR. Homeowners throughout Europe use the extra rooms in their homes to provide lodging for travelers. More Americans are using that extra room as a way to earn money and meet interesting people. A single room in a small house will do, or a large old home can be converted into an "Inn" capable of housing several travelers at a time. Business people who must frequently be on the road enjoy getting away from motels, and they provide repeat business for enterprising "country inn" operators. A country inn isn't necessarily located in the country but is identified by the decor, feel, and treatment of guests. If no extensive refurbishing is needed, this business requires very little money to start. Resource: *How to Start and Run Your Own Bed and Breakfast Inn.* Ripley Hotch and Carl Glassman, 1992. Stackpole, Harrisburg, PA 17105.

BUTCHERING AND SAUSAGE MAKING. Custom butchering, proven to be a good cottage industry, requires a knowledge of basic butchering techniques, but little equipment. It could include both game and farm animals. (City folk like to hunt game, but rarely know how to properly prepare the meat.) Resource: *Home Butchering and Meat Preservation.* Geeta Dordick, 1986. TAB, P.O. Box 40, Blue Ridge Summit, PA 17294-0850.

CANING CHAIRS. Since homes now reflect a fascination with "country styles," the cane-bottom chair could be the seat of a thriving business.

CANNING SPECIALTY FOODS. Every country shop worth its name carries a line of homemade jellies and jams and an array of pickled products from okra to watermelon rind. Someone is making those items, and it could be you. You might also grow the products you prepare.

CATERING. This is another growing field that can range from baking and decorating wedding cakes to putting together complete menus for large or small groups. This requires equipment and cooking expertise. A good catering service is quickly established through the recommendations of those who attend catered events. Resource: *Cater from your Kitchen — Income from Your Own Home Business* by Marjorie P. Blanchard, 1981. Macmillan, 866 Third Ave., New York, NY 10022.

CHEESE MAKING. Homemade foods are mentioned at several places in this list because there is a strong market for these items. Cheese making is a skill that can be converted into a home business. Resource: *The Art of Home Cheesemaking.* Anne Nilsson, 1979. Woodbridge Press, P.O. Box 6189, Santa Barbara, CA 93160.

CHILD CARE. With increasing numbers of mothers returning to work (while others are discovering the pleasure of working from home) child care is a growing field. A single child might be cared for, but this will yield little income. A child-care center or nursery is much more profitable and time-efficient. It can be operated from a portion of your home and will require little more than basic equipment and toys to get started, plus a hefty liability insurance policy. Resources: *Start Your Own At-Home Child Care Business.* Patricia Gallagher, 1989. Doubleday, 666 Fifth Ave., New York NY 10103. *Family Day Care: How to Provide It in Your Home.* Betsy Squibb, 1986. Harvard Common Press, 535 Albany St., Boston, MA 02118.

CHIMNEY SWEEP. The need for chimney sweeps is increasing as woodburning stoves and fireplaces become more common. Little equipment is needed to get started in this occupation. Resource: *Chimneys and Stove Cleaning* (Bulletin), Storey Communications, Pownal, VT 05261.

COMPUTER-ORIENTED OCCUPATIONS. Computers are changing the way work is done. They have made a huge impact on the business world, and are allowing much work previously done in an office to be done at home. Classes are offered in the evening by public schools and by computer retailers to make computers a part of everyday life. It is worth taking a class to learn what all the fuss is about and to prepare yourself for computer-based occupations.

For the advanced computer operator, writing computer programs to meet specific business needs is profitable work. These should be written on contract just as a book is written on contract. Other occupations are available for the less sophisticated computer worker, and most of these use programs that were written to fill a specific need. It takes only modest expertise to operate programs that maintain inventories and financial records. The information can be relayed through a process called telecommunicating, whereby a telephone line connects your home computer with the company's office computer.

A word processing program takes much of the labor out of writing articles, newsletters, and books, and is a prime reason there has been a proliferation of desktop publishing. It is a useful tool for secretarial work, easing the tasks of writing letters and other paperwork. A business can be built around a word processor, with stenographic services offered on a "piece work" basis to other small businesses that do not need a full-time secretary. (See FREELANCE WRITING below.) Resources: *Exploring Computer Careers at Home* by Scott Southworth, 1986. Rosen Publishing Group, 29 E. 21st St., New York, NY 10010. *Computer Business Ideas: Starting a Business and Making Money With Computers*. 1992. Gordon Press, P.O. Box 459, Bowling Green Station, New York, NY 10004. *Home Office Computer Book*. Steve Rimmer, 1991. Sybex, 2021 Challenger Dr., Alameda, CA 94501. Also see the monthly, *Home Office Computing*, available on newsstands.

CONSULTANT. After gaining experience and a reputation in a specific field (political, academic, agricultural, business, etc.), one can function as a consultant working from a home office. In order to attract a clientele, you must be very knowledgeable in a particular field. Name recognition is helpful. Resources: *How to Start and Operate Your Own Profitable Consulting Business*. Irwin Nathason, 1990. Worldwide Mktg., 1544 Deer Point Way, Reston, VA 22094. *How to Become a Successful Consultant in Your Own Field*. Hubert Bermont, 1991. Prima Publishing, P.O. Box 1260, Rocklin, CA 95677-1260.

COPY MAKER. This business would require an initial outlay for a copy machine, but thereafter the business works virtually by itself. There is a growing need for copies of letters and reports as our society becomes "paper bound." Adding pickup and delivery would greatly increase the market for this service.

COUNSELLING. One can offer counselling in practically any field with the most obvious ones being psychological, scholastic, and medical counselling, but this type of work requires the appropriate education and background. Less extensive education is required to counsel on such things as dressing for success, farm advice, animal care, etc.

CRAFTING. Making creative things at home is a wonderful way to make a living. Crafts that might be pursued include woodwork, pottery, stained glass, quilt making, needlepoint, leather work, rug making, and weaving, to name a few. Some of these crafts require a substantial investment in equipment, while others require very little to get started. The items can be sold at fairs, in shops, through sales reps, or out of your home. Resources: *Start and Run a Profitable Craft Business*. William Hynes, 1992. ISC Pr., P.O. Box 10192, Costa Mesa, CA 92627. *Selling Arts and Crafts by Mail Order*. Allan Smith. Success Publications, 2812 Bayonne Dr., Palm Beach Gardens, FL 33420.

* DELIVERY SERVICE. A delivery service can range from delivering groceries to shut-ins to delivering newspapers. Many shops offer free delivery but do not have a staff delivery person and rely on a freelance delivery service. Another profitable service, that can bring in a reliable income, is delivering older people who have given up their cars but want to visit friends, shop, and do business transactions at the bank or post office.

DESKTOP PUBLISHING. The time and energy-saving features of the computer have made newsletter and report publishing easy and efficient. Almost all churches, schools, private and public organizations issue newsletters. Newsletter writing is usually a regular assignment that provides a continuing income. Resource: *How to Start Your Own Desktop Publishing Business*. Robert Brenner and Scott Olson, 1992. Brenner Info Group, 9282 Samantha Ct., San Diego, CA 92129.

FARMING. Farming is the traditional cottage industry. Besides farming your own property, you can farm other people's property on a rental basis with a portion of the crop profit going to the landowner.

FREELANCE COMMERCIAL ART. Freelancing means a business does not keep you on the payroll, but pays for individual jobs as they are performed. Freelance artists find work with publishers and businesses that put together special projects. Artists are also needed to make advertising copy. Creating logos is a good way to earn money and contact new companies. Resources: *Artist's Market*. Writer's Digest Books, 1507 Dana Ave., Cincinnati, OH 45207. A new edition is published each year. Lists 2,500 buyers of all types of artwork. *How to Survive and Prosper as an Artist: A Complete Guide to Career Management*. Caroll Nichels, 1988. H. Holt and Co., 115 W. 18th St., New York, NY 10011.

FLY TYING. A small amount of inexpensive equipment

and a bit of experience is all that's needed to get started in this business. The products can be sold in fishing and sporting goods stores.

FURNITURE REFINISHING. A good furniture refinisher will always have customers. It takes both knowledge and work to bring old pieces back to life, but people are willing to pay a good price to have their treasures restored.

* GARDEN TILLING. Many people want to garden but lack the equipment to turn the soil. While this provides work only briefly during the Spring, it can supplement another job.

GARDENING AND TRUCK FARMING. You can sell directly to the consumer through a produce stand or to local groceries who need reliable suppliers of fresh garden products.

GIFT SHOP OPERATOR. Many successful gift shops operate out of a home or in a building erected near the home. A craftsperson can do crafting while tending shop, and this frequently draws customers. Be sure to check the local zoning if you are contemplating this type of business.

GREENHOUSE AND FLORAL ARRANGEMENTS. One doesn't necessarily lead to the other as you might raise plants to sell, or you might buy flowers to make into floral arrangements. Silk flowers can also be used in floral arrangements, and dried floral arrangements and wreaths are very popular and should bring a good profit. A healthy summer crop from your backyard or the roadsides will yield the dried plants you'll need to work with throughout the winter.

HERB FARMING. This is a growing field because of the potpourri that is being used for everything from scenting the home to keeping skin youthful looking. Herbs are being used in wreaths and floral arrangements, teas, and for medicinal purposes. The market includes craft shops, flower shops, and country stores. A gardening area is needed, and space for drying, mixing, and arranging. Resource: *Herbal Treasures for Gardening, Cooking and Crafts.* Phyllis Shaudys, 1990. Storey Communications, Pownal, VT 05261.

* HOME CLEANING AND MAINTENANCE. Home maintenance may include house painting, carpet installation, wallpaper hanging, carpet cleaning, and roofing to mention but a few. Resource: *How to Start Your Own Cleaning Business With as Little as Five Dollars: A Step-by-Step Guide for the Housecleaning Business.* Vikki Wachuku-Stokes, 1990. Vikkis Creative, 119 E.

Grand River, Suite 6, East Lansing, MI 48823.

IMPORTING AND EXPORTING. A large number of corporations import products from lands where labor is cheap and the merchandise inexpensive. Many of these products come from Japan, Korea, Sri Lanka, and Taiwan, but merchandise is also being imported from European countries. You will find library books that address this subject, and they will lead you to specific companies with whom you might deal. Importing goods is only part of this business. You would also need to develop a marketing plan and either sell the products yourself or hire sales representatives to sell the goods for you. See Chapter 18, Marketing Methods. A garage or spare room in a home with ample storage space could accommodate this type of business. Resources: *Importing: A Practical Guide to an Exciting and Rewarding Business.* Anne Curran and Glen Mullett, 1992. ISC Pr. 243 Kearny St., San Francisco, CA 94108. *Importing as a Small Business.* John Spiers, 1988. Five Star, P.O. Box 11451, Winslow, WA 98110. *Export-Import: Everything You and Your Company Need to Know to Compete in World Markets.* Joseph A. Zodl, 1992. Betterway Books, 1507 Dana Ave., Cincinnati, OH 45207.

INCOME TAX PREPARATION. Classes and books that teach the preparation of tax returns are available. Many of the people who prepare taxes for some of the well-known tax firms learned through these classes and books, but this knowledge can also be converted into a home business.

* INSURANCE SALESPERSON. If you plan to work as an insurance salesperson, your membership in various organizations will help to make contacts. Another asset in this business is name recognition; thus, if you are/were in sports as a player or coach, a politician, or in some other highly visible position, take advantage of your name's ring of familiarity to make appointments with prospective clients.

* INTERIOR DECORATOR. You may have a natural flair for decorating but have confined your work to your own home. Use your home to demonstrate your decorating prowess to customers who seek your services. Many community colleges and public schools offer courses in interior decorating and design. Resource: *Interior Design Business Handbook: A Complete Guide to Profitability.* Mary Knackstedt and Laura Haney. 1992. Van Nos Reinhold, 115 Fifth Ave., New York, NY 10003.

KENNEL OPERATOR. A substantial investment is needed to establish a small animal kennel, but this is a good home business because of our on-the-go society and the popularity of pets.

* LAWN SERVICE. This seasonal occupation includes not only cutting and trimming but also weed control and fertilizing. It can be combined with SNOW REMOVAL to assure income over a greater part of the year. Snow removal from shopping center parking lots, gas stations, and other businesses usually yields better income than snow removal from the walks and drives of private homes. Have all contracts in place before the first flake falls in order to make the best use of your time. Resource: *How To Make Big Money Mowing Small Lawns.* Robert Welcome, 1984. Brick House Publishing Co., Francestown Turnpike, New Boston, NH 03070.

LAWYER. It's not necessary to maintain an elaborate office and staff to operate an effective law firm. The minimum prerequisite is, of course, a law degree and access to a law library. You will need a private area to meet clients, preferably one with an outside entrance.

MAIL-ORDER BUSINESS. A mail-order business can be promoted either through advertisements in magazines and other publications or through direct mail. See Chapter 18. Resource: *Sell Anything by Mail.* Frank Jefkins, 1990. Adams Inc., 260 Center St., Holbrook, MA 02343-1074. *How to Start a Mail Order Business.* Edward Allyn, 1987. Allyn Air, 17 Millstream Rd., Woodstock, NY 12498.

* MEALS ON WHEELS. This is an invaluable service to people who are unable to prepare their meals, perhaps because they are aged, ill, physically impaired, or mentally deficient. The business would involve both cooking and delivering the meals.

MUSIC. Music can earn you money in a variety of ways including writing and selling compositions, performing, teaching, and promoting other performers. Resources: *Making Money Making Music,* James Dearing, 1990, and *Songwriter's Market,* 1994, both from Writer's Digest Books, 1507 Dana Ave., Cincinnati, OH 45207.

PET BREEDING. Pets for pet shops are always in demand. Gerbils, hamsters, birds, dogs, and cats are the usual animals bought by pet stores. Or, you can breed dogs and cats and sell directly to the public, earning a larger portion of each sale.

* PHOTOGRAPHER. Weddings, passports, class plays — many occasions call for a photographer. This might be a high stress occupation for some because there is often but one opportunity to take a photograph. A substantial investment is needed for equipment, but if you are already a photographer, you will probably have much of the necessary equipment. Resource: *How to Start and Run a Successful Photography Business*. Gerry Kopelow, 1992. Images Press, 7 E 17th St., New York, NY 10003.

PROFESSIONAL OCCUPATIONS. Many of the professional occupations adapt well to a home office. These include such healthcare fields as dentistry, nursing, psychology, and mid-wifery (which is becoming popular again) as well as professions such as architectural design and engineering.

* REALTOR. Although most realtors are associated with large organizations, some are self-employed and work from home. The independent realtor may have difficulty in getting listings, but for the person with community contacts or name recognition, this may not be a problem. A realtor's license is required for this occupation. Resource: *Real Estate Agent*. Jack Rudman, 1991. National Learning Corp., 212 Michael Dr., Syosset, NY 11791.

RENTAL PROPERTY MANAGER. Managing rental property is a good home business if you live in or near the property you manage; e.g., living in an apartment in the building you oversee. Resource: *How to Become an Apartment Manager and Live Rent Free*. Robert Stuart, 1991. Pro-Guides, 3045 Tower Ct., Tallahassee, FL 32303.

REPAIR PERSON—APPLIANCES AND HOME EQUIPMENT. This is a vast field with work opportunities assured because of the automated age we live in. Repair work is needed for televisions, small and large appliances, lawn and garden equipment, and automobiles, to name a few. Most people in this business concentrate on a particular area such as electronic devices, small kitchen appliances, or gasoline-engine powered machines. A skilled repair person attracts repeat business.

* SALES REPRESENTATIVE. This is a very large field, and there are many people functioning as sales reps. See Chapter 18.

SECRETARIAL SERVICES. These services are needed by many small businesses and can be rendered from a tiny nook housing basic office equipment. Resources: *How to Start Your Own Secretarial Services Business at Home*. Stephen G. Kozlow, 1980. SK Publications, 7149 Natalie Blvd., Northfield, OH 44067. *How to Start Your Own Home Typing Business*. Joan Cate, 1984. Calabasas Pub., P.O. Box 9002, Calabasas, CA 91301-9002.

SEWING AND ALTERATIONS. Sewing and clothing alteration continues to be a good way to earn money at home. Resource: *Sewing for Profit* by Judith and Allan Smith. Success Publications, Palm Beach Gardens, FL 33410.

SHARPENING HAND TOOLS AND SCISSORS. Many hardware stores and fabric shops offer sharpening services. These tools and scissors are usually serviced by a home worker who picks up the implements on a weekly route, sharpens them at home, and returns them and picks up more business.

SIGN DESIGN AND SIGN PAINTING. Signs are the hallmark of America. We use them to identify our homes, home businesses, campers, and commercial enterprises. This can be an excellent home business.

SMALL ANIMAL BREEDING. Rabbits, poultry, squab, earthworms, fishes — all can be bred to satisfy local markets that range from pet shops to grocery meats and fish food. Resources: *How to Raise Rabbits for Fun and Profit*. Milton Faive, 1973. Nelson-Hall, 111 N. Canal St., Chicago, IL 60602. *How to Raise Earthworms for Profit*. Jack Frost, 1991. R. Longhurst, 1322 W. 7125 S., West Jordan, UT 84084-3434. Storey Communications, Pownal, VT 05261, publishes many books on raising small animals. Write for a free catalog.

TAXIDERMY AND TANNING. A service that is not readily available in many rural areas, tanning can be a good business venture that combines well with taxidermy. Fishermen and hunters are the main customers, but tanning pelts for fur apparel adds diversity to this type of business. Resource: *How to Make Extra Profits in Taxidermy*. John E. Phillips, 1984. New Winchester Press, RR 1, Box 384C, Rte. 173W., Hampton, NJ 08827.

TEACHING AND TUTORING. Lessons for children have become an obsession in our society. There's your market. Lessons for music, dance, baton twirling, reading, writing, and arithmetic are all in demand. Organize the lessons to earn maximum profits while delivering excellent service. Group lessons work well for subjects such as dance, while the student is better served by private lessons for subjects such as the three R's.

TELEPHONE ANSWERING SERVICE. "Call Forwarding" is a service of the telephone company that allows phone calls from one line to be transferred to another number. Receiving calls for small businesses, whose personnel are away from the office, is a good way to earn money without making an investment in equipment. This is an especially good way for physically handicapped people to earn a living at home. The client is charged for each call you intercept.

WRITING, FREELANCE. Freelance writing takes many forms. Large businesses, local governments, schools and churches use freelancers to put together special projects, brochures, etc. These same groups also use editing services for in-house written material.

Freelancers write articles for magazines and books. Which of the two provides a better income? It depends. If you aren't determined to write the "great American novel," you can probably make more money writing books on subjects that fill a need. Books provide an ongoing income with royalties paid every year, while articles are paid for only once, although they can be resold after a little rewriting. Good marketing procedures are essential to surviving in this business. Resource: *How to Start and Run a Writing and Editing Business*. Herman Holtz, 1992. Wiley, 605 Third Ave., New York, NY 10158-0012. The *Writer's Market* and other writing guides can help you find outlets for your work. See Chapter 18, Marketing Methods.

There is an abundance of books on the market that describe a diversity of small businesses, many of which would be adaptable to the home environment. A few books are mentioned below, but check your local library for a more extensive list.

Earn Money at Home. Peter Davidson, 1981. McGraw-Hill, 1221 Avenue of the Americas, New York, NY 10020.

How to Pick the Right Small Business Opportunity. Kenneth J. Albert, 1980. McGraw-Hill, New York.

Homebased Businesses. Beverly Feldman, 1989. Fawcett, 201 E. 50th St., New York, NY 10022.

100 Ways to Make Money in Your Spare Time, Starting With Less Than One-Hundred Dollars. John Stockwell and Herbert Holtje, 1986. Prentice-Hall, 15 Columbus Cir., New York, NY 10023.

100 Ways to Make Money at Home, 1991. Gordon Press, P.O. Box 459, Bowling Green Station, New York, NY 10004.

1001 Business Profit Making Ideas. Success Publications, 2812 Bayonne Dr., Palm Beach Gardens, FL 33420.

About the Author and the Artist

Jo Frohbieter-Mueller is part owner and operator of Printed Tree, Inc., a home-based manufacturing business, and is the author of over 500 articles on topics ranging from general interest to scholarly scientific research. She is also the author of *Growing Your Own Mushrooms*, Garden Way Publishing, *Practical Stained Glass Crafting*, David and Charles and *The Business of Writing*, Glenbridge.

About the Artist:

The artwork is by Jon Michael Siau. Jon teaches art and cartooning and is known for his portraits and caricatures of sports figures. He is equally adept at capturing an idea in pen and ink, as illustrated in this book. His freelance artwork is a good example of how one might use a skill to develop a home business.

Index